P9-DNI-427

Successful
Investing
with
Fidelity
Funds

Successful Investing *with* Fidelity Funds

Revised & Expanded 2nd Edition

Jack Bowers
Editor, Fidelity Monitor

PRIMA PUBLISHING

*To my family, whose love and support
made this project possible.*

© 1997 by Jack Bowers

All rights reserved. No part of this book may be reproduced or transmitted in any form or by any means, electronic or mechanical, including photo-copying, recording, or by any information storage and retrieval system, without written permission from Prima Publishing, except for the inclusion of a quote in a review.

PRIMA PUBLISHING and colophon are registered trademarks of Prima Communications, Inc.

Library of Congress Cataloging-in-Publication Data

Bowers, Jack. 1958–
    Successful investing with Fidelity Funds / Jack Bowers. — Rev.
    p.   cm.
    Includes index.
    ISBN 0-7615-0842-2
    1. Mutual funds—United States.   2. Fidelity Funds (Firm)
I. Title.
    HG4930.B69   1996
    332.63'27—dc21   96-47767
                                                            CIP

97 98 99 00 01 RRD 10 9 8 7 6 5 4 3 2 1
Printed in the United States of America

How to Order:
Single copies may be ordered from Prima Publishing, P.O. Box 1260BK, Rocklin, CA 95677; telephone (916) 632-4400. Quantity discounts are also available. On your letterhead, include information concerning the intended use of the books and the number of books you wish to purchase.

Visit us online at http://www.primapublishing.com.

CONTENTS

v

11

12

13

14

15

INTRODUCTION

This book summarizes my philosophy on mutual fund investing in general and on Fidelity funds specifically. It shows how a long-term approach with Fidelity funds can help you reach your financial goals.

What I hope to establish is a framework for investing with Fidelity, one that takes away some of the uncertainty and confusion that can exist when trying to make investment decisions on your own.

The opinions presented here represent an independent viewpoint. I have no financial ties with Fidelity, nor do I have any friends or relatives who work at Fidelity (other than the helpful contacts who have provided me with information). Still, I do admit to being a long-time fan of Fidelity mutual funds, an affliction that developed in the mid-1980s when I was doing independent research on mutual fund performance.

In this updated version, I have made an effort to present a balanced view of Fidelity, one that keeps long-term performance in perspective. Too many financial journalists saw Fidelity through rose-colored glasses in 1993, and too many have an overly pessimistic view in 1996. The truth is somewhere between those extremes. One thing is certain: Fidelity didn't get where it is today without working hard and focusing on customers. In the long run, the company is likely to do what it takes to remain a leader in the industry.

Jack Bowers

Note: Jack Bowers is editor of *Fidelity Monitor,* an independent advisory newsletter that makes Fidelity fund recommendations. For information, call 800-397-3094 or write to *Fidelity Monitor,* P.O. Box 1270, Rocklin, CA 95677. He is also chief investment strategist of Weber Asset Management, an independent money management firm that invests in Fidelity Funds for clients with large accounts. For information call 800-438-3863.

1

About Mutual Funds

The Investment Company Act of 1940 defined the structure of present-day mutual funds. This relatively strict act, designed to prevent abuses, requires mutual funds to maintain a separate custodian (usually a bank holding company) as the holder of a fund's assets. It also sets rules governing conflict of interest and requires funds to disclose many different aspects of their operation. It even requires shareholders to vote on any changes to a fund's strategy, a practice that doesn't even exist with regular corporations.

No doubt there was a bit of grumbling among mutual fund industry leaders at the time. Little did anyone know in 1940 that this legislation, which survives today with only minor modifications, would set the stage for the industry's financial dominance in the 1990s. After an era of insider trading, defaulted limited partnerships, corruption among savings and loan executives, overleveraged insurance companies, and a nearly insolvent FDIC, the public has readily embraced the relatively clean record that mutual funds have maintained.

In a country where almost every business leader shuns regulation of any kind, several key players in the mutual fund industry (including Fidelity's Ned Johnson III) met on Capitol Hill in 1993 to deliver a message to a congressional subcommittee. The message: "Please spend more money to regulate our industry!" Over the years the Securities and Exchange Commission (SEC) had assigned several thousand regulators to banks, brokerages, savings and loans (S&Ls), and other investment companies. Only a few hundred had been allocated to the mutual fund industry. The industry's leaders, who play by the rules, wanted to be sure that all mutual funds remain in compliance with SEC regulations. The industry's high level of public trust rests on such compliance.

Some benefits of mutual funds are almost taken for granted. Among the most important is the ease in following a fund's performance. Imagine trying to obtain the average five-year return for a stockbroker's clients. Because mutual funds disclose their performance to the public, they have no choice but to act in the interest of their shareholders. Maximizing returns and keeping expenses reasonable is good for both the investor and the fund. In contrast, having a stockbroker make your investment decisions is like having a real estate salesperson decide where you should live and how often you should move! Brokerage companies make their living from commissions and stock underwriting. Other factors being equal, a brokerage portfolio will usually exhibit higher turnover, higher fees, and mediocre security selection. All of these factors reduce long-term returns. Granted, there are many brokers who ignore the inappropriate incentives and act in the interest of their clients, but in many cases these folks are constantly at odds with their employer.

Other benefits of mutual funds are more obvious. If you've ever tried to build a portfolio by picking your own securities, you know it can be a lot of work. Doing the proper research takes time—lots of it. Even if pouring over quarterly reports doesn't keep you up late at night, you can still lose sleep worrying about whether or not you've bought the right stocks and bonds. Many investors tend to be either too conservative or too aggressive when picking their own securities. Some keep everything in certificates of deposit (CDs) or government bonds. Others, seeking aggressive growth, dive into the latest technology stock; sooner or later it becomes evident that the stock can go down as fast as it goes up. Eventually, most investors realize that mutual funds offer a well-balanced approach to building wealth without tying up all of their free time.

ADVANTAGES OF MUTUAL FUNDS

The main advantages of mutual funds lie in diversification, professional management, liquidity and convenience, shareholder disclosure, economy of scale, easy access to foreign markets, protection from insolvency, and services.

Diversification

Suppose you put $5,000 into a stock fund such as Magellan. You have automatically purchased a small position in several hundred different stocks. Let's say Magellan has 1 percent of its portfolio in Megachips, a semiconductor company with a promising future in computer memory chips. Suppose Megachips now announces that it has fallen behind on shipments because of a quality problem, and the stock price falls 50 percent. If you had put $5,000 into Megachips, it would now be worth $2,500. But in Magellan, where Megachips is only 1 percent of your $5,000 investment, the impact of this event is only $25. Additionally, it's possible that the decline would be offset by some upside surprises in Magellan's other stock holdings.

Although diversification protects against surprise events affecting a single security, it does not protect against events that affect the entire market. In a stock fund, diversification spreads equity risk but does not protect against a market sell-off. In a bond fund, diversification spreads credit risk but does not protect against the impact of an upturn in interest rates.

Diversification does not provide any significant benefit to investors buying government bonds or insured municipals, both of which have near-zero credit risk (although both can have substantial interest-rate risk). A mutual fund offers other advantages for those who wish to invest in these securities, but diversification isn't really an issue.

Professional Management

When you buy a mutual fund, you are, in effect, hiring a full-time manager to look after your money. The objectives and limitations of the fund provide a framework, but within that framework your manager will be trying to maximize performance for you and thousands of others who own shares in the fund.

Liquidity and Convenience

Mutual fund companies agree to buy back your shares if you decide to sell (the exception being closed-end funds that are traded on the exchanges like individual stocks); this agreement creates a liquid market by definition. Although the law allows funds to extend their settlement dates or even repay shareholders "in kind" with actual securities, these measures are rarely invoked unless liquidity dries up in the financial markets. (Fidelity and many other fund companies extended settlement dates by five days in the wake of the 1987 crash.)

Fund families like Fidelity offer many conveniences. If you open a money market fund and set up checkwriting, that fund can be used as the basic account from which other funds are bought and sold. Suppose you've got $40,000 in Equity-Income II and you need $5,000 for your daughter's tuition. Just call Fidelity's 24-hour 800 number and give instructions for moving $5,000 from Equity-Income II to Cash Reserves. Wait until the trade is executed at the close of the next trading day, then verify your account balance and write the check.

Shareholder Disclosure

Making mutual fund performance a matter of public record creates healthy competition. Providing an attractive return for shareholders becomes a major priority for any fund that wants to survive and prosper. Because a mutual fund's track record includes the impact of expenses, fund companies know that if their expenditures are too high, their long-term performance will suffer. (Management, administrative, trading, and 12b-1 marketing costs are deducted before calculating performance.) Funds with high expense ratios also attract negative attention in the media.

Economy of Scale

Because mutual funds serve thousands of shareholders, they trade securities in large blocks. Not only does this reduce transaction costs for their shareholders but it can also reduce the price spread between buyers and sellers in the over-the-counter markets. Transaction costs are further reduced because, on a daily basis, mutual funds are able to match up investors wanting to buy fund shares with those wanting to redeem shares. Fund families such as Fidelity also realize some benefit when one fund sells or buys securities from another fund in the family.

Easy Access to Foreign Markets

It used to be that investors faced insurmountable obstacles when trying to buy securities through a foreign exchange, but investing globally is now inexpensive and convenient— thanks to mutual funds. Fund companies, acting on the behalf of thousands of shareholders, can afford to deal with the complexities of international research, exchange rates, hedging, and administrative requirements imposed by foreign exchanges. Even as ADRs (American Depository Receipts—foreign stock equivalents) become more common in the United States, mutual funds still offer the best approach for international investing.

Protection from Insolvency

Because a mutual fund is an independent financial entity owned by the shareholders, the collapse of a management company such as Fidelity would not wipe out any shareholders. Instead, each fund's assets would remain intact and safe from creditors in the hands of the fund's custodian (typically a bank holding company). The fund's board of directors would have to hire a new manager and probably deal with heavy redemptions, but the shareholders—unlike customers of a failed bank or insurance company—would not have to stand in line behind other creditors. In essence, a mutual fund is as sound as the assets in which it invests.

Services

The law allows mutual funds to engage in a broad range of services. Checkwriting is commonly available on money market funds, and many investors use this feature to avoid the delay of redeeming shares by mail. Direct deposit of a paycheck, making wire transfers, and automatic savings plans are all features that are commonly available. Fund families like Fidelity provide direct exchanges between funds, and in most cases investors can call an 800 number to make trades.

THE MECHANICS OF MUTUAL FUNDS

Simply put, a mutual fund is an investment pool. In an open-end fund, shareholders purchase shares from the fund company, and the purchase goes into the fund's asset base. The manager of the fund purchases securities that are consistent with the fund's objectives and limitations, and the fund company obligates itself to buy back (redeem) shares for shareholders who decide to sell.

Every mutual fund has a share price that is determined by dividing the fund's total assets by the number of shares held by shareholders. The share price is often referred to as the net asset value, or NAV. Most funds calculate their share price once a day after the markets close. The value of an individual's investment in a fund can be determined simply by multiplying the number of shares owned by the NAV. A mutual fund's share price does not imply anything about the securities in its portfolio, so it should not be a factor in selecting a fund. (A mutual fund with a low share price could own high-priced stocks, or vice versa.)

A fund's prospectus is a legal document that defines how the fund will be managed and operated. The prospectus spells out fees, investment objectives and limitations, account features, and historical performance. It is required reading, and a mutual fund company is not allowed to let you buy shares until you acknowledge that you have read the prospectus (this doesn't apply to brokerage accounts).

A fund's prospectus may seem overwhelming at first glance, but the important information covering the fund's objectives and limitations will usually be only a few pages long. (In the future the SEC may allow a profile prospectus that lists only key information.) Consider the prospectus for Fidelity Equity-Income II. It states that the fund's objective is to seek income by investing primarily in income-producing equity securities (dividend stocks), considering the potential for capital appreciation. It also notes that the fund seeks a yield exceeding the S&P 500, although it is not required to meet this goal.

Like other funds, Equity-Income II has a set of fundamental and nonfundamental restrictions. The fundamental limitations, which can be changed only by a vote of the shareholders, include restrictions on how much the fund can borrow or lend against its asset base (in Equity-Income II's case, 33.3 percent), along with more complex restrictions to prevent too much of the portfolio from being concentrated in any one company or industry group. There is also a fundamental limit for illiquid or restricted securities

(10 percent for Equity-Income II). Nonfundamental fund restrictions are less formal and can be changed by the fund's board of directors. These can usually be found in the prospectus, but sometimes they are not included. One of Equity-Income II's nonfundamental policies is the requirement that the fund invest at least 65 percent of assets in income-producing securities.

Once you purchase shares in a fund, you are considered a shareholder of the fund as long as you own shares. Shareholders have certain rights, which include attending shareholder meetings, electing board members, and voting on changes to the fund's prospectus. Few shareholders ever travel to shareholder meetings, but it is a good idea to vote when you receive a proxy in the mail. Without enough votes, the fund might incur additional expenses in order to obtain the required number of votes. (Fidelity actually calls larger shareholders and reminds them to vote if it looks as if a fund will come up short on proxy votes.)

A mutual fund hires a management company (or advisor) to make the investment decisions for its pool of assets. For example, Fidelity funds hire and pay their management fees to Fidelity Management & Research Company, or FMR. FMR, in turn, is responsible for managing the portfolios for all of the Fidelity funds. In this book I am usually referring to FMR whenever I mention Fidelity.

A fund's custodian (a bank holding company in most instances) accounts for a fund's assets and shields them from creditors. In this regard, mutual funds offer better protection than other types of investments. At a bank or insurance company, your investment is exposed to the tiny but significant risk of being allocated to creditors if the firm becomes insolvent. In a mutual fund, the risk to principal is defined by the securities in the fund and not by the financial health of the management company.

A mutual fund is considered an investment company, and as such it is required by the IRS to distribute essentially all of its income and capital gains realized in the course of buying and selling securities. These payouts can take two basic forms: regular income and scheduled distributions.

Regular Income

Money market funds and bond funds accumulate interest on their holdings, which is calculated daily and usually paid out monthly. (A fund's yield can give you an idea of the rate at which the monthly income will be paid out.) Unlike a CD, which has a "locked-in" rate, the income stream in a mutual fund fluctuates according to market conditions. A fund's payout of regular income can go toward purchasing additional shares (reinvested dividends) or can be returned to you through such options as getting a check in the mail or having the proceeds deposited to a money market account. In either case, taxes are due on these dividends, unless they come from a tax-free municipal fund or if the fund is held in a retirement account.

Scheduled Distributions

Mutual funds are required to disburse accumulated dividends and capital gains. Stock funds usually make these payouts in December, but they can occur in other months as well, depending on how the fund is set up. Growth and income funds usually distribute capital gains in December, but most schedule dividend payouts on a quarterly basis. Unlike regular income, a scheduled distribution lowers the share price by an amount equal to the payout. For example, suppose Equity-Income II pays out a $0.10 dividend on its Ex-date (the date of record for distributing assets from the fund) and closes at $20.00. The share price is then $0.10 lower than it would have been without the payout. Distributions like this do not change the value of an investment, but they do lower the share price.

Many investors set up their accounts so that the distributions are automatically reinvested in additional shares. Suppose you own 500 shares of Equity-Income II in an account that is set up for automatic reinvestment. In the example just given, your total payout would be $50 ($0.10 per share times 500 shares), which would be reinvested at $20 per share. That means an additional 2.5 shares would be purchased, raising your position to 502.5 shares. In the end, the value of your Equity-Income II holdings is unchanged by a distribution. You simply own more shares at a lower share price.

Now the bad news. Unless your shares are in a retirement account such as an IRA, Keogh, 401(k), or 403(b), the IRS requires you to report and pay taxes on the distribution—regardless of how long you have owned the fund.

For that reason, it's usually a good idea to delay the purchase of a fund that is nearing its distribution date. Consider what happens if you invest $10,000 in a stock fund in early December, only to get a 5 percent distribution a few days later. You now have to pay taxes on $500 without any investment gains to show for it.

Scheduled distributions can have three components: dividends, short-term capital gains, and long-term capital gains. You are responsible for the taxes on each of these when filing your 1040, no matter how long you have owned the fund. Dividend payouts come from the fund's accumulated stock dividends, and they usually occur only on stock funds or on funds that mix stocks and bonds. Short-term capital gain payouts represent the fund's profits on securities sold less than a year after purchase, and the long-term capital gain component is from profits on securities sold after being held for more than a year. Capital gain payouts can occur on both stock funds and bond funds. Even municipal bond funds can generate small capital gain distributions (although their regular income is tax-free).

MUTUAL FUND EXPENSES

Compared to other investment vehicles, the advantages of mutual fund investing come at relatively modest expense—particularly if you are dealing with a no-load or low-load fund (typical low-load funds charge a fee of 3 percent or less). Funds are very cost-efficient when compared with the alternative of building a diversified portfolio on your own. The cost of owning a fund breaks down into two basic components: internal expenses (which are already reflected in the NAV) and external costs (such as loads, transaction fees, and annual account fees). I'll start with the internal expenses because they are common to all funds (including those that are no-load).

Internal Expenses

A typical domestic stock fund will incur expenses and brokerage fees ranging between 0.5 percent and 1.5 percent. In other words, the fund's assets will be reduced by such a percentage each year. The costs that make up this figure occur continuously and are usually deducted before calculating the share price each day—resulting in performance that takes into account all internal expenses. A breakdown of a mutual fund's internal expenses follows.

Management Fee Sometimes called the advisor fee, this fee is charged by the fund's management company for the job of security selection, and it is often the largest piece of the expense pie. The management fee is the primary source of profits for the management company. Among other things, it pays for the salaries of the fund managers and the analysts who support them. Large firms like Fidelity pool the advisor fees from many different funds and use the money to pay for an entire staff of managers and analysts. Management fees usually range from 0.3 percent to 1.0 percent for a stock fund (although foreign funds can be higher), from

0.3 percent to 0.8 percent for a bond fund, and from 0.3 percent to 0.6 percent for a money market fund.

Administrative and Overhead Expenses The cost of 800 numbers, shareholder reports, statements, quote services, proxy mailings, legal filings, and even the daily cost of calculating a fund's share price come under this category. Fund families will sometimes combine all of their administrative costs and then allocate them to each fund they serve, based on assets under management. Typically these costs run 0.1 percent to 0.3 percent of assets.

12b-1 Fees The SEC allows funds to take a small percentage of fund assets each year to pay for advertising, marketing, or even commissions for brokers selling the fund. Often called the hidden load fee, the 12b-1 category is by far the most controversial because there is no direct benefit to existing shareholders. Fund companies that have 12b-1 fees claim they must expand their asset base to remain competitive, but this category is often used just to increase management company profits. Some fund companies avoid the stigma of a 12b-1 charge by inflating their management fee, but either approach has a negative impact on performance. If a fund company is taking too much for itself, the fund's long-term performance will be less competitive.

In Fidelity's case, retail funds have the option of charging a 12b-1 fee but are not presently doing so.

Trading Costs Whenever a stock fund buys or sells assets, it must pay brokerage commissions. Funds that do a lot of trading (high turnover, as it is called) incur more brokerage expenses, whereas the more stable portfolios spend less. International funds come with a higher burden in this area because of the greater cost in carrying out foreign transactions. Most domestic funds have costs of 0.1 percent to 0.5 percent for trading expenses, whereas international funds typically range from 0.5 percent to 1.5 percent. A fund's brokerage expenses are relatively hidden because they are reported only in an obscure document called the statement of additional information. For many funds, trading expenses include more than just commissions on the purchase of securities. Through the use of "soft dollars," many fund companies have their brokerage companies provide computers and quote systems. The cost of the equipment is buried in the brokerage commissions. This is a sneaky but legal practice, and it enjoys widespread use in the industry.

Determining Expense Burden   My favorite source for getting an idea of a fund's overall expense burden is *Morningstar Mutual Funds* [Morningstar, Inc., 225 West Wacker Drive, Chicago, IL 60606; (312) 696-6000]. Take the expense ratio percentage and add the annual brokerage cost percentage to get overall expenses. (Trading costs are not included in the expense ratio.) Keep in mind that some fund companies don't accurately report commissions, in which case there's really no way to get a precise number. Sometimes the cost of brokerage commissions and soft-dollar purchases are buried in the security price spreads, and the fund company reports a near-zero figure. Fidelity appears to reflect the full cost of transaction fees and soft dollars but credits back brokerage discounts against its expense ratio. This tends to slightly understate the expense ratio.

In any case, recognize that the final figure for internal expenses may only be approximate. Expenses for international stock funds typically range from 1.5 percent to 2.5 percent for this number. Domestic stock funds are usually between 0.6 percent and 2.0 percent, and bond funds (which do not break out brokerage expenses) run from 0.4 percent to 1.0 percent. Money market ratios are usually between 0.3 percent and 0.8 percent. Fund companies are particularly motivated to hold down internal expenses on bond funds and money markets because of the direct impact on the fund's yield. Consider a money market fund holding a portfolio of 4.5 percent notes. A 0.4 percent expense ratio will produce a yield of 4.1 percent for the fund, but if the expense ratio is 0.8 percent, the resulting yield will fall to 3.7 percent.

Sometimes a fund company will waive or cap fund expenses on a new fund to encourage new money to flow in. This practice is popular on bond funds and money markets because it allows the fund to state a higher yield as long as the waiver is in place. These funds often provide above-average returns, but the benefit can be short-lived. Once the waiver is removed (often without any formal notice), the fund's income stream will edge lower. Although the decline is usually not large, it can sometimes make the difference between an outperforming fund and one that's subpar.

External Expenses

All expenses discussed so far are internal to the operation of the fund and are fully reflected in a fund's total return figures. External expenses are the fees you can incur when buying or selling a fund and include the front-end load (or sales charge), redemption fees, exchange fees, brokerage commissions, and account fees.

Front-End Load or Sales Charge   This fee comes off the top of your investment before the money ever goes to work. For example, if you invest $10,000 in a fund with a 3 percent front-end load, $300 will go straight to the management company and $9,700 will be invested in the fund. Load funds collect this fee by charging a higher share price (usually called the offering price), which includes the sales charge. Front-end loads can be as high as 8.5 percent, but a broker is probably getting a commission on the sale at that rate. Some fund families (Fidelity included) do not charge a front-end load if you have already paid a load previously. Suppose you buy into Magellan and pay 3 percent on the purchase. As long as you keep that money in a Fidelity fund, you won't have to pay a second time around. This rule applies even if you move into a no-load fund and later move back to a 3 percent fund. (See Chapter 12 for more information.)

Redemption Fees Also known as back-end loads, these fees are deducted from your balance when you sell shares. Some fund companies, including Fidelity, use a 0.5 to 1.5 percent charge to discourage investors from frequently switching in and out of a particular fund. Some broker-sold funds in the industry are now being structured with no front-end load but with a 4 or 5 percent load on the back side. Many of these redemption loads are dropped if you stay in the fund for a specified period of time, which can be as short as 30 days or as long as five years.

Exchange Fees Most fund families allow you to switch between funds without cost, although limits are imposed to prevent abuse of the privilege. Other funds charge for redemptions or exchanges. In Fidelity's Select family, there is a $7.50 fee for exchanges (which is currently being waived for automated trades) and a redemption fee of $7.50 if you've been in the fund for at least 30 days (otherwise you pay 0.75 percent of assets).

Brokerage Commissions If you buy a mutual fund through a brokerage account instead of purchasing it directly from the fund company, you'll pay a commission on the transaction unless you are part of a network program where transaction fees are waived on participating funds. (Schwab, Fidelity, and Jack White are the major players offering a wide selection of industry funds.)

Account Fees Some accounts are charged a fixed annual fee. Fidelity, for example, charges $12 per year on balances of less than $2,500 (more on this in Chapter 12). It pays to be aware of these charges if you have a small account. A $2,000 balance in an IRA account that is charged $30 annually will forfeit 1.5 percentage points in performance on an annual basis.

Fund companies like Fidelity commonly waive external or internal expenses for competitive reasons or to encourage growth in a given fund. Temporary waivers are popular because they retain the flexibility to return the fund to load status when the fund company decides it's appropriate. (Fidelity has some "temporary waivers" that have been in place for years.) Exchange fees are sometimes waived if the exchange is an automated one. Account fees are often waived if the balance in the fund (or the total of all accounts) is above a certain level.

MUTUAL FUND PERFORMANCE

The percentage that a fund gains or loses in value over time is called total return. In the industry, total return figures are computed with the following assumptions:

- All distributions and regular income payouts are reinvested in additional shares of the fund.
- The impact of income taxes is not included. (This would be difficult to determine because every investor's situation is unique.)
- The impact of front-end loads, redemption fees, exchange fees, and account charges is not included. (Because investors buy and sell at different times it would be hard to include the effect of external expenses.)

Total return figures are usually expressed as a cumulative percentage (total gain or loss) or in annualized form (average compound growth rate). Say that you invest your

$10,000 IRA account in Fidelity's Blue Chip Growth fund and three years later your balance is $15,000 with reinvested distributions. In this example, Blue Chip Growth had a cumulative total return of 50 percent, or an annualized total return of 14.5 percent.

In this example, the effect of compounding explains why three years of 14.5 percent growth "adds up" to a 50 percent total return. As the investment grows over time, gains in later years are realized not only on the original investment but also on the gains achieved in earlier years. Over the long run, realizing gains on gains has a dramatic effect. Over 20 years, a 14.5 percent growth rate translates into a 1,400 percent cumulative total return. That original $10,000 IRA balance would grow to $150,000 under such a scenario.

The mathematically inclined can convert between annualized and cumulative total return with a calculator that can raise a number to a power. First, convert the percentage increase (or decrease) to a *gain factor* by dividing it by 100 and adding 1. Taking the previous example, 14.5 percent becomes 1.145. Next, raise the gain factor to the number of years in the period (for 20 years, raise 1.145 to the 20 power), and you will get a cumulative gain factor (15.000638 for this example). Finally, convert back to a percentage by subtracting 1 and multiplying by 100. You should get 1,400 percent. (Normally it's not a round number.) You can also use this approach to convert from cumulative return to annual return; just follow the same steps but raise the gain factor to the power of 1 divided by the number of years (in this case, 1 divided by 20, or 0.05). If you do the steps correctly you should be able to convert a 1,400 percent cumulative return to a 20-year annualized rate of 14.5 percent.

Total return figures are usually available from the mutual fund companies themselves and are also tracked by industry service firms like Morningstar and Lipper. (Most newspaper and magazine reports on mutual funds will cite one of these two sources.)

When dealing with stock funds, you can calculate total return directly from the share price if the fund has not made any distributions over the period being measured. (Just divide the current share price by the starting share price for a gain factor, then subtract 1 and multiply by 100 for a percentage figure). Beware, however, that you could be fooling yourself. If a midyear distribution has occurred without your knowledge, your calculations will be meaningless. It's better to figure from the dollar value of your account—provided that your distributions are being reinvested and you haven't redeemed shares or added new money.

Distributions are sometimes omitted in charting services and in newspapers that report year-to-date gain/loss figures, although in recent years many publishers have started relying on firms like Lipper and Morningstar to supply total return figures. Here's how the tracking services correctly adjust for distributions and regular income:

- When a fund makes a distribution, all share prices prior to that date are divided by an adjustment factor to create what is called an adjusted share price (or adjusted NAV). The adjusted share prices are lower than the original prices, and any previously adjusted share prices are further reduced. The adjustment factor is computed by dividing the distribution amount by the reinvestment price and adding 1. As an alternative, it is possible to approximate the effect of the adjustment by subtracting the distribution from prior share prices, but this approach is highly inaccurate when used over longer time periods.
- For bond and money market funds, prior shares prices are also divided by an adjustment factor that includes the regular income. This factor is computed by taking the fund's monthly mil rate figure (a figure that's avail-

able from the fund company), dividing by the X-price (the share price on the date the income payout is computed), and adding 1. The 30-day yield figure is not used because it does not represent a fund's actual monthly income; rather it is an approximation based on the SEC's yield-to-maturity guidelines.

- Once an up-to-date database of adjusted share prices is established, total return figures can be determined. This is done by taking the most recent monthly closing price and dividing by the adjusted share price at some point in the past. For example, if a fund's current price is $12 and its adjusted share price was $10 one year ago, the division will result in a factor of 1.2, which yields a one-year total return of 20 percent after you subtract 1 and multiply by 100.

UNDERSTANDING YIELD

Investors who are new to mutual funds can be misled by the yield figures that are quoted for money market and bond funds. In the world of savings accounts and CDs, yield and total return are essentially the same thing. This is not the case for mutual funds.

For a money market fund, the yield that is quoted is based on annualizing the fund's last seven days of income. However, this figure changes with time and market forces. If interest rates were to stay frozen, the total return of a money market fund would be pretty close to its quoted yield at the time you bought in. In the real world, however, stable interest rates are the exception rather than the rule. Over a one-year period, the total return you obtain in a money market fund is likely to be different from the original quoted yield. It may end up a bit higher or lower (due to changing interest rates) than the yield at the time of purchase. In either case, however, the total return will be equal to the monthly income that is reinvested in the fund.

For a bond fund, the total return includes not only the regular income but also the fluctuation of principal that occurs as the fund's holdings rise and fall with the bond market. If rates were frozen and the market's perception of credit risk did not change, most bond funds would have a total return similar to their 30-day yield over a one-year period. However, if rates move up or if credit risk increases, the value of a bond fund will decline (although the income stream would probably go up). Fluctuations in principal usually dominate a bond fund's total return in the short run, because higher interest rates can reduce principal by an amount equal to many months of income. Of course, market forces can also work in the investor's favor if rates decline or if the perception of credit quality improves.

EVALUATING FUND PERFORMANCE

When comparing performance figures between different funds, it's best to examine funds with similar objectives. Comparing one growth fund to another is a logical comparison, but judging a growth fund against a bond fund is not. (The two invest in completely different markets that have different characteristics.)

Most funds aim to outperform a specific index of securities. For example, many domestic stock funds try to exceed the Standard & Poor's Composite Index of Stocks (or S&P 500), a broad-based stock index made up from 500 of the largest public companies in the United States. The S&P 500 is popular among mutual funds because it provides a better picture of the overall market than does the more narrowly focused Dow Jones Industrial Average. When examining fund performance, it's a good idea to examine periods of at least a year. On a daily or monthly basis, the short-term "noise" of the market's random movements tends to mask the underlying trends. Consider a growth fund with an outstanding manager who is outperforming similar funds by ten percentage points per year. Day by day, this fund's advantage amounts to only about one penny per share. Over a week or even a month this manager's advantage is virtually invisible because it is buried in daily price fluctuations of 10 or 20 cents. If, however, you measure this fund over a year or more it will become more obvious that something good is going on.

In recent years many studies have focused on risk-adjusted performance. Most have found significant correlation between historical risk-adjusted performance and future performance. In other words, a fund that performs well on a risk-adjusted basis has a good chance of outperforming its peers in the future. In contrast, the correlation between historical total return and future performance is relatively weak. A fund manager who has simply delivered high total returns is only slightly more likely than others to continue the good record.

Most techniques for determining risk-adjusted return are based on the Sharpe ratio or some variation of it. For a given measurement period with a specified number of data points, the Sharpe ratio defines risk-adjusted return as the difference between a particular investment's average gain and a riskless investment's average gain, with the result being divided by the standard deviation of the specified investment's gains and losses (standard deviation is a statistical calculation that describes how much variation exists in a set of data).

When applying the Sharpe ratio to mutual funds, the usual approach is to use a monthly interval and to pick a period of time that goes back somewhere between 24 and 60 months. Suppose a growth and income fund has an average monthly gain of 0.9 percent over 24 months, and during the same period 90-day T-bills average 0.4 percent per month (90-day T-bills are considered a riskless investment). If the standard deviation of the monthly gains and losses is 1.84 percent, the Sharpe ratio would compute a factor of

0.27 for risk-adjusted return. By itself this figure is not significant. However, once calculated the same way for other funds, it can be used to identify funds that have higher risk-adjusted returns.

Generally speaking, funds that seem to migrate to the top of a risk-adjusted scoring system tend to be "sure and steady" performers. Many funds ranking high only on a total return basis often drop down on a risk-adjusted list because they take on too much risk in obtaining their high returns.

OTHER MEASUREMENT TERMS

Aside from those already discussed, there are a few other technical terms that are used in describing mutual fund characteristics.

Relative Volatility

Relative volatility is a measure of risk that is usually computed from the standard deviation of a fund's gains and losses and normalized to an index such as the S&P 500. For example, if the S&P 500 is assigned a relative volatility of 1.0, a typical growth fund might carry a score of 1.2, a growth and income fund could be 0.7, and an average bond fund would probably be around 0.4. A fund's price fluctuations are usually a pretty good indicator of how risky its portfolio is; a higher volatility means the fund has a greater risk of loss. Still, a relative volatility figure shouldn't be used to predict how much a fund will fall in a bear market. Market declines affect stocks and bonds differently; a particular fund's response to them cannot be reliably computed from a relative volatility number. Instead, use beta to help understand bear-market risk.

Turnover

Turnover indicates how actively a manager buys and sells securities in a fund. It is usually computed by dividing the dollar amount of securities sold (over a one-year period) by the fund's asset base. The result is then expressed as a percentage. Funds with turnover above 200 percent can expose shareholders to higher trading expenses, an effect that is particularly significant for foreign funds. They can also trigger larger capital gain distributions at year-end if the increased trading activity results in capital gains. By itself, high turnover is not necessarily bad. If the manager is doing a good job of selling high and buying low, a high turnover fund can provide superior long-term results. On the other hand, a fund with high turnover that has lagged behind its respective index for more than a year or two can be a sign of poor judgment on the part of its manager.

Beta

To the extent that a fund moves with an index, beta measures the degree of the movement. Typically the S&P 500 is used and is defined as having a beta of 1.0. If, on average, a fund moves up 2 percent when the index moves up 1 percent, it will have a beta of 2.0. On the other hand, if it moves up just 0.5 percent, it will have a beta of 0.5. Beta is useful for assessing the impact of a market sell-off (or rally) on a fund, but many investors incorrectly treat it as if it were an indicator of risk. Beta works like relative volatility if a fund correlates well with the S&P 500, but it can be deceiving at other times. As an example, an aggressive foreign fund or a gold fund may carry a beta of only 0.3 or 0.4 while maintaining a risk level twice as high as that of the S&P 500.

R-Squared

This figure measures correlation between a fund and an index, typically the S&P 500. (It can also be used to compare one fund to another.) If a fund always moves up or down in direct proportion to the S&P 500, it has an R-squared of 1. If a fund never moves with the index, it has an R-squared of 0. If a fund moves opposite to the index more often than not, it will have a negative R-squared figure. Most funds range between 0 and 1 for most situations. Some investors use R-squared to build a portfolio. By choosing several funds that correlate loosely to each other (usually indicated by an R-squared of less than 0.7), it is possible to create a portfolio that has less overall risk than the funds it includes.

DERIVATIVES

Simply put, a derivative is a financial instrument with returns linked to, or derived from, an underlying asset such as a stock, bond, commodity, or index. Options and futures, which have been around for decades and trade on established exchanges, are derivatives in their simplest form.

Many of these exchange-listed derivatives are more popular and more liquid than the underlying asset they are pegged to. Consider S&P Stock Index futures, which are a convenient way to obtain a diversified equity position. The alternative is to buy all of the individual stock positions and pay a lot more in brokerage commissions. Another kind of derivative commonly used is the foreign currency contract. These securities enable a fund manager to reduce the currency risk that exists whenever a foreign stock is purchased. For example, if a fund manager has ten percent of his portfolio in Japanese stocks, he can protect against a decline in the yen by purchasing a contract to sell yen at some future date. If the yen declines, the contract will increase in value to offset the currency-related loss on the Japanese stock holdings. Suppose a fund manager buys $1,000,000 of Sony stock when the yen is trading at 100 to the dollar. Then the manager hedges against a decline in the yen by purchasing $1,000,000 in contracts to sell yen at 100 to the dollar. Suppose the yen declines to 105 to the dollar and Sony stock remains unchanged in Japan. In dollar terms the manager has seen about a 5 percent decline on his or her Sony position, but the $48,000 loss is offset by a similar gain on the currency contract. In effect, foreign currency contracts allow a manager to match the performance of a stock in its home country (minus the cost of the currency contract).

Indexed securities, another kind of derivative, can add unique risks to a portfolio. Sometimes referred to as structured notes, these derivatives fluctuate in a defined way against a specified index. They are often used to profit from a particular viewpoint. For example, suppose a fund manager expects interest rates to decline in Sweden. He or she could purchase a structured note indexed to the value of two-year Swedish bonds, multiplied by 8.5. If the view is correct and Swedish interest rates fall by one percentage point, this structured note would gain 15 to 20 percent. On the other hand, if Swedish interest rates go up one percentage point, if could lose 15 to 20 percent. A fund manager cannot lose more than the original investment with an indexed security, but because of high volatility this type of derivative can add risk to a portfolio. Many funds lost money on indexed securities in 1994 because their manager's viewpoint was incorrect.

It was mortgage-backed derivatives and inverse floaters that gave derivatives a bad name when interest rates went up in 1994. Many of these exotic securities were held in what were supposed to be conservative funds. A few well-publicized bond funds and money market funds paid the price for excessive positions in these securities because many inverse floaters and mortgage-backed derivatives failed to follow their computer pricing models when markets for these securities became illiquid.

Business page headlines in 1994 brought a lot of stress to some mutual fund investors. Many reacted with alarm upon discovering that a fund they trusted owned some derivatives in its portfolio, as if any and all derivatives were a ticket to future losses.

The fact is that lots of money managers were betting on declining interest rates, and derivatives just happened to be the most efficient vehicle for doing it. If derivatives had never existed, 1994's headlines would probably have told tales of massive losses on zero-coupon bonds and the overuse of margin in bond-oriented portfolios.

You don't need to be excessively concerned about derivative use in mutual funds. Fund managers are now exercising more caution in their use of structured notes, mortgage derivatives, and inverse floaters after 1994's lesson. Public pressure has also forced mutual fund companies to be more forthcoming about their use of derivatives. In Fidelity's case, you can call and find out the current derivative exposure on any of their funds.

2

Fidelity's Strengths and Weaknesses

When you evaluate a mutual fund company, there are three basic factors to consider. In order of importance, these factors are performance, available choices, and service.

Most mutual fund companies do well in at least two of the three, or they don't stay in business very long. Fidelity and other successful firms in the industry have strengths in all three.

Fidelity's attractiveness has not gone unnoticed by the investing public. About one of every eight dollars in the mutual fund industry resides in a Fidelity fund—by far the largest market share in the industry. The company has a similar lead among 401(k) providers as well as in the variable annuity business.

Many companies tend to become less competitive as they get big, but Fidelity continues to search aggressively for new opportunities. The firm seems determined to be a key player in the brokerage business and is always trying to lure customers from key rivals such as Schwab. Becoming a leading financial services firm in overseas markets is also one of Fidelity's key goals, although trade barriers and cultural differences have kept the firm from growing very fast in foreign markets. The company is even testing its customer service advantage in some different domestic industries that complement its role in financial services. Two examples include corporate benefits administration and institutional software products.

But Fidelity's retail fund business remains its bread and butter, and the company hasn't stopped trying to improve. Current areas of internal focus include the use of company-specific financial models to improve earnings forecasting, increased investment in foreign research to boost performance in overseas markets, developing an advantage through quantitative techniques, and developing easy-to-use automated services for customers.

This chapter focuses on Fidelity's retail fund business and how it stacks up against the competition.

FIDELITY PERFORMANCE

If you've had a chance to flip through *Morningstar Mutual Funds,* you may have noticed the higher concentration of five-star ratings that show up about five pages into the alphabetical listings. In the issue of August 2, 1996 (which lists data through June 30, 1996), a total of 173 out of 1,492 industry funds had earned the top badge for risk-adjusted performance. (Morningstar uses a bell curve to establish where each fund ranks relative to others in its class; only 12 percent of the funds listed in this issue were awarded five stars.) Skip to the Fidelity section, and you'll find that 19 percent (20 out of 107 Fidelity funds) receive the high honor. Clearly, Fidelity's emphasis on research produces statistically significant results in the real world.

There's nothing special about that particular issue of *Morningstar Mutual Funds;* it just happens to be the latest one available as of mid-1996. You can probably find a similar ratio in Morningstar's latest issue, even several years after the fact.

Comparison with the Industry Average

Fidelity's performance lead over the industry is not limited just to five-star ratings but also shows up when you compare total return averages. Using the Morningstar database, I grouped Fidelity's funds to compare performance against the eight industry-wide benchmarks that are published in each issue of *Morningstar Mutual Funds*. I used a trailing period of five years, ending June 30, 1995. This period is long enough to provide a clear picture of Fidelity's recent performance, which includes a generally favorable period in the first half and a generally unfavorable period in the second half. I excluded any funds that did not have a five-year history. Keep in mind that these five years were bullish for stocks. In the future, rates of return are likely to be lower for the Domestic Stock, Specialty Stock, and Hybrid categories.

Domestic Stock This category, which includes domestic stock funds and stock-oriented growth and income funds, is one where Fidelity shows a clear advantage. The 23 Fidelity funds in this group had an annualized return of 17.8 percent, versus 15.3 percent for the average of 725 industry funds with a five-year return. A lead of 2.5 percentage points may not seem huge, but it is significant when you consider that it is an average of 23 funds and it occurred over a five-year period.

International Stock This is the only category where Fidelity failed to beat the industry average. The seven Fidelity funds in this category returned 10.7 percent per year, versus 11.3 percent for the 146 industry funds for which Morningstar has a five-year history. Fidelity is investing heavily in international research, and results in this category could improve over time.

Specialty Stock   Reserved mainly for sector funds, this category includes Fidelity's Select funds, a real estate fund, and a utilities fund. Most of these funds are domestic and many of them have a focus on small stocks, an area where Fidelity's research capability makes a bigger difference. The average of 36 Fidelity funds came out at a strong 18.7 percent per year, versus 14.4 percent for the 126 industry funds in the category. Many of the first-time managers heading up the Selects started out as analysts, so these numbers are a testimonial to Fidelity's effective recruitment and promotion process.

Hybrid   This is the category Morningstar assigns to funds that blend stocks and bonds. The six Fidelity funds in this group averaged 13.8 percent annually, compared to 12.0 percent for 235 industry funds that had a five-year record. Generally speaking, it appears that Fidelity's advantage in this group comes mainly from stockpicking, whereas bond holdings appear to have played a less significant role.

Specialty Bond   For this group Morningstar tracks 141 funds, mainly those that invest in junk bonds, convertibles, and foreign debt. Fidelity has a significant lead in this group owing to its research strength in junk bonds and convertibles. The average of four Fidelity funds came out at 12.7 percent per year, versus 11.2 percent for the industry average.

Corporate Bond   Fidelity could have done better here, but a tough 1994 took a heavy toll on funds that held foreign debt. As a result, the four Fidelity funds tracked here had an average return of 7.8 percent annually, the same as the 7.8 percent return registered for Morningstar's 176 industry funds.

Government Bond   The average of seven Fidelity funds was 7.4 percent per year, versus 6.9 percent for 217 industry funds. Fidelity's advantage seems to come from trading on short-term pricing inefficiencies in the government bond market, a practice that the company has refined over the years.

Municipal Bond   The 20 Fidelity funds with a five-year history averaged 7.4 percent annually, compared to 7.1 percent for the 536 industry funds. Four-star and five-star funds are common in this group, suggesting that Fidelity adds value in the form of risk reduction as well.

How Fidelity Outperforms the Competition

Beating the industry performance averages in six of the eight major fund categories is no small feat, but for Fidelity it is business as usual. That's because performance is part of the Fidelity corporate culture, and the Fidelity organization is set up to foster it. The way that funds are managed and the way that fund managers are supported is clearly unique in the industry.

Commitment to Research   Fidelity's hundreds of in-house analysts and the variety of markets that are covered are simply unmatched by any other mutual fund company. Many investors think the fund manager is the main factor that determines performance, but in Fidelity's case all fund managers are backed up by teams of analysts who have a vested interest in the quality and accuracy of their recommendations. In other words, Fidelity managers are set up for success because they pick and choose from a pool of securities that have been extensively researched.

Knowing the Real Story   Fidelity analysts and managers meet with thousands of company executives every year to ask questions about sales, margins, competition, cost cutting, and industry trends. Some of the meetings occur when the fund managers or analysts go on the road; some occur on the phone (fund managers often call and chat with several companies every day). Many companies travel to Boston to tell their story directly to Fidelity. On a typical day Fidelity managers and analysts can pick from an agenda of several different meetings without ever leaving their work location. All this communication is very significant because it allows Fidelity managers to base investment decisions on information that is more up-to-date than the latest quarterly report. Company executives are surprisingly honest when discussing their situation. If they paint an overly rosy picture, they risk losing credibility with Fidelity down the road. If they downplay their situation, their stock price may not reach its full potential. As such, most give an accurate account of business just as they would to any major shareholder. Of course, there are a few companies that won't talk to Fidelity. But most public companies will not ignore a major (or potentially major) shareholder.

Hard Work   Fidelity managers, many of whom are young workaholics, put in the extra hours that make a difference. The more you know, the better your decisions are. Fidelity managers spend a lot of time trying to know as much as possible. In reference to working Saturdays at Fidelity, Peter Lynch (the former Magellan manager) often mentioned that there were usually enough fund managers for a game of basketball. Morningstar said in the March 1993 issue of *5-Star Investor* (now *Morningstar Investor*) that Fidelity managers are far more likely to be at the office during off-hours than are their competitors. This comment was based on Morningstar's own experience in trying to reach managers for telephone interviews.

Hands-off Management   Despite some new controls, Fidelity fund managers still have plenty of freedom to execute their strategies without facing management scrutiny every time they make a move. It makes a big difference when your bosses let you live with your own mistakes instead of second-guessing your decisions all the time. As a result, most Fidelity managers are highly motivated, independent thinkers.

Performance-Based Hiring and Promotion   Fidelity understands well that some people are naturally talented when it comes to picking securities. The ability to accurately assess opportunity and risk seems to be a personality trait, and regardless of education or background there are some who are better at it than others. Accordingly, new hires usually start out as analysts. Once they have proved their worth, they get a chance to run a Select portfolio or become an assistant at a larger fund. If they excel in that role, they may eventually run a mainstream fund. This system of promotion tends to weed out the candidates who are well-educated but would otherwise be less than successful at running a fund. It works particularly well at Fidelity because the managers of large, important funds are selected from a large base of analysts and smaller funds.

Is Fidelity Getting Too Big?

The negative side of being big and successful is that at some point you become too big a fish for the pond. Fidelity is clearly a big fish. The company's stock fund assets are equivalent to about 3 percent of the U.S. market capitalization (as of mid-1996). If the company were 30 times larger, Fidelity funds could not outperform the market because they would be the market.

Here's how size can hinder Fidelity's fund managers:

- Large funds, such as Magellan and Contrafund, can't move too quickly when accumulating or liquidating a large position in a particular stock. If they do, they risk moving the stock's price in a way that works against the fund over the long run.
- Large Fidelity funds can't benefit when they find attractive small-cap stocks. Suppose Magellan buys $30 million of a small company stock that has a market capitalization of $300 million. Let's say this stock

doubles over a one-year period. In a small fund a move like that would make for a good year. But in Magellan's $50 billion portfolio the total return for the period would increase by less than one-tenth of one percentage point. The fund would have to find 100 such stocks just to boost its return by about six percentage points—and that's not a realistic scenario. In effect, larger funds are unable to realize gains from the small-cap arena. Instead, they must focus on finding the best large-cap and mid-cap investment opportunities.

- Fidelity funds that focus on small-caps are sometimes "shut out" of a stock by Fidelity's internal limits on ownership (these limits exist for liquidity reasons). The limits, which are usually set at 10 percent for smaller companies, stipulate the maximum percentage of a stock that all Fidelity funds can own. So if a given fund manager wants to buy a particular stock, but other Fidelity funds already own 10 percent of the company, the manager is forced to look for some other opportunity. In practice, Fidelity managers are usually not limited much on large-cap and mid-cap stocks, but in the small-cap universe there can be "lock-outs" on hundreds of stocks.

Together these constraints may seem somewhat alarming, but you have to realize that most Fidelity managers have been dealing with them for years. While there is clear evidence that size tends to hamper performance to some degree, there is no evidence to suggest that size *prevents* Fidelity funds from outperforming.

The best example of this is Fidelity's Low-Priced Stock Fund. Manager Joel Tillinghast has been battling ownership limits and other stock restrictions almost since inception, and because he focuses on small-caps it can be hard to find enough places to invest new money. His fund has lived with cash positions ranging from 20 to 50 percent for most of the past five years, and he currently holds over 700 stocks—not because he wants to, but because it's the only way to put $4 billion to work and not own more than 10 percent of any one company. The situation sounds like it would be hard to manage, but then you look at the fund's five-year return and discover that it has outperformed more than 90 percent of industry stock funds. The fund's size allows a dedicated team of analysts to support Tillinghast, helping to keep better tabs on all those companies. That's in contrast to other small-cap funds in the industry where the manager usually has to go it alone.

Another example is Magellan, the fund of choice for the media to pick on. For ten years, article after article has been critical of the fund's huge size, yet Magellan still beat 85% of industry growth funds for the period. Magellan is big, but Fidelity has always put strong managers in charge, and these leaders have done quite well focusing on mid-cap and large-cap stocks. Even as of mid-1996, with the fund at about $50 billion, Magellan is less than 1 percent of the U.S. stock market capitalization. It will probably take much longer than a decade to reach 2 percent—even if it does outperform. While Magellan may be too big for the kind of rapid industry moves that Vinik was making, there's no reason it can't beat the S&P 500 with Stansky's sure and steady approach to picking large-cap stocks (see Chapter 4 for more on Magellan).

Many investors have wrongly concluded that Fidelity's large size is responsible for the high percentage of funds that have lagged the S&P 500 in 1994, 1995, and 1996. In reality, this is an issue of investment style. Compared to the rest of the fund industry, Fidelity managers usually place more emphasis on mid-cap, small-cap, and foreign issues. Even for funds that invest mainly in the S&P 500 universe, Fidelity managers tend to focus on less expensive stocks. Traditionally this approach has provided a significant advantage over the S&P 500, but during most of these three years the S&P 500 has outperformed everything else. That's unusual, and it isn't likely to last. The high valuation on S&P 500 stocks should tilt the odds in Fidelity's favor in the coming years.

Fidelity's large size will slow its funds down a bit, but not for 15 years or more will size become a serious hindrance to performance. Between now and then, the company is likely to expand and improve its foreign research, sharpen its domestic forecasting models, and realize some benefits as its quantitative (computer-based number crunching) techniques are refined.

AVAILABLE CHOICES

With about 160 retail funds directly available to the public, Fidelity quite clearly provides the largest selection of any mutual fund company. As of this writing, you can invest directly in any of 20 domestic growth funds, 14 growth and income and asset allocation funds, 35 sector funds (Select portfolios), 19 international and foreign funds, 20 taxable bond funds, 26 municipal bond funds, and 24 taxable and municipal money market funds. More than 80 funds are available with no front-end or back-end load, so no-load enthusiasts can find plenty of diversified funds to choose from.

If you decide to invest in a load fund, the most you will pay at the time of purchase is 3 percent, and your mutual fund shares will be tagged by Fidelity's computers so that you don't pay the 3 percent again on a future exchange involving those shares. All you have to do to retain the load credit is keep the investment in a Fidelity fund. (The details of Fidelity's load credit system are discussed in more detail in Chapter 12.)

Even though Fidelity's fund lineup is impressive, there are some bases that aren't covered. The only index fund offered on the retail side is Market Index, which tracks the S&P 500. Fidelity doesn't offer any index funds for mid-cap, small-cap, foreign, or bond markets. Fidelity is also missing a socially conscious fund (one that avoids companies involved in alcohol, tobacco, weapons, or environmentally damaging practices), although Select Health Care makes a good stand-in for this objective. Although there are plenty of municipal bond choices, Fidelity doesn't have one for every state that has an income tax.

Some investors would argue that you don't need a broad-based lineup from any one fund company now that mutual fund networks are available through Fidelity, Schwab, Jack White, and others. After all, if you can access hundreds of funds from your brokerage account, what does it matter?

It may not matter, but the mutual fund networks come with some drawbacks that can make them less attractive than staying with a single fund family. For one, the networks usually come with greater restrictions on trading if you plan to stay with no-load, no-transaction-fee funds. If you play the full field, you can pay multiple transaction fees and loads— something that doesn't usually happen in a single fund family. Finally, you may not help your performance. Conventional wisdom says the more choices, the better. However, from the standpoint of probabilities you may be worse off in a network as opposed to confining your money to a research-advantaged group like Fidelity or a cost advantaged group like Vanguard.

FIDELITY SERVICE

Many American companies could learn a few lessons about customer service by observing Fidelity's practices. Many of Fidelity's competitors had to, whether they wanted to or not.

In the mid-1970s, Fidelity was the first fund company to make checkwriting available on money market funds, and by the end of the decade it was selling no-load funds directly to the public via newspaper and magazine ads. (Before then Fidelity funds were sold through brokers with a hefty 8.5 percent load to cover the commission.) By the mid-1980s Fidelity had expanded the staffing of its 800-number phone lines to provide around-the-clock coverage for exchange orders, quotes, fund information, and general questions.

Fidelity also began a major initiative to establish investor centers in all major cities around the nation. By 1992 this network of investor centers had been expanded to most large cities, and automated phone systems were in place allowing investors a faster way to get fund pricing and account balances and make exchange orders.

Over the years Fidelity's competitors have matched many aspects of Fidelity's high level of customer service, but the large number of investor centers serve as a reminder that Fidelity is still ahead in the game. Walk into any of the 80 or so centers around the country, and you can talk with knowledgeable professionals who are willing to help—without the typical sales pressure. You can pick up a prospectus or attend an educational seminar. You can even get help with an application form or work directly with a representative to resolve a problem with your account. All without any extra charges.

The investor centers are particularly reassuring for first-time Fidelity investors who are a little nervous mailing off a check to a company they have never dealt with. For these investors, it's reassuring to deal directly with Fidelity employees who live and work closer to home.

One-Stop Shopping

One of the benefits of dealing with just one mutual fund company is that it can simplify your paperwork. One set of statements. One set of phone numbers. One set of money market checks. One set of year-end tax forms.

When you choose a mutual fund company with a wide array of financial services and products, you have the added advantage of going with one company for all of your financial needs. For example, with a Fidelity Brokerage Ultra Service Account (USA) you can consolidate your investments and perhaps even eliminate the need for a bank account. Following is a rundown on the many services available from Fidelity.

Checkwriting on a Money Market Fund   Writing a check on a money market fund is an easy and convenient way to redeem mutual fund shares, because it saves the time of waiting for Fidelity to send a check through the mail. A simple phone call can move money out of a stock fund and into your money market fund. At that point, all you have to do is wait a day, verify the trade was executed properly, then write the check. Most Fidelity money market funds have a checkwriting minimum of $500 and do not charge for the service, except for the Spartan funds—which stipulate a $1,000 minimum amount and cost of $2 per check unless you maintain a high balance. Checkwriting is also available on bond funds, but I don't recommend it. Unlike a money market fund, each check written against a bond fund is a taxable transaction.

The Bank Alternative   If you're out to replace your bank checking account, Fidelity Brokerage's enhanced USA plan is the best bet. You get a variety of features for a flat $5 per month—services that would probably cost much more at a bank. You need $25,000 in investments to establish the account, but you can satisfy the requirement if you have that much in non-retirement Fidelity fund accounts. It takes some time and paperwork to move these holdings into a USA brokerage account, but the fee structure and exchange privileges on Fidelity's brokerage side are virtually identical to its mutual fund group. If $25,000 is too much, you can open a streamlined account with $10,000 in assets—but you'll end up paying a bit more in fees.

The core account in the USA plan is the one that works similar to an interest-bearing checking account. For a flat $5 per month with the enhanced option, you get unlimited checkwriting (checks can be written for any amount), returned check images, stop payment and wiring services at no added cost, expense coding to track where you spend your money, and check reordering without an added fee. The regular core account pays just slightly less than a money market fund, and you even have the option of a municipal core account. You can also get a VISA "check" card, which allows cash from an ATM or debit purchases at various stores that accept VISA.

Of course, there are some drawbacks to substituting a Fidelity USA for a checking account. The more common problems include ATM fees that get tacked onto cash withdrawals, and the seven- to ten-day mailing and clearing time on deposited checks. In the latter case you can avoid the delay on paychecks by setting up direct deposit.

Charge Cards and Credit Cards If you have the USA plan, you can link a charge card (VISA or MasterCard) to your account, and all charges will be automatically deducted from your account around the 25th of the month. You can also use the charge card for getting cash at an ATM.

If you want a regular credit card for carrying a running balance, Fidelity offers these too (VISA and MasterCard). You don't even need a USA or other brokerage account to apply. Once established, you just mail in your payment each month as you would for any other credit card. Unfortunately, the APR isn't very competitive, at least under Fidelity's mid-1996 fee structure.

IRA, Rollover IRA, Keogh, and SEP-IRA Accounts Retirement accounts allow you to invest in the full range of Fidelity mutual funds (except municipals) while deferring any taxes until you start taking withdrawals (usually after age 59½). In these retirement accounts the front-end load is waived on all funds except Magellan, New Millennium, and the Selects. Also, the minimum initial investment on non-Spartan funds is reduced to $500 (as opposed to $2,500 for most funds in a taxable account). Retirement accounts are discussed in more detail in Chapter 11.

Moneyline Transfers The Moneyline service allows transfers between a given fund and a bank account, and these transactions usually take two to three business days to occur. The minimum amount for redemptions into a bank account is $10. For additional purchases of an existing fund, the minimum is typically $250 (except for Spartan funds, which have a $1,000 minimum). The Moneyline feature must be set up before you need it, because it can take about ten business days to be established.

Automatic Purchases or Withdrawals Automatic Account Builder piggybacks onto Moneyline and will transfer money from your bank account into a fund on a monthly or quarterly basis. (The minimum additional fund purchase drops to $100 with this program.) Personal Withdrawal Service offers the ability to do automatic redemptions on a monthly basis (or less often). The redemptions must be at least $25, and the proceeds can be placed in another fund (such as a money market) or into your bank account via Moneyline, or they can simply be mailed to you in the form of a check.

College Savings Plan Fidelity's College Savings Plan allows you to transfer money to a child's own account under rules specific to the state you reside in. Five fund choices are available with a $1,000 minimum: Blue Chip Growth, Growth & Income, Asset Manager, Puritan, and Cash Reserves. Loads are waived, and for Cash Reserves you can even start with as little as $100. Purchases can be monthly or quarterly and must be at least $100. Other funds are available too, but loads are not waived and the regular minimums apply.

FundsNetwork Available with any Fidelity brokerage account, FundsNetwork allows you to purchase any of over 3,000 industry mutual funds. There are three classes of funds: those with loads, those with a fixed transaction fee, and those with no load or transaction fee. FundsNetwork has been one of Fidelity's faster growing programs, but as I mentioned before more choices does not necessarily mean better performance.

Bill Paying Service   Available with the USA program, bill payments can be scheduled 24 hours a day and can be made to almost any party through a secure system using a telephone, a personal computer, or both. Fixed payments, such as a mortgage, can be set up to occur at a specific time each month. One-time bill paying can be scheduled for a specific time in the future. Fidelity guarantees the timely delivery of all properly scheduled payments, paying any late fees up to $50.

Portfolio Advisory Service   Fidelity's money management program, Portfolio Advisory Service, allows an investment team to choose your funds and make your trades for you. The cost can be up to 1 percent of assets per year, and the minimum account size is $200,000 for regular accounts and $100,000 for retirement accounts. The fee for this service is probably less than you would typically pay for an independent money manager to manage your account, but the strategies are generally more diversified and may not offer as much growth for aggressive investors.

Variable Annuities   Discussed more in Chapter 14, variable annuities resemble mutual funds but are sold as life insurance in order to qualify for special tax treatment. They function somewhat like a nondeductible IRA account because investment gains are tax-deferred, but the options are limited and the fees are a bit higher than those of regular mutual funds. Nevertheless, Fidelity's lineup of variable annuities is more competitive than what most other insurance companies offer.

Charitable Gift Fund   This Fidelity-created organization is recognized by the IRS as a public charity. As with a private foundation, your contributions are tax-deductible at the time you put money into an account. Once inside the Charitable Gift Fund, what happens to the money you donate is still your decision. You arrange how it is invested by allocating between four Fidelity mutual fund pools, and you (or a beneficiary) recommend grants to the charities themselves. The Gift Fund requires a minimum grant of $250 and will make payouts only to IRS-recognized charities (this includes many educational institutions and other nonprofit organizations). Donations to the Gift Fund are irrevocable, and once in your Gift Fund account there is no tax liability on investment gains because the account is not considered part of your estate.

Some families may find the Charitable Gift Fund a simpler alternative to creating a private foundation because it eliminates the need for tax and legal filings. For others, it is a way to take a deduction on contributions now and pass on a legacy of charitable giving to heirs. The minimum to get started is $10,000, and additional contributions must be at least $2,500. The Gift Fund takes 1 percent of assets per year for services.

Trust Services Available in most states through the investor centers, Fidelity Personal Trust Services provides services for the full range of trusts, including living, revocable, irrevocable, and charitable trusts. The program provides fully tax-sensitive portfolio management for each individual account. In addition to mutual funds, Fidelity incorporates and manages the individual securities clients already own. Fidelity Personal Trust Services also manages general investment and rollover IRA portfolios.

The minimum account size for this service is $400,000 in cash, funds, or individual securities for living, revocable, and irrevocable trusts. It drops to $200,000 for charitable trusts. In both cases an annual fee is charged based on the total assets of the account.

On-Line Services Fidelity Brokerage offers its Windows-based FOX + trading software to investors who want to trade on-line. Among other things, the package allows you to review your investment holdings, get quotes, and place stock trades at a discount.

Fidelity also runs a state-of-the-art home page on the World Wide Web (http://www.fidelity.com). Investors can get the latest news on the market, review fund performance and portfolio holdings, and download prospectuses.

Service Problems

Mistakes are rare when dealing with Fidelity, but they can be frustrating when they occur. It's easy to get edgy when significant amounts of money are involved, and Fidelity's phone system doesn't make it very easy to deal with a single person in resolving the problem. Often you end up waiting for someone at Fidelity to get back to you, and it can sometimes take longer than you would like. If things aren't going well, one option is to enlist the help of a Fidelity contact at your nearest investor center. This usually doesn't speed up the resolution of the problem, but it can relieve the stress because you have a key person who "owns" your problem.

The other service issue with Fidelity is mail volume. Even though the company has sharply reduced promotional mailings, there's still a lot material that arrives in your mailbox: annual reports, proxies, prospectuses, transaction statements, quarterly statements, tax statements, manager changes, Fidelity magazines, and more. Having a brokerage account or an annuity account can further increase the volume. Much of what is sent is legally required, meaning that Fidelity can't stop sending it even if they wanted to. In this respect, the volume of mail you get from Fidelity is no worse than what you would receive from any other fund company. I suspect that in future years fund companies will be allowed to post legal information on-line and avoid the costs of printing and mailing documents.

The Benefits and Risks of Long-Term Investing

The Dow Jones Industrial Average will reach 10,000 in the year 2013. Does that sound like an insightful prediction based on years of research and confidential forecasting models? Hardly. It's based on the simple knowledge that the Dow Average grows at a long-term rate of about 5 percent per year. In all likelihood, this "no-brain" prediction will be accurate within a few years of the actual date that the Dow crosses the 10,000 mark.

If you held a portfolio of the Dow Stocks you would be even better off. That's because you would probably earn 7 to 8 percent per year with the inclusion of the dividend income that the Dow stocks provide. (I'm assuming it would be reinvested in additional shares of stock.) If the Dow Jones Industrial Average were to start reflecting the dividend income, it would be much higher by the year 2013—probably around 20,000.

The omission of dividends in the Dow index and the Standard and Poor's 500 index is one of the reasons that many would-be investors have taken so long to understand how well a portfolio of stocks can do over time. The financial media haven't helped much—many newspapers still don't include the income stream when calculating returns for the Dow and the S&P 500, and I'm not just talking about the local business section. Granted, it isn't as big a deal today because dividend yields are lower, but just over a decade ago dividends added 5 percent per year in total return.

The Dow Jones Industrial Average has some other peculiar characteristics. Owing to its design in 1896, it is calculated by adding up the prices of its stocks and dividing by an adjustment number that reflects stock splits. (When invented, the index had to be something that could be calculated quickly and easily; tabulators were not yet in widespread use.) As a result of this price-weighting approach, stocks with higher share prices affect the index many times more than stocks carrying a lower price per share. When a stock splits, the Dow index gives it only half the weight it had before the split, making it a smaller part of the index. In reality, stock splits have no impact on market value. Imagine trying to run a Dow index fund. As certain stocks rise in price, you would have to buy more shares, selling shares of those with smaller gains. Every time a stock split came along, you would have to immediately sell one-half of the position.

The Standard and Poor's Composite Index of stocks, now known as the S&P 500, was established in 1926. Today it includes 500 stocks to the Dow's 30, providing a better representation of the overall market. Unlike the Dow, it is capitalization-weighted, meaning that the companies with the largest market value carry the most weight. Thus, stock splits have no affect on a particular stock's weighting.

The NASDAQ index has gained popularity in modern years. As an index of over-the-counter stocks, it is fully adjusted for splits and reinvested distributions. Until 1990, the NASDAQ index was a good representation of small-cap stocks. Today, however, there are a handful of large technology firms that haven't moved to the New York exchange. Because these firms carry a large market capitalization, they tend to

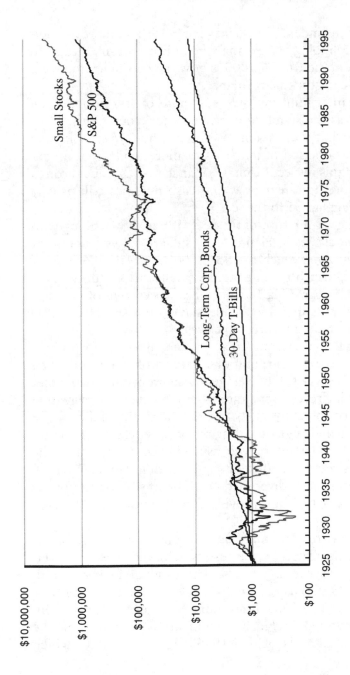

Figure 1 Growth of $1000 invested at the end of 1925 in four basic asset classes.
Source: Ibbotson Associates, Inc.

dominate the index. This makes the NASDAQ more an indicator of technology stocks than an indicator of small-caps. In my opinion, the Russell 2000 is now the best index to watch for small-cap stock performance.

The mutual fund industry has more or less adopted the S&P 500 as the standard benchmark for stock funds. Most domestic equity funds aim to exceed it but typically lag the index over a period of ten years or more. (Fidelity is an exception in this respect.) Unless a manager adds value through stockpicking, fund expenses and cash holdings will usually result in lagging performance.

The long-term return of the S&P 500 is shown along with other asset classes in Figure 1. This chart shows a period of 70.5 years, over which the S&P 500 returned 10.6 percent annually. During the same period, small stocks returned 12.5 percent per year. Clearly stocks have been one of the best long-term investments available, having outperformed inflation by more than 6 percent per year.

The total return from stocks exceeds inflation in a stable economy because corporations earn profits by providing goods and services. On average, those profits are used either for increasing revenue at a rate faster than inflation, increasing the value of company assets at a rate faster than inflation, or for paying dividends and buying back stock. In the latter case, shareholder return will usually exceed inflation if the company's revenue and profits grow with inflation. What all this means is that a diversified portfolio of stocks held for the long run will typically provide a total return that exceeds inflation.

The power of compounding at a rate faster than inflation is clearly illustrated by the results achieved by some of Fidelity's longer-running funds. The original Fidelity Fund, started in 1930, has returned 10.7 percent annually for over 66 years; had retirement accounts been around back then, $1,000 invested in Fidelity Fund at inception would be worth $839,000 as of mid-1996. Or take Puritan, which has gained 12.3 percent per year since 1947; in just over 49 years, $1,000 would now be worth $300,000. Trend has delivered an annual return of 13.9 percent since 1958; a $1,000 investment in Trend would be worth $142,000 after 38 years. Even Equity-Income, a relative newcomer of just over 30 years, would have turned a $1,000 investment into $56,000 with its 14.3 percent annual growth. All of these examples illustrate the potential benefits of long-term investing. While there is no guarantee, it is reasonable to expect that stocks will continue to exceed inflation over the next 20 years.

THE ARGUMENT AGAINST MARKET TIMING

If anyone asks you if the stock market is headed up or down, always say up. You'll be right about two-thirds of the time. Based on a monthly history of the S&P 500, stocks have out-performed cash about 67 percent of the time over a one-year period. Increase your investment horizon to three years, and stocks exceed cash 76 percent of the time. Over ten years the favorable odds increase to 83 percent. Invest for 15 years and you would have been ahead 93 percent of the time. Over 20 years the S&P 500 has always exceeded the return on a cash investment.

Nevertheless, new investors often look at a historical chart of the market and reach the obvious conclusion that holding cash during declines would have boosted returns. Along the same line of thinking, you could do better at the race track if you would take care to bet on the winning horses. The whole idea of timing the market is based on the false assumption that predicting the future will be as easy as observing the past.

I estimate that over a ten-year period fewer than 5 percent of market timers will actually exceed the S&P 500 return, and those who do will beat it by only a small margin. Many first-time investors do not appreciate how hard it is to predict the market until they have tried a few times. Here are the reasons I do not recommend jumping in and out of the market, either with stocks or stock funds:

- By their very nature, financial markets move in the direction that surprises or disappoints the maximum number of participants involved. If the majority wants to buy, prices are higher. If the majority wants to sell, prices are lower. If the majority are content, trading volume becomes small and liquidity dries up, setting the stage for a surprise move up or down. The only way to win at this game is to ignore the short-term volatility and benefit from the long-term trend.
- Because stocks move up twice as often as they move down, a cash position will be the wrong choice by a two to one margin when applied randomly over any long period of time. Many investors think they can make up for this statistical disadvantage by outsmarting the rest of the investment population, but over a long period of time no amount of intelligence can overcome those odds.
- More opportunity exists in picking funds than in timing the market. Imagine two farmers. The first studies the weather and tries to figure out the best years to farm and then plants several crops when the time looks right. The second ignores the weather and plants every year but tries to pick crops that will bring the most profit. Which farmer do you think will be better off in 20 years? Figure 2 compares the hypothetical return of perfectly timing the market versus perfect fund selection in Fidelity's domestic growth category. No one can do this well in the real world, but clearly an investor who focuses on fund selection has a better shot at maximizing returns than one who ponders whether the investment should even be made.

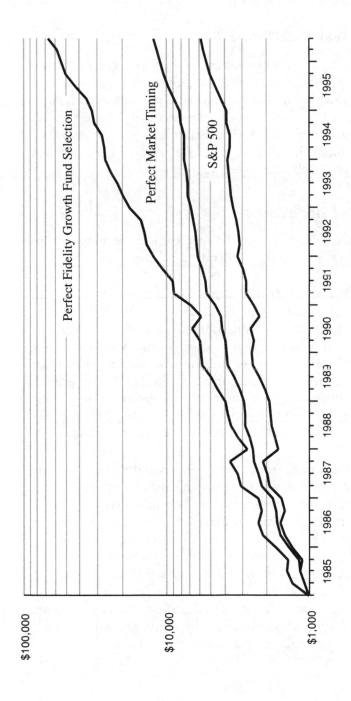

Figure 2 Perfect fund selection versus perfect market timing, quarterly over an 11.5-year period.

CHARACTERISTICS OF STOCKS

Stocks, or equities, represent ownership in a corporation—entitling the stockholder to a proportional claim on the corporation's net worth and its dividend payouts. Shareholders also have a right to influence the company's direction on strategic issues, either through a shareholder vote, by providing inputs to the board of directors, or by expressing a point of view at the shareholders' meeting.

Stocks and Stock Values

Stocks have value based on the corporation's earnings (or future earnings potential), dividends, and assets.

Earnings In a mature company, earnings are necessary to continue paying out dividends and/or to repurchase existing shares of stock. In a growing company, earnings provide capital for expansion. In either case, a company's earnings (or anticipated future earnings) are the best indication of what future shareholder compensation might be. Many growth stocks do little to reward shareholders during their growing years, but shareholders anticipate that these firms will pay dividends or buy back shares at some point in the future.

Dividends and Stock Buybacks Companies that are making money but are not growing usually reward shareholders with direct compensation because there isn't much potential to grow their business by reinvesting profits. In essence, shareholders are better off receiving dividends instead of having the company retain its earnings for internal use. The income stream of a dividend stock (or the ongoing increase in earnings per share for a company that is buying back its stock) can make it attractive even when earnings are flat or declining, provided the slump is not permanent and is not bad enough to force a dividend cut.

Assets   A stock can have value without earnings or dividends if the company owns property, equipment, patents, licenses, or other valuable assets. Many companies trade above their book value per share because the accounting methods for determining book value do not usually reflect the appreciation of assets such as real estate.

Fundamental Indicators

Stocks are often compared on the basis of their price-to-earnings ratio (P/E ratio), which can often provide an indication of how expensive or cheap a particular company may be. For example, if a given stock has a $20 share price and earnings of $2 per share over the prior 12 months, it has a trailing P/E ratio of 10. Generally speaking, P/E ratios are lower for dividend/value stocks and higher for growth stocks. Many Fidelity managers consider a stock to be undervalued if the anticipated earnings growth rate is higher than the P/E ratio. For example, a stock with a P/E ratio of 25 may seem expensive on an absolute basis, but if the company can grow earnings at a 30 percent rate the stock can still be attractive. Nevertheless, stocks with high P/E ratios are vulnerable. At some point the earnings growth slows down, and the stock usually gets clobbered. Suppose a company with 30 percent annual earnings growth encounters some new competition, and earnings growth slows to a 20 percent rate. Suddenly, the "fair market" P/E ratio for the stock is 20 instead of 30—a potential decline in price of 33 percent.

A company's price-to-book ratio (which compares the stock price to the company's net worth per share on an accounting basis) is also a useful indicator, especially when earnings are depressed. P/E ratios are undefined if a firm is losing money, and they tend to be very high if the company is near breakeven. In these situations the price-to-book ratio can be useful. Generally speaking, value stocks have price-to-book ratios of less than 2, whereas growth stocks are often above 4. But the price-to-book ratio isn't perfect either. Occasionally a company that has been through some tough years will be relatively cheap but still carry a high price-to-book ratio due to its heavy debt load. Furthermore, book value for smaller companies tends to be less accurate than for the larger blue chips and foreign companies follow a different set of rules for establishing book value.

That's when the price-to-sales ratio can be useful. You can look at the price-to-sales ratio to see how cheap the stock is relative to current business levels (most stocks range between 0.5 and 2.0). You can even compare the ratio to companies in the same industry to see what the stock might be worth with normal profits. Price-to-sales is also a dead giveaway for expensive stocks, which usually trade with ratios above 4. When evaluating foreign companies, price-to-sales generally cuts through the accounting differences that can cloud comparisons of P/E or price-to-book. The only problem with price-to-sales is that it isn't well defined for some businesses, such as banks and other financial entities.

One other fundamental indicator for stocks is dividend yield, although this long-time indicator is less useful today. The increasing trend toward stock buybacks has prompted many companies to slow the growth of dividends and instead use the money to reduce the number of shares outstanding. Shareholders like it that way, because dividend income is taxed every year and can carry a higher tax rate than capital gains. Stock buybacks produce capital gains, the favored form of shareholder compensation. Still, if you can find a company with a high dividend yield, it is probably a good value unless the company's future earnings (and thus its dividend) are in jeopardy.

One popular investment strategy uses the dividend yield on the Dow stocks to identify the best values. There are several variations, from holding the second-highest yielding stock to holding the top ten highest dividend stocks. Now that there are billions of dollars following this approach it isn't likely to

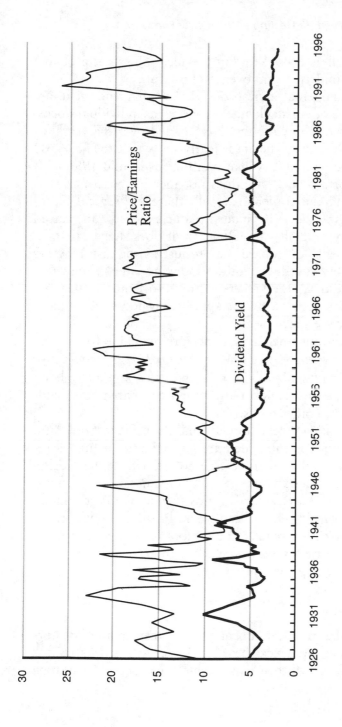

Figure 3 S&P 500 price/earnings ratio and dividend yield.
Source: **Standard & Poor's.**

work as well as it used to, but the nice thing is it probably won't ever underperform over the long run.

Two fundamental indicators, P/E and dividend yield, are often calculated for stock indexes as well as individual stocks. Figure 3 shows how the two have varied over the years for the S&P 500 index. The lines clearly show that the S&P 500 is at the high end of its valuation range as of mid-1996.

A high-priced S&P 500 does not mean a bear market is right around the corner. After all, there are several places along the chart where the index became expensive and stayed that way for several years. However, it does suggest that future gains will not be nearly as robust as the last 15 years (more on this in a discussion on indexing later in the chapter). After a long period where a growth-oriented strategy realized the best returns, a value approach is now looking more prudent for the years ahead.

Aggregate fundamental statistics are available for mutual funds. My favorite source is *Morningstar Mutual Funds*. Not only can you find a fund's overall P/E ratio and price-to-book ratio, but you can see how these figures compare to the major indexes and to other funds.

When tracking Fidelity funds, I find the price-to-book ratio to be the most useful in determining whether a fund leans more toward value or more toward growth. Some Fidelity managers favor cheap turnaround companies, but their funds can show above-average P/E ratios if they purchase companies where earnings have been weak. In these situations, the price-to-book ratio tends to be a more reliable indicator because it will usually be low when a manager is heavy into turnaround companies.

Bear Markets

Fear of being caught in a bear market keeps many investors out of stocks. A typical bear market causes stocks to lose about one-third of their value, which may seem devastating to some. However, time is on the mature investor's side. The average bear market sell-off lasts about a year, and the recovery period averages about 14 months. Most of the time, the entire cycle runs less than three years. Bear markets usually occur with an economic event that has a broad-based negative impact on corporate earnings for an extended period of time. Most bear markets are triggered by one or more of the following three factors: higher interest rates, surging oil prices, and trade restrictions.

Higher Interest Rates When rates go up, the economy can slow and earnings can decline. Companies with debt suffer the most because they are hit with an increase in borrowing costs and a drop in revenue. Higher interest rates are the most common cause for bear markets, but this is widely known and the stock market is quick to adjust to changes that may affect corporate earnings. In the past, the Federal Reserve has set off many bear markets by raising short-term interest rates to fight inflation and then failing to wait long enough for results before making additional tightening moves. Usually the Fed had gone too far by the time there were visible signs that inflation was in check. Today's Fed is trying to act earlier and wait longer for results, a process that seems to have worked well in recent years. Time will tell if this approach succeeds over the long run.

Surging Oil Prices Directly or indirectly, the price of crude affects the cost of doing business for just about all corporations. When oil goes up, it costs more to travel, it costs more to ship goods, it tends to raise the price of commodities, and it increases the trade deficit because most of our oil is imported. Except for wages, it is the single most influential factor affecting inflation. In 1973–74 the price of crude quadrupled as the OPEC cartel took advantage of its dominant position in the world oil markets. In the U. S., this caused the worst bear market in the last 50 years and set off an eight-year wave of inflation that caused the consumer price index (CPI) to double. By the mid-1980s, OPEC's pricing tactics had encouraged the development of other worldwide oil reserves, and competition finally broke the cartel's stranglehold. Still, as Iraq demonstrated in 1990, it is possible to see major worldwide supply disruptions. (Prices doubled after Kuwait was invaded and remained high until the Gulf War began.)

Today the main concern for oil is the growing demand from emerging countries, which for several years was masked by sharp declines in Russian demand. Technology has helped to expand supply and satisfy growing world demand. No doubt it will play a key role in keeping the price of crude from appreciating sharply over the long run. Still, there may be times when oil prices surge in the short term. During these periods the negative impact on the domestic stock market could be significant.

Trade Restrictions   Government policies can devastate an economy if exports or key imports are restricted in a major way.

Country by country, national economies are good at some things and not so great at others. For example, the U.S. excels in developing new technology and providing top-notch entertainment; it also boasts the world's most productive farms and accounts for some 25 percent of global farmland. Japan's economy, with few natural resources, has emphasized high-volume manufacturing; be it memory chips, photocopiers, cars, or VCRs, the Japanese have some of the world's best factories and can mass-produce with exceptionally high quality. China has labor and can produce simple goods like toys at low cost. The list goes on: the Arab countries have low-cost oil; Canada has timber and minerals; Europe does well with mass transit, industrial machinery, food products, fashion, and performance automobiles.

When trade is free, it raises the average standard of living for everyone by allowing each country to profit from what it can do best. When trade is restricted, consumers lose out and corporate earnings can be hit hard. The worst bear market of this century occurred in the early 1930s when isolationism was essentially legislated by Congress.

Imagine what our economy would be like if trade had been cut off 15 years ago. Gasoline would be over $4 per gallon, color TVs would cost $1,000, cars would be unreliable, and computers would be running on kilobytes instead of megabytes. Food would be cheap, but mortgages would probably exceed 12 percent because no foreign capital would be available to absorb the federal debt.

The point is that a breakdown in trade can wreak havoc with the economy. These days a trade-driven bear market seems less probable, but skirmishes between the U.S. and other major trading partners could still escalate into a bear market.

However bad they seem at the time, bear markets are temporary. Ultimately, things change for the better, and the financial markets are quick to react as the first evidence of recovery surfaces.

Many risk-averse investors buy only CDs or Treasury bills, feeling much better about a guaranteed 5 percent than about taking a chance on a 10 percent return with the possibility of a loss. With an investment horizon of less than three years it's hard to argue with this approach. However, if you don't have plans for your money for eight years or more, you're selling yourself short if you're not in the stock market. The long-term risk of owning stocks is much lower than the short-term risk. Over an eight-year period, there's about an 85 percent chance that stocks will do better than CDs or Treasury bills. Although a cash strategy might realize 50 percent growth over eight years, an equity-income fund would probably double over the same period.

Indexing to the S&P 500—No Longer a Great Idea

One constant of financial markets is that any investment that becomes too popular will eventually disappoint. Such is the case today for indexing to the S&P 500. After years of being promoted as a foolproof way to beat the pros and hold down taxes, some $600 *billion* is now estimated to be following this strategy (mostly through various index funds and trusts). That's over ten times as much money as Magellan!

Having all this capital chasing a fixed number of companies has made for some very expensive stocks. Take Coca-Cola, with a mid-1996 P/E of 37. Coca-Cola is a great company with great growth prospects, but is it really worth almost $20 for every man, woman, and child on the planet? Index mania has prompted some mid-cap companies to try and get "promoted" into the S&P 500. Once your company is adopted by the index, you become a small piece of an immensely popular investment strategy. Such an event can significantly boost a company's stock.

As of mid-1996 the S&P 500's price-to-earnings ratio is almost 20, and earnings growth over the last ten years has averaged about 9 percent. Most analysts agree that if a stock has a P/E ratio above its earnings growth rate, it isn't cheap. Suppose that a rising dollar and competition reduces the S&P 500 earnings growth to 7.5 percent over the next decade and suppose that the P/E ratio for the index slides to 14 over the same period. The likely result would be a decade where the S&P 500 total return slides to around 6 percent per year.

Under such a scenario, mid-caps, small-caps, and foreign issues will be the better choice over the next ten years. That being the case, actively managed stock funds should do much better relative to the S&P 500. Instead of just 30 percent of industry stock funds beating the index, it may be more like 60 or 70 percent over the next decade.

At any rate, Fidelity funds should do quite well in the years ahead. Fidelity managers generally look outside the S&P 500 for their best stocks, and they tend to seek value even when they are buying growth companies. Although this approach didn't work well in 1994, 1995, and 1996, I suspect it will be rewarded in the years ahead.

CHARACTERISTICS OF BONDS

When you buy a bond, you are lending money to either a corporation, a municipality, or to the government. In any case, you are purchasing a promise to return your principal with interest.

A bond's value is influenced by many factors, but interest rates and credit risk are the two basic factors that are dominant.

Interest Rates

Because most bonds have a schedule of payments over a specified length of time, they have an inherent sensitivity to interest rates. If prevailing interest rates go up, a bond is worth less because its schedule of payments has become less attractive relative to the yield available on newly issued bonds. Other factors being equal, the value of the bond will fall until its yield-to-maturity (the yield of the remaining payments compared to the current value) is equal to prevailing market rates.

Suppose a ten-year bond pays a fixed coupon rate of 6 percent and is sold for $1,000. Later, the prevailing yield on similar ten-year bonds moves up to 7 percent. The market value of the bond would decline to about $950 so that a new buyer would realize an effective yield of 7 percent if the bond is held to maturity (the coupon rate is still 6 percent, but because the bond is bought at a discount the effective yield is higher). Conversely, a decline in prevailing interest rates will cause the value of the bond to rise until its yield-to-maturity is similar to the market rate.

The degree of interest rate sensitivity of a bond is determined by its repayment period. Long-maturity bonds fluctuate the most with interest rates because the schedule of interest payments goes on for a long time, leaving the bond holder with a substantial advantage or disadvantage, depending on whether rates go down or up. Short-maturity bonds, on the other hand, fluctuate less because the principal and interest will be available to reinvest at market rates in relatively short order.

Credit Risk

The other significant factor affecting bond pricing is the ability of the bond issuer to repay (although this tends to be less significant in a bond fund). U.S. government bonds are considered to have near-zero credit risk because they are backed by the government's authority to raise taxes if push comes to shove. Top-rated corporate bonds and high-grade municipal bonds carry a little higher yield and a little more risk but are usually considered fairly safe. Investment-grade bonds, usually a broad range of corporate debt, are the next step down because business conditions can play a small role in the ability of the issuer to service its debt. At the bottom rung are high-yield bonds, otherwise known as junk bonds. In this group the default rate can be significant, and business conditions play a major role in the ability of the issuer to service its debt. Yields in this group are typically several percentage points higher than government bonds.

Bonds are often rated by agencies such as Standard and Poor's and Moody's. These firms review the health of the issuer and cast their judgment on credit risk. Standard and Poor's ratings (in descending order of risk) are AAA, AA, A, BBB, BB, B, and CCC. BB and higher are generally considered to be investment grade. Moody's ratings (again in descending order) are Aaa, Aa, A, Baa, Ba, B, and Caa. Ba and higher are considered investment grade. U.S. government bonds are considered to be at or above AAA or Aaa bonds.

Bonds usually carry less risk than stocks, but over the long run they have not exceeded inflation by as much. Since the start of 1926 (a period of 70.5 years), the annualized total return for long-term investment-grade bonds has been about 5.5 percent per year. Real growth (net of inflation) was about 2 percent for the period.

In modern years bond investors have done better. Starting in the early 1980s, investors began to understand how inflation factors into long-term returns. Since then, the inflation premium on long-term investment-grade bonds has risen to around three to four percentage points, almost double the long-term average. There are signs that this adjustment is a permanent one. It could mean that the difference in annual return between stocks and bonds may be only a few percentage points in the years ahead. Given the relatively high premium on the S&P 500 (as of mid-1996), large-cap stocks may not provide much of an advantage over bonds in the decade ahead.

There have been many bear markets for long-term bonds over the years, but most were only half as bad as a major sell-off in stocks (10 to 15 percent losses are typical). For short-term bonds, the sell-off was about half again as bad (usually 5 to 7.5 percent). Bonds are clearly safer than stocks, but they are far from being risk-free.

Bear markets usually occur at different times for stocks and bonds. In the typical economic cycle, interest rates will usually move upward as the economy expands and borrowing increases to meet expansion needs. Under these conditions, stocks are usually benefiting from earnings growth, but bonds are sliding as interest rates edge up. At some point the economy peaks, and growth begins to slow. Corporate earnings start to slide, causing stocks to decline. Borrowing demand slacks off, causing long-term interest rates to fall. This is a period when bonds benefit. Near the bottom of the cycle, stocks start to rise because of falling interest rates and future economic potential. Bonds continue to do well because there is not yet any upward pressure on long-term interest rates.

Because stocks and bonds are usually somewhat "out of phase," a portfolio that includes both is subject to less volatility. A mix of 60 percent stocks and 40 percent bonds is pretty close to ideal; it carries less risk than a bonds-only approach yet provides a higher total return. For this reason, the 60-40 mix has long been popular with conservative growth and income funds as well as balanced funds.

CHARACTERISTICS OF CASH AND GOLD

Since 1926, cash-type investments (represented by the 30-day Treasury bill) have returned an average of 3.7 percent per year, just slightly ahead of the long-term 3.1 percent for inflation. If government money market funds had been around since 1926, the advantage over inflation would have been offset by the management fee. When investing for the long term with a money market fund, the best you can hope for is to break even after inflation and taxes. Most of the time you won't even do that.

Investors who bought CDs and money funds in the early 1980s remember when risk-free double-digit returns were available. By contrast, today's rates seem low. They aren't. The 1980s were unique because short-term interest rates reflected the inflation rates of the late 1970s, yet inflation had subsided to less than 5 percent early in the decade. For about ten years, riskless cash investments delivered the kind of real returns that would normally be associated with long-term bonds. Then the recession in 1991 showed how low the return on cash can go in a soft economy. Short-term interest rates have risen since then, but it's unlikely that cash investments will ever again provide the kind of real returns that existed between 1981 and 1991.

Gold is sometimes considered the perfect inflation hedge. From the standpoint that it holds its value against inflation, it is. However, its real return over the long run is usually zero, just like cash investments. What is different about gold is that it tends to surge when inflation escalates and decline when inflation recedes. The volatility of gold is similar to the S&P 500, but the volatility of gold stocks (and gold funds) is typically twice as great as the metal itself.

Gold and gold stocks are sort of like inflation insurance. The long-term return usually isn't very good, but if inflation runs out of control (either in the U.S. or in other mature economies), gold-oriented investments tend to perform well.

Gold and bonds are somewhat inversely correlated, meaning that gold (and gold stocks) often move up when bonds are declining. A small 5 percent position in gold stocks or a 10 percent position in the metal itself can actually reduce the volatility of a bond portfolio because of this offsetting effect. However, it can also reduce the long-term return of the portfolio by a small amount.

The same is not true for stocks. When the economy is expanding and interest rates are edging up, cyclical stocks and gold are usually moving up together. If the Fed raises short-term interest rates too far, stocks and gold can both be declining at the same time. Many investors ran for gold after the stock market crashed in 1987, only to see their gold holdings drop sharply a few days later.

After being in a bear market for over a decade, gold now seems in position to move up slowly over the long run. Jewelry demand in emerging countries is on a long-term growth trend, whereas world gold-mining capacity is relatively fixed. Still, you don't want to bet the farm. Gold isn't like other commodities where a large and growing shortfall would imply sharply higher prices. Most of the gold ever taken out of the ground is still around. With some 100,000 tons in "circulation" as jewelry, coins, and central bank reserves, the price of the metal doesn't need to rise very much to fill the void between supply and demand.

Gold stocks remain very expensive as of mid-1996. Many have P/E ratios over 50, without earnings growth to match. Some of these stocks will be cheaper in the years ahead even if gold does rise modestly over the long run.

INFLATION

Over the last 70 years there have been two periods when inflation rose at an 8 percent clip for almost a decade. The first was right after World War II began, when the economy strained to support a massive military buildup. The second began right after the 1973 Arab oil embargo, when the price of crude quadrupled in U.S. dollar terms. Between those two unusual periods, inflation usually averaged about 2 to 3 percent per year.

Many investors today worry a bit too much about inflation. Perhaps because so many experienced it directly in the 1970s, inflation has permanently biased the attitudes of an entire generation, just as the Depression did in the 1930s.

But the economy today is nothing like the 1970s. Low-cost technology has triggered massive changes in the world economy, and the resulting competition here and abroad should keep inflation at moderate levels for years to come:

- Low-cost technology increases competition by reducing barriers to entry. Small firms are able to compete effectively with large established companies because the low cost of computers and telecommunications provides good access to information and customers. For better or for worse, technology allows high-quality manufactured goods to be produced anywhere in the world. With increased domestic and global competition, monopoly powers are being stripped away. Companies today have very little pricing power. That's a far cry from the 1970s when firms like AT&T, Xerox, IBM, and Kodak could raise prices whenever they wanted. Not even OPEC has much control today. Expanded oil production in non-OPEC countries has reduced the cartel's share of the world market from 60 percent in the 1970s to less than 35 percent today. Without technology to help find new oil deposits, this wouldn't have happened.

- Technology increases competition for jobs among wage earners, putting a damper on wage growth. Computers and automation allow companies to get by with fewer people. Technology also makes it easier for firms to use outside help for high-wage projects. Facing tough competition, businesses are doing what they have to do, and employees are bearing the burden. Granted, there is evidence that wage growth will be higher in the years ahead after a long dry spell, but wage growth is inflationary only if it consistently exceeds productivity growth, and so far that hasn't happened. Furthermore, most of the current increase comes from an uptick in low-wage jobs where the overall impact on inflation is very low.

- Innovation and competition within the technology industry itself means that prices for technology-related goods and services will continue to fall, just as they have throughout the industry's 50-year existence. In the general economy, most businesses are spending more on computers and telecommunications as time goes on. Over the long run, deflation in technology-related goods and services should have a greater impact on the overall economy.

Some investors still believe that inflation will run out of control, not because of pricing pressures but because government debt will force the government to print massive amounts of new money to avert a budget disaster. Guess again. Total federal debt is now growing at a slower rate than Gross Domestic Product (GDP), which means that interest payments on the debt are shrinking as a percentage of the overall budget.

Increased exports of food commodities and technology-driven products are likely to keep GDP growing faster than 2.5 percent per year in the years ahead. That means an annual federal deficit of less than $150 billion is sustainable and will probably not undermine the economy over the long run.

Of course, it would be better if the deficit were zero and taxes were lower. Then the economy could grow even faster without inflation, bringing up the standard of living over the long run.

No doubt Congress will be working to reduce government spending and entitlement outlays for years to come, but the current mood in Congress and the line-item veto are likely to keep things on the right track. I suspect the U.S. will continue to be a model to follow as European countries and Japan struggle with mounting debts of their own.

4

Domestic Growth Funds

Growth funds aim for growth of capital, and most maintain portfolios that hold 80 percent or more in stocks. Some hold stocks that pay dividends, but generating dividend income is usually not a priority for this group. The typical fund in this group will have a lower dividend yield and higher P/E than the S&P 500. These funds usually carry more risk than the index, although there are a few exceptions. During a market decline, it is normal for these funds to decline more than the market. For this reason, you should invest only if your investment horizon is eight years or more and you are willing to accept a short-term loss of 25 to 30 percent if a bear market comes along.

Chances are you'll find Fidelity's best long-term performers in this group of funds. As I mentioned earlier, Fidelity's research advantage in domestic stockpicking puts it ahead in the game. Unlike the rest of the industry, Fidelity's domestic growth funds usually outperform the S&P 500 over a period of ten years or more.

Many funds in this group have a portion of their portfolio dedicated to foreign stocks, which is consistent with Fidelity's philosophy of looking for growth and value wherever it may exist. With a few exceptions, you can usually figure that foreign holdings will be less than 25 percent in a given fund. Fidelity managers sometimes hedge against foreign currency declines when holding a foreign stock position in a domestic fund. That way, the fund's risk level doesn't increase due to exchange rate fluctuations.

DOMESTIC GROWTH FUND CHOICES

Following is a fund-by-fund look at Fidelity's domestic growth choices. For all funds in this group, Fidelity reserves the right to block additional purchases after four trips in and out of the same fund in a 12-month period. Calendar-year performance for the group is listed in Appendix A. For suggested portfolios of growth funds, see Chapter 10.

Blue Chip Growth

Blue Chip Growth was started at the end of 1987. The fund's objective is to seek growth of capital over the long term by investing primarily in a diversified portfolio of common stocks of well-known and established companies. Distributions can occur in September and December. The front-end load is 3 percent and is currently waived for retirement accounts and the College Savings Plan.

Blue Chip Growth performed well during 1991 and 1992 under manager Steven Kaye; manager Michael Gordon also beat the S&P 500 in 1993 and 1994. Current manager John McDowell seems quite capable, but I have a slight preference for Large Cap Stock over this fund. Large Cap has the same basic objective, but its asset base is much smaller and should afford more flexibility. For investors in Fidelity's college savings program, however, this fund is the best pick for long-term growth when you consider the choices available with reduced minimums.

Capital Appreciation

Capital Appreciation's objective is capital appreciation from common stocks. It may invest in other securities such as preferred stocks and bonds as well as smaller, less well-known companies both here and abroad. Dividends and payouts of capital gains can take place in February and December. It carries a 3 percent front-end load, which is currently waived for retirement accounts.

Because of a manager change in 1996, this fund has become a bird of a different feather. Ex-manager Tom Sweeney used to go after cheap, out-of-favor cyclical companies. The fund often held down-and-out cyclical stocks as well as some unique utilities. *Forbes* magazine once described Sweeney's stockpicking approach as "roadkill with a pulse." All that went out the window when Harry Lange took over in early 1996. Lange is an ardent technology bull and a true believer in growth stocks.

Time will tell how Lange does at this fund, but I suspect that over time Capital Appreciation will take on the characteristics of Growth Company Fund. If you liked the old Capital Appreciation, your best bet is to move to Canada Fund, which is Tom Sweeney's current assignment (see Chapter 5).

Contrafund

Like other funds in this group, Contrafund's objective is capital appreciation. This broad-based fund tries to seek out undervalued companies undergoing positive changes and turnarounds. Distributions can occur in December and in February. It is sold with a 3 percent load, which is currently waived for retirement accounts.

Contrafund has been under the guidance of many different managers since it was started in May 1967. However, performance was subpar until Jeff Vinik became manager in 1988. Will Danoff, the fund's current manager, extended Vinik's winning streak after he took over in October 1990. Most of Danoff's great performance was achieved while running Contrafund like a traditional growth fund. Starting in late 1995 Danoff has been acting more like a contrarian (one who goes against the crowd). Fidelity has been encouraging managers to stick closer to their objectives and Danoff has picked up Contrafund's theme while continuing to do a great job in picking stocks.

For several years Contrafund was Fidelity's best five-year performer, and it became a popular favorite in the media. Unfortunately, this caused its asset base to reach the same league as Magellan. It won't be as easy for the fund to outperform in the future.

Still, Contrafund is an attractive fund because of Will Danoff's stockpicking skills, and Fidelity analysts have a good record with contrarian plays in other funds. To the extent that Danoff becomes a true contrarian, he'll certainly be backed up with some good research on the stocks he chooses from.

Disciplined Equity

Disciplined Equity is headed up by Brad Lewis, who has been with the fund since it started in December 1988. This fund seeks capital growth by investing among the S&P 500 stocks while maintaining an industry mix that is similar to the index. Distributions occur in December; the fund is sold no-load.

Disciplined Equity has outperformed the S&P 500 by about 1.5 percentage points per year since inception, and it seems likely to outperform the index in the future. Fidelity has been trying to establish this fund as an active alternative to a market index fund, but on a year-to-year basis there has been considerable variation from the S&P 500.

The fund was the first introduction in what is now a small family of quantitative "neural network" funds. Advanced methods of computer screening are used to identify stocks that are inefficiently priced. The computer programs were developed by Brad Lewis, and currently both Brad Lewis and other Fidelity researchers continue to make advancements in this area.

The computer-driven approach to stock selection is a bit like having a highly skilled fund manager sit down and review the fundamentals and pricing trends of hundreds (or thousands) of companies every day of the year. The approach works because it tends to identify opportunities as they emerge and not after the fact.

There are positive and negative arguments for screening stocks by computer. On the plus side, quantitative techniques take emotion out of the picture, and they are quick to detect changes in the market. They also evaluate all holdings on a continuous basis. But there are drawbacks. Quantitative screens only look at numbers. A computer program can't call up a company president and ask about plans to increase market share or cut costs in the next fiscal year. It can't detect an optimistic or sobering tone in a company's presentation. Traditional Fidelity managers and analysts do these things extremely well.

Over time, Fidelity's quantitative funds could provide a competitive edge for other funds that are currently run by traditional means. Don't look for Disciplined Equity to steal the show, however; its charter is too restrictive. If you are interested in the quantitative approach, go with Stock Selector, which has more flexibility and is likely to beat the S&P 500 by a wider margin over time.

Dividend Growth

Dividend Growth was started in April 1993 and seeks capital appreciation. Distributions can occur in September and December. It is sold no-load. This fund looks for companies that have the potential to raise their dividends over time, but many of its holdings are growth companies whose dividends are small to begin with. Although its risk is below average for the group, it is not a safer fund just because the word "dividend" is in its title.

Abigail Johnson (daughter of Fidelity chairman Ned Johnson) managed this fund with good results during its first year. Johnson adopted a strategy that could best be described as conservative growth. After moving over to head up OTC Portfolio in April 1994, she was replaced by Fergus Shiel, who took on a large technology position and benefited from the technology rally in 1995. Current manager Steve Wymer took over in May 1995 and gradually moved the fund back to a broadly diversified position with an emphasis on mid-caps.

Dividend Growth has posted strong results since inception, but some of its attractive performance stems from having the right management style at the right time. Still, Wymer has exceeded the S&P 500 over a period when most other funds have lagged. The combination of good Fidelity research and a focus on mid-cap stocks could make this fund one of Fidelity's better long-term performers.

Emerging Growth

Started near the end of 1990, Emerging Growth seeks long-term capital appreciation by investing primarily in stocks of emerging growth companies. Distributions are usually made in January and December. The fund carries a 3 percent front-end load (currently waived for retirement accounts), and there is a 0.75 percent redemption fee on shares held for less than 90 days.

Emerging Growth's price volatility alone qualifies it to be the riskiest choice in Fidelity's diversified growth arena, mainly because of its heavy position in technology stocks. Since inception, the fund has averaged about 1.8 for relative volatility, meaning that its price swings are about 80 percent greater than the S&P 500. Clearly this is not a fund for the faint of heart.

In theory, Emerging Growth should wind up with the group's best long-term returns because it takes on the most risk. It did in 1991, when the fund was up 67.1 percent, although 1991 was an unusually strong year for growth stocks. Since then, the rewards of taking the high risk path haven't been as clear-cut.

As of this writing, manager Larry Greenberg has recently been assigned to Growth Company in addition to his responsibilities at Emerging Growth. There's a reasonable chance he'll be replaced at this fund in the future. Aggressive investors may want to keep a close eye on any developments because a fund like this is heavily dependent on the skill of the manager.

Export Fund

A new introduction in late 1994, Export Fund invests in smaller, less well-known companies that may be sensitive to foreign economic and political conditions. Payouts of capital gains and dividends can occur in October and December. The fund carries a 3 percent front-end load, which is waived for retirement accounts.

Fidelity notes with interest that U.S. companies exporting a higher percentage of their business than the national average have outperformed the market on a historical basis. The theory is that any firm capable of producing products domestically and selling them in foreign markets must be doing things right because they are able to overcome language barriers, shipping costs, and duties while still making a profit. As trade barriers fall around the world, these types of companies stand to do well.

What really sets Export apart, however, is the fund's small-cap focus. Under manager Arieh Coll, the fund represents a relatively pure play on small-cap growth stocks. This makes Export's volatility relatively high, but in combination with its export strategy the fund could realize attractive returns over the long run. As of this writing, Export is still somewhat undiscovered with an asset base of about $250 million.

Fidelity Fifty

One of Fidelity's more unusual funds, Fidelity Fifty is run by Scott Stewart and was started in September 1993. Its objective is long-term capital appreciation; it invests primarily in equity securities of both domestic and foreign growth companies. Distributions can occur in August and December. It's sold with a 3 percent load, but as of this writing, the sales charge is being waived.

Fidelity Fifty differs from other funds in that it holds just 40 to 60 stocks instead of buying hundreds of companies like other diversified funds.

Like the funds that Brad Lewis runs, Fidelity Fifty relies heavily on a quantitative approach (see the earlier section on Disciplined Equity). In Fidelity Fifty's case, the final stocks selected for the portfolio are carefully considered by a review board and by Stewart himself.

Because this fund is less diversified than its peers, Fidelity takes extra trouble to assure a balanced industry mix. Sector by sector, this fund does not overweight industry groups the way some of Fidelity's other funds do. The result is that the fund's overall risk profile is actually less than some funds with more diversified portfolios.

To understand why this is, consider an earnings surprise in one of Fidelity Fifty's stock holdings. Even if an individual stock plummets 25 percent, the impact to the fund's share price is only about 1 percent. On the other hand, consider an overweighted sector position by a fund that owns hundreds of stocks. If a fund has a quarter of its portfolio in technology stocks and that sector declines 10 percent on unfavorable economic news, the fund could lose 2.5 percent with other factors being equal.

Fidelity Fifty's long-term performance is dependent on the quantitative models and the review process itself. So far, results have been mixed. The fund's approach dictates that most of its holdings be large-cap stocks for liquidity purposes, and that could shut out a lot of good mid-cap and small-cap stocks. If you want to go with the quantitative approach, Stock Selector is more diversified and has more long-term opportunity.

Growth Company

Introduced in January 1983, Growth Company seeks capital appreciation by investing primarily in common stocks and convertibles of companies believed to have above-average growth potential. Known in its early years as Mercury Fund, Growth Company distributes dividends and capital gains in January and December. It is sold with a 3 percent front-end load, but as of this writing, the load is being waived.

Ex-manager Bob Stansky made this fund a winner by outperforming the S&P 500 by about three percentage points per year over a nine-year period. New manager Larry Greenberg is likely to maintain the fund's focus on blue-chip growth stocks, although he seems to be more comfortable with faster-growing, higher-priced stocks. That could mean a higher risk level and larger declines during bearish periods.

Growth Company remains a solid choice but may be harder pressed to outperform the S&P 500 in the years ahead. Investors may want to consider Large Cap Stock, which follows a strategy similar to how Bob Stansky used to run this fund.

Large Cap Stock

Started in June 1995, Large Cap Stock seeks long-term growth of capital, investing mainly in equity securities of companies with large market capitalizations. The fund can distribute dividends and capital gains in June and December. It is sold no-load.

In some respects, manager Tom Sprague is emulating the strategy that Bob Stansky used with Growth Company: pick large, well-known companies that have consistent earnings growth and a stock price that isn't too expensive. It's a time-tested strategy at Fidelity, and Sprague has the advantage of running a relatively small portfolio. The only drawback to this fund is that it doesn't generally invest in mid-cap and small-cap stocks, a market segment that includes many faster-growing companies.

As of this writing, Large Cap doesn't have much of a track record, but I suspect that over the long run it will outperform the S&P 500 by several percentage points per year.

Low-Priced Stock

This fund was started in December 1989 and has a colorful history. Manager Joel Tillinghast has been running the fund since it started, and he has a dedicated team of analysts. As its name suggests, Low-Priced Stock seeks capital appreciation by investing primarily in a portfolio of low-priced stocks. Dividend and capital gains payouts can occur in September and in December. The fund carries a 3 percent front-end load (currently waived for retirement accounts), and there is a 1.5 percent redemption fee on shares held for less than 90 days.

Low-Priced Stock's focus on small-cap value has been a mixed blessing. While it has helped the fund to generate impressive returns with only moderate risk, it has also attracted too much capital. Since inception, the fund's cash level has often ranged 20 to 50 percent for the simple reason that it takes time to find attractive small-caps that comply with the fund's value-oriented restrictions.

Low-Priced has been closed twice in the past: once between March 6 and May 28 in 1992 and again between February 9 and September 20 in 1993.

The fund is less risky than others in this group for three reasons. First, it usually has a higher cash position than other growth funds. Second, it typically holds around 750 or more stocks, meaning that a large decline in any one stock has little overall impact. Third, small-cap value stocks don't usually react as much to the various economic events that often play havoc with S&P 500 stocks.

Provided that cash levels stay under 30 percent, Low-Priced has the potential to remain one of Fidelity's better long-term performers. Keep in mind that Fidelity may close this fund again someday. It may not be a bad idea to own a small position so that you can add to it in the event that new investors are shut out.

Magellan

Magellan's objective is capital appreciation by investing primarily in common stocks and securities convertible into common stock. Distributions are paid out in May and December. It carries a 3 percent load, except for 401(k) and 403(b) plans, where the sales charge is usually waived.

This famous stock fund got its start as Fidelity International fund in 1963, but shortly after inception Congress slapped a 15 percent tax on foreign investments, forcing the fund to change its charter. It was closed to new investors and did not reopen until 1981 after two other funds (Essex and Salem) were merged into it. Peter Lynch became manager in 1977, and his legendary stockpicking (coupled with the fund's small size at the time) resulted in about ten years of "golden" performance, in which annualized returns exceeded 30 percent. Investors took notice, and the fund grew by leaps and bounds after being reopened in 1981. By early 1986 it had crossed the $5 billion mark, and performance began to cool off, although it continued to do well. By the late 1980s, Lynch's workaholic schedule had begun to take its toll. In April 1990 Lynch announced his plans to "retire," and Morris Smith took over. Smith navigated the fund for about two years, then announced plans to move his family and live in Israel. Jeff Vinik replaced Smith and outperformed the S&P

500 while running the fund between July 1992 and June 1996. Vinik was widely criticized by the media for his "gunslinger" style, his personal trading habits, and an upbeat comment on Micron that was made right before he sold out $20 billion in technology stocks (Micron included).

Current manager Bob Stansky took the helm amid widespread media speculation that Magellan was too big to outperform. As of this writing, Stansky is slowly repositioning Magellan's portfolio, and he appears to be sticking with the bottoms-up stockpicking approach that served him well at Growth Company.

For ten years the media has been saying that Magellan is too big, and during the same ten years Magellan outperformed 85 percent of all other domestic growth funds in the industry. Magellan may be too big for the massive sector moves that Vinik was making, but under Bob Stansky it is not unreasonable to expect that Magellan will outperform the S&P 500 by two to three percentage points annually. After all, the fund is currently less than 1 percent of the U.S. stock market capitalization, and even if it outperforms it could take ten or twenty years before it becomes 2 percent of the domestic market. If Stansky does nothing else but avoid the overpriced stocks in the S&P 500 over the next decade, he'll easily be ahead of the game.

Along this line of thought, I continue to recommend Magellan. I don't think it's worth the 3 percent load charged on retail accounts, but for 401(k) investors (who usually don't pay the sales fee) it is still one of the best choices around.

Mid-Cap Stock

Mid-Cap Stock was started in March 1994. It aims for capital appreciation by investing in companies with medium-sized market capitalization. Managed by Jennifer Uhrig, the fund's goal is to outperform the S&P Mid-Cap Stock index. Distributions can occur in March and December. The fund is sold no-load.

Mid-Cap companies are generally known to have a market capitalization between $300 million and $3 billion, although the fund may include firms that are larger or smaller than those limits. Recent long-term studies have shown that mid-caps keep up with small-caps but incur less risk. This makes sense when you consider that many mid-cap firms are doing the right things and would not have grown to their present size otherwise. Many successful mid-cap companies are likely to become blue-chip stocks in future years.

Fidelity is likely to do well with this fund. I think Fidelity stands a good chance of beating the S&P Mid-Cap 400 index, and the mid-cap index itself is likely to outperform the S&P 500. Mid-Cap Stock stands a good chance of outperforming the S&P 500 over time.

New Millennium

New Millennium was started at the end of 1992, and it is currently closed to new investors. The fund's objective is capital appreciation, investing in all types of equity securities, favoring small- to medium-capitalization companies that show growth potential or that have the potential to exceed current earnings expectations. Distributions occur in January and December. Additional contributions for existing shareholders are subject to a 3 percent front-end load.

Manager Neal Miller is charged with using "change analysis" to identify stocks for his portfolio, the idea being to observe long-term trends in society and government and then figure out which companies will benefit. For example, the aging baby boom population will start to enter retirement in about ten years, pushing up demand for travel and leisure activities. Ideally, change analysis would uncover such trends just before they become widely recognized by the market. To date, the fund's largest position has been technology stocks.

New Millennium has produced a very good record while holding a unique blend of growth stocks, although some of the fund's strong 1995 gains appear to be a result of getting in on some attractive Initial Public Offerings (IPOs). Still, manager Neal Miller seems to keep overall risk lower than expected for a portfolio rich in high-priced stocks. Over the long term New Millennium should remain a good performer, but the fund's technology holdings make it one of Fidelity's more risky choices.

If you aren't currently a shareholder but you like the New Millennium concept, consider Export Fund instead. Export carries a slightly different theme, but like New Millennium it invests mainly in growth-oriented small-caps.

OTC Portfolio

OTC's objective is capital appreciation by investing in primarily in stocks traded in the over-the-counter securities market. The fund was introduced right at the end of 1984. Distributions can occur in September and December. The fund charges a 3 percent load, which is waived for retirement accounts.

OTC had an outstanding first year in 1985, achieving a 68.6 percent return. It went on to outperform the NASDAQ index until Alan Radlo took over from Morris Smith in mid-1990. Unfortunately, Radlo's sector bets were not the best, and OTC lagged the NASDAQ index during his tenure (although it was still slightly ahead of the S&P 500). Abigail Johnson took over in April 1994 and delivered performance comparable to the NASDAQ before turning the fund over to Charles Mangum in June 1996.

Mangum is off to a good start, and I suspect he will do well at this fund. Keep in mind that OTC tends to carry a relatively high risk level because it closely resembles the technology-heavy NASDAQ. Although it holds plenty of small-cap stocks, it also has exposure to many of the larger companies that dominate the index.

Retirement Growth

Formerly known as Freedom, Retirement Growth was started in March 1983 as a restricted fund available only for tax-deferred retirement accounts. The fund's objective is capital appreciation from investing primarily in common stocks, both domestic and foreign. Distributions occur in January and December, but in retirement accounts the payouts are simply reinvested with no tax impact. It is sold no-load.

The original concept behind Retirement Growth was to create a fund that could trade actively without creating large capital gain distributions. Fidelity must have felt that higher turnover would lead to better performance at the time, but it never followed through on the idea. Typically, Retirement Growth has maintained a lower turnover than its peers, and capital gain payouts have been average except in 1987 and 1992.

In recent years, this fund has been a poor performer. Ex-manager Harris Leviton was too defensive in late 1994 and 1995, and Michael Gordon's short tenure didn't help much. Current manager Fergus Shiel joined the fund in June 1996 and has been increasing its risk level. Investors may want to wait until Shiel is able to demonstrate good performance over a period of 18 months before buying this fund.

Small Cap Stock

Small Cap Stock has an objective of long-term capital appreciation, investing primarily in companies with a market capitalization of $750 million or less. It was introduced near the end of June 1993 and can distribute dividends and capital gains in June and December. Its 3 percent front-end load is waived for retirement accounts. There is a 0.75 percent redemption fee on shares held less than 90 days.

Small Cap is one of Brad Lewis's quantitative funds (see the earlier section on Disciplined Equity). In this particular version, the computer's eye is on domestic small-company stocks. Small Cap was launched with a conservative mix of industries, but changes to the fund's models have made it more growth oriented in recent years. Small Cap's flexibility and the greater volatility of smaller stocks make it one of the more risky funds in this group.

Like the international quantitative model, the small-stock model may need to be refined for a few more years before Small Cap Stock consistently outperforms. Once at its potential, the fund should be a good long-term performer, since opportunities abound in the small stock universe. Until then, investors may want to consider Export Fund for small-cap exposure.

Stock Selector

This fund is Disciplined Equity's more flexible cousin. Managed by Brad Lewis since its inception in September 1990, Stock Selector's objective is capital growth by investing in common stocks determined to be undervalued relative to their industries' norms. Distributions of dividends and capital gains occur each year in December. There is no load.

As with Disciplined Equity, Lewis runs a quantitative computer model to screen for attractively priced stocks (see the earlier section on Disciplined Equity). Stock Selector, however, is allowed more latitude to overweight industry groups, and it may invest up to 35 percent of holdings in foreign stocks. Until 1994, Lewis kept Stock Selector's focus on the S&P 500; after some improvements to an international quantitative model, Lewis began to include foreign stocks in the fund's portfolio. A 10 to 20 percent foreign position now seems to be the norm for the fund.

Stock Selector's extra freedom has allowed the fund to outperform the S&P 500 by about four percentage points per year, about three percentage points better than Disciplined Equity over the same period. If Stock Selector continues to outperform, and I suspect it will, it may end up one of Fidelity's better long-term performers.

Trend

Trend's stated objective is capital appreciation; it invests in securities of well-known, established companies as well as smaller, less prominent companies. The fund's manager tries to interpret trends in security prices and fundamental values. Trend pays out dividends and capital gains in February and December. The fund is sold no-load.

Created in 1958, Trend is Fidelity's oldest growth-oriented fund. It was one of Fidelity's high flyers during the "go go" years of the 1960s, when it was run by Fidelity chairman Ned Johnson. The fund hasn't done as well since then, lagging the S&P 500 most of the time.

Current manager Abigail Johnson could bring this fund back into the limelight. Johnson has a bias toward growth but tends to pick less expensive stocks. She will probably run Trend similar to how she ran Dividend Growth during its first year of operation. Trend is still a relatively small fund in the Fidelity universe, and could perform well under Johnson.

Value

Started in December 1978, this fund has also been known as Asset Investment Trust and Discoverer. Value seeks capital appreciation by investing in companies with valuable fixed assets or in companies believed to be undervalued based on company assets, earnings, or growth potential. Payouts of dividends and capital gains can occur in December. There is no load.

Partly because of its lower-risk style, Value was a laggard up until late 1990; then a string of successful managers began to turn things around. Brian Posner, Rich Fentin, Jeff Ubben, and Bettina Doulton all proved that a value approach has its rewards. Rich Fentin is now back again, and he has made this fund more value-oriented than ever. Fentin did well during his nine years at Puritan (see Chapter 6), and his appointment is particularly timely in consideration of the S&P 500's high valuation as of mid-1996.

Value is a good choice for taking the less risky path to growth-oriented investing. Even though it had a weak record in 1987 and 1990, the fund would normally hold up better than its peers during a market decline. Value has special appeal for investors who would otherwise index to the S&P 500. By going with Value instead, you can lower your risk level and perhaps improve upon your total return. Value owns many of the less expensive S&P 500 stocks, and I suspect it will be able to exceed the index by several percentage points per year over the long run.

5

International Growth Funds

Foreign investing has not been a strong area for Fidelity, but that could be changing as time goes on. The company is investing heavily in foreign research, as evidenced by an increasing number of foreign analysts—many of whom are located in the countries they are covering. In some ways, this buildup of a solid "research infrastructure" resembles Fidelity's expansion of domestic research in the late 1980s. Over time it could favorably impact the performance of Fidelity's international funds.

ADVANTAGES OF FOREIGN INVESTING

There are two main arguments in favor of investing outside the U.S.:

- Investing internationally adds an element of diversification to your portfolio. About half the time the U.S. markets move with the major foreign markets, and about half the time they move in the opposite direction. By blending foreign and domestic stocks together, the volatility of a portfolio can be reduced. (This is the same effect that occurs when you blend domestic stocks and bonds.)

Studies show that a blend of 70 percent in the S&P 500 and 30 percent in the Morgan Stanley EAFE (Europe Australia Far East) index will result in less volatility than either index by itself.

- The potential for faster growth exists in emerging market regions (although risk is substantially higher too). Emerging countries account for less than 10 percent of global stock market capitalization. Their share of world GDP is about 20 percent, and they include about 85 percent of the world's population. As emerging economies embrace free trade and privatize government-owned companies, their share of the world GDP will increase, raising the market capitalization of their stocks. The key question, of course, concerns how fast this will happen. At this point there appears to be enough sustainable economic growth to support the argument that stocks in emerging countries will grow faster than the S&P 500.

DISADVANTAGES OF FOREIGN INVESTING

Less known is the fact that foreign securities (and foreign funds) generally perform worse than their domestic counterparts on a risk-adjusted basis:

- Even in a large mutual fund, expenses are higher when investing internationally. Higher expense ratios are the norm, and brokerage expenses (which don't show up in the expense ratio) can be double or triple those of a domestic stock fund. Add the two together, and many international funds run with an annual performance drag of two percentage points or more.
- Funds investing in emerging markets are exposed to significant political risk. An ignorant leader or an offbeat political party can inflict significant damage to a small economy in a short amount of time, and any worldwide setbacks in the trend toward free trade and democracy

can take a significant toll on emerging market stocks. It's not unusual for this group to fall 50 percent in a bear market. Corrections of 20 percent are common even during expansion periods. In some respects, emerging market stocks behave like the U.S. stock market prior to World War II.

- In some foreign countries, a strengthening dollar could offset gains that occur in the local markets. After declining against the yen and mark for 25 years, the dollar's slide is coming to a close. Government debt and balance of trade figures are improving in the U.S. but are deteriorating in Japan and Germany due to years of stalled deregulation and restructuring efforts. The stage is now set for a long, steady rise in the dollar.

INTERNATIONAL GROWTH FUND CHOICES

Following is a review of Fidelity's international choices. (Calendar-year performance is listed in Appendix A.) As with other equity fund groups, Fidelity reserves the right to block additional purchases after four trips in and out of the same fund in a 12-month period.

Generally speaking, I tend to favor broad-based funds that depend on Fidelity managers to pick the countries. It's difficult to do well on your own when rotating through the world trying to pick the hot countries or regions. As with market timing, the odds of success are higher if you pick one or two diversified funds and stay with them for a while.

Canada

Canada's objective is long-term capital growth; it invests primarily in securities of issuers that have their principal activities in Canada. The fund was started in November 1987. Dividends and capital gains are paid out each year in December. The fund's 3 percent load is waived for retirement accounts. There is a redemption fee of 1.5 percent in the first 90 days.

Of all the single-country funds, Canada is the least risky because the U.S. dollar and the Canadian dollar have relatively high correlation (a natural result of proximity and the fact that the United States is Canada's largest trading partner).

About half of Canada's economy is based on natural resources, and this is reflected in the fund's portfolio. Canada's timber, natural gas, and various mining operations are likely to prosper over the long run, offsetting concerns over high government debt (per capita) and the Quebec separatist movement.

Performance for the Canada fund in the future is likely to be similar to the past (the fund's lifetime return is about 10 percent per year), but it could pick up under manager Tom Sweeney. Keep in mind that you don't have to own this fund to have a stake in Canadian stocks. Many of Fidelity's domestic growth funds maintain significant Canadian exposure from their position in energy or mining stocks.

Diversified International

Diversified International was started at the end of 1991 and seeks capital growth from investing primarily in countries that are included in the Morgan Stanley EAFE index. The fund focuses on companies with a market capitalization of $100 million or more and seeks to outperform the GDP-weighted EAFE index. Distributions are paid in December, and the fund is sold no-load.

Manager Greg Fraser has run the fund since inception at the end of 1991. Working with Brad Lewis, Fraser adapted the quantitative models used for Disciplined Equity and Stock Selector (see Chapter 4) for use in this fund. Initial results were disappointing, but after major changes in early 1995 the fund began to outperform. Fraser and Lewis appear convinced that they have a solid approach, because they added a foreign component to Stock Selector—also around early 1995.

I think Diversified International will outperform the GDP-weighted EAFE index over the long run, and it stands a good chance of becoming one of the better performers in this group.

Emerging Markets

Emerging Markets started in November 1990 under the name International Opportunities. In early 1993 it was renamed Emerging Markets and began focusing specifically on developing countries. It seeks capital appreciation aggressively by investing in emerging markets, emphasizing countries whose GDP is relatively low compared to that of the world's major economies. Distributions can occur in December. The fund carries a 3 percent front-end load (currently waived for retirement accounts), and a redemption fee of 1.5 percent is charged on shares held for less than 90 days.

Current manager Richard Hazlewood has been at the helm since June 1993. Although Emerging Markets Fund has focused mainly on the regions of Southeast Asia and Latin America, the fund is permitted to pursue opportunities anywhere on the globe. For this reason, it is a more diversified fund than Latin America, Hong Kong & China, or Southeast Asia Funds because it includes stocks from all of those regions.

In the long run, the performance of Emerging Markets will depend on the growth of stocks in developing countries, the manager's skill, and expense control. The fund aims to exceed the Morgan Stanley Emerging Markets Index, a group of world stocks that has the potential to exceed the S&P 500 by several points per year over the long run. Emerging Markets is likely to remain one of Fidelity's better-performing international funds.

Still, emerging market funds are not for the faint of heart. A short-term sell-off of 33 percent or more is possible if political or economic events take a turn for the worse. Because these types of funds are on the higher end of the risk spectrum, you have to be aware that a monthly gain or loss of 5 to 10 percent is a regular event. In order to control your risk, I recommend limiting your position in this fund (and other emerging market funds) to 15 percent of your overall portfolio.

Europe Capital Appreciation

Europe Capital Appreciation was introduced at the end of 1993 and seeks long-term growth of capital from companies that have their principal activities in Eastern and Western Europe. Distributions occur in December, and the fund's load structure is identical to Europe Fund.

Manager Kevin McCarey has tended toward a cyclical focus, but because of the region's sluggish economic conditions his performance has been slightly behind Europe Fund. Europe Capital Appreciation hasn't taken on more than a small position in the emerging markets of Eastern Europe as of mid-1996, but its stake could increase if better opportunities begin to emerge.

Absent of any significant emerging market opportunities, Europe Fund is probably the better choice of the two because of its lower turnover and its focus on the region's blue-chip stocks.

Europe Fund

Europe Fund is one of Fidelity's longer-running foreign funds, having started in October 1986. The fund aims for long-term capital growth by investing in the securities of issuers with their principal activities in Western Europe. Dividends and capital gains are distributed each year in December. The fund comes with a 3 percent front-end load (currently waived for retirement accounts), and a redemption fee of 1 percent is charged on shares held for less than 90 days.

Sally Walden has been running Europe Fund since July 1992. Before then, the fund was run by John Hickling and Penny Dobkin. Through mid-1996, Europe Fund has returned 11.4 percent per year for almost ten years, about even with the Morgan Stanley Europe index. Walden invests mainly in Europe's blue-chip growth companies, a group that could benefit if shareholders become more of a priority in the years ahead.

European securities involve currency risk, and Walden doesn't do much hedging in this fund because of the drag it creates on long-term performance. As a result, it is not unusual to see the fund's share price move up or down 2 percent in a day due to the combined action of exchange rates and stock prices.

Europe is a solid fund with a solid track record, and it may be one of the first funds to benefit from Fidelity's increased commitment to foreign research.

France Fund

Introduced in November 1995, France seeks long-term growth of capital by investing in equity securities of French issuers. Annual payouts can occur in December. The fund is sold with a 3 percent load (currently waived for retirement accounts), and there is a 1.5 percent redemption fee on shares held less than 90 days.

Manager Renaud Saleur has outperformed his respective French stock index during this fund's first year. Currently Fidelity is capping the fund's expense ratio at 2 percent, which is a good thing since its asset base is rather small.

Like other European countries, France's economy has been constrained by high tax rates, too many government regulations, and an abundance of government-provided or government-mandated social services. Driven by prolonged economic stagnation, the country's political leaders now seem determined to turn things around. If their reforms are successful, France's stock market could end up being one of the better long-term performers in the European region.

Germany Fund

Germany Fund began in November 1995. Its objective is long-term growth of capital by investing in equity securities of German issuers. Annual payouts can occur in December. The fund carries a 3 percent load (waived for retirement accounts at this time), and there is a 1.5 percent redemption fee on shares held less than 90 days.

Manager Simon Roberts is betting on an economic rebound in Germany, but so far his bet has not paid off. Part of the problem is the country's sky-high currency. The deutsche mark climbed against the dollar for decades, and in recent years the currency's strength has inflicted serious damage on the country's export businesses.

Relief may be coming. The German government has been running up large deficits trying to modernize former East Germany and in trying to stimulate the country's economy in general. Eventually, the currency markets could push the deutsche mark lower, giving a boost to exporters and the economy in general.

Unfortunately, Germany Fund may not see the full benefit of a lower deutsche mark. Suppose the deutsche mark falls 10 percent against the dollar, and the fund's stocks jump 20 percent in the German market. Unless the fund is hedged against a decline in the deutsche mark (unlikely with Fidelity's current policy on hedging), Germany Fund would only realize a 10 percent total return.

Unless Germany Fund can consistently outperform the the German stock index over the long run, I suggest that investors go with a more diversified fund.

Hong Kong and China

Introduced in November 1995, Hong Kong and China seeks long-term growth of capital by investing mainly in equity securities of Hong Kong and Chinese issuers. Distributions can occur in December. There is a 3 percent load (currently waived for retirement accounts), and a 1.5 percent redemption fee applies on shares held less than 90 days.

Almost all of this fund's assets are invested in Hong Kong, owing to the liquidity problems and foreign restrictions of China's small stock exchange. As of mid-1996, the Hong Kong market is cheap relative to other emerging markets because of the uncertainty surrounding the end of British rule. However, Hong Kong companies are quite healthy and are likely to remain that way. Unless the Chinese government restricts the Hong Kong stock market or strips away free-market privileges (neither seems likely), Hong Kong stocks are in a position to do well over the long run. Limit your total position in emerging market funds to 15 percent of your overall portfolio.

International Growth & Income

One of Fidelity's longer running funds, International Growth & Income was introduced at the end of 1986. The fund's objective is capital growth and current income consistent with reasonable investment risk. The fund invests principally in foreign securities. Dividends and capital gains can be paid out in December. The fund is sold with no load.

John Hickling is once again managing International Growth & Income. Hickling exceeded the EAFE index by an impressive four percentage points per year while running this fund during its first seven years. After running other foreign funds between December 1993 and March 1996, he is back at the fund where he built his reputation.

Hickling's success in international markets stems from the fact that he maintains a low turnover (which keeps trading costs low) and because he doesn't overweight specific countries or regions excessively. Hickling adds value through basic stockpicking, an approach that is likely to work as well in the future as it has in the past. If your main goal is to diversify your portfolio with some international exposure, this fund is a good choice.

International Value

Introduced in November 1994, this fund seeks long-term growth of capital by investing in securities of foreign companies believed to be undervalued in the marketplace or that possess valuable assets. Distributions can occur annually in December. The fund is sold no-load.

International Value is managed by Rick Mace, who also runs Overseas and Global Balanced (see Chapter 6). Mace has done well with this fund to date. His large moves in and out of Japan bear some resemblance to the big sector bets Jeff Vinik made with Magellan, but so far he has been right more often than wrong. Even when his mix of countries wasn't the best he did okay by picking the right stocks.

With Mace at the helm, I suspect this fund will outperform the EAFE over the long run, but it will probably be a bit more volatile than Fidelity's other diversified international funds.

Japan Fund

Japan Fund was started in September 1992, and it seeks long-term capital growth by investing primarily in securities of issuers that are organized under Japanese law or have their principal activities in Japan. Payouts for the fund usually occur in December; it carries a 3 percent load and a 1.5 percent redemption fee for the first 90 days. The load is currently waived on retirement accounts.

John Hickling managed this fund between June 1993 and September 1994. Since then, it has been run by Shigeki

Makino, who lives and works in Japan (Makino was an analyst for the fund while Hickling was manager).

The Japanese economy is in a unique situation. After years of restricting imports and building up domestic capacity to fuel its economic "export machine," Japan now has to deal with a strong currency that has made the country an expensive place to produce goods. Unlike Germany, which has been living with a strong currency for many years, the transition has forced big changes for all of the country's major export firms. Many have responded by moving their manufacturing operations into lower-cost countries. Few have restructured at home, and profits have nose-dived as a result.

The country's government has been trying hard to keep the yen from going any higher for fear it will bring dire economic consequences. Imported products are finally being allowed in, and the central bank accumulated a massive position in U.S. treasuries, which was somewhat successful in weakening the yen.

Once Japan's trade surplus is eliminated (which could occur in the next few years), the yen could begin a long, slow decline against the dollar. The Japanese government has taken on a lot of debt in its efforts to revive the country's economy, and without a positive trade balance the currency markets would start to see the same risk in the yen that has been seen in the dollar over the last decade.

A lower yen would be good news for the country's large exporters because domestic manufacturing utilization would rise, sales on the home front would pick up, and profits earned on overseas manufacturing would be worth more when translated into yen. Japanese stock prices, which are cheap relative to sales revenue, would see significant gains.

Although it could lose out from a declining yen, Japan Fund should still benefit enough from gains in Japanese stocks to perform significantly better than the S&P 500 over the next decade.

Japan Small Companies

Japan Small Companies began in November 1995, and it seeks long-term capital growth by investing mainly in equity securities of Japanese companies with a market cap of 100 billion yen (about US$1 billion) or less at the time of investment. Distributions occur in December, and the load structure of this fund is identical to Japan Fund.

Many of my assumptions for Japan Fund hold true for this fund as well, but keep in mind that small Japanese companies don't have a level playing field like small U.S. companies do. Political interests, heavy-handed regulations, and traditions still pose significant barriers to would-be entrepreneurs. Furthermore, until Japan's financial system gets back on its feet (which could take years), smaller Japanese companies will be starved for expansion capital as well.

If the yen drops sharply against the dollar, this fund could end up ahead of Japan Fund, but under normal circumstances I suspect that Japan Fund will be the better place to be over the long run.

Latin America

This fund was started in April 1993 and seeks high total investment return. The fund invests in the equity and debt securities of issuers that have their principal business activities in Latin America. The fund carries a 3 percent load (currently waived for retirement accounts), and there is a 1.5 percent redemption fee on shares held less than 90 days. Distributions typically occur in December.

As an emerging-market region, Latin America carries a lot more risk than other funds, but it also has the potential to deliver a higher long-term growth rate. Manager Patti Satterthwaite has done a good job of stockpicking but has sharply lagged the Morgan Stanley Latin America Index because of being in the wrong countries at the wrong time.

Latin America's high risk level comes from political and economic factors. Inexperienced leaders can make bad decisions, antireform movements can block progress, and expansion programs are highly dependent on foreign capital. As the Mexican peso devaluation demonstrated, a fund like Latin America can lose 50 percent of its value in months if things go the wrong way.

Nevertheless, this fund has good long-term potential. Under NAFTA and GATT many Latin American countries are seeing increased export opportunities, and Mexico in particular should enjoy many years of export growth as a result of the 1995 peso devaluation. Aggressive investors may want to include this fund in their portfolio, provided their total emerging market exposure doesn't exceed 15 percent. A less risky approach is to go with Emerging Markets Fund, which typically invests about one-third of its assets in Latin America.

Nordic

Introduced in November 1995, Nordic Fund seeks long-term growth of capital by investing mainly in equity securities of Danish, Finnish, Norwegian, and Swedish issuers. Distributions can occur in December. There is a 3 percent load (currently waived for retirement accounts), and a 1.5 percent redemption fee applies on shares held less than 90 days.

The companies in this region have generally given more priority to shareholders than others in Europe, even though the region suffers from some of the economic stagnation that has been a problem for Europe in general. A stable base of exporting companies and government deregulation could make for good long-term results. In the first year of operation, manager Colin Stone has outperformed the Nordic index he competes with.

Overseas

Introduced in December 1984, Overseas was Fidelity's first international fund. Its objective is long-term capital appreciation from investing primarily in foreign securities of issuers whose principal activities are outside of the United States. Payouts are made in December. The fund is sold no-load.

Overseas racked up strong gains under George Noble in 1985 and 1986 (78.7 percent and 69.3 percent, respectively) when the U.S. dollar made a major move down. Since 1987, however, performance has been less impressive.

As a mainstream international fund, Overseas is a solid way to invest in foreign markets, primarily Europe and Japan. Current manager Rick Mace has shown good stock-picking skills at International Value but is sticking with a more diversified approach for this fund. Over time, I suspect Overseas will perform slightly better than the EAFE index.

Pacific Basin

Pacific Basin started in October 1986. The fund aims for long-term capital growth, investing primarily in securities of issuers having their principal activities in the Pacific Basin. Countries within the fund's charter include Australia, Hong Kong, Indonesia, Japan, Korea, Malaysia, Singapore, Thailand, and others. Distributions can occur in December. The fund has a 3 percent load, and a redemption fee of 1 percent applies to purchases of less than 90 days.

Pacific Basin is a mix of mature and emerging markets, with Japan being the dominant equity market in the region. Manager Shigeki Makino (who also runs Japan Fund) took over the fund in May 1996 and has increased holdings of Japanese companies to almost 75 percent of assets.

From a risk standpoint, Pacific Basin Fund is slightly less volatile than either Japan or the developing nations of Southeast Asia, but it can still be characterized as an aggressive fund. Makino has a good handle on Japanese securities, but his ability to pick stocks in emerging Asian markets is not yet established.

Southeast Asia

Started in April 1993, Southeast Asia seeks capital appreciation. The fund invests primarily in securities of issuers having their principal business activities in Southeast Asia. The fund does not anticipate investing in Japan and so far has not taken on positions in Australia or New Zealand either. Dividends and capital gains are typically paid out in December. A 3 percent load is charged (currently waived for retirement accounts), and a redemption fee of 1.5 percent is charged on shares held less than 90 days.

As an emerging-market fund, Southeast Asia is more diversified than Hong Kong and China but more narrowly defined than Emerging Markets. The fund invests in countries that are likely to prosper through increased trade in the region (Hong Kong, Malaysia, Thailand, Korea, Philippines, and Singapore).

Manager Allan Liu has done reasonably well, when you consider the large amounts of money that have flowed in and out of his fund, but I see little benefit to choosing this fund over Emerging Markets. Both funds should provide similar long-term growth, but Emerging Markets doesn't have quite as much risk. In either case, limit your total holdings in emerging-market funds to 15 percent of your overall portfolio.

United Kingdom

Fidelity's original United Kingdom fund was introduced in November 1987 and later merged into Europe Fund in 1989. Today's United Kingdom fund was introduced in November 1995. It seeks long-term growth of capital by investing mainly in equity securities of British issuers. Distributions can occur in December. There is a 3 percent load (currently waived for retirement accounts), and a 1.5 percent redemption fee applies on shares held less than 90 days.

So far, this fund hasn't caught on any more the second time around. Its asset base is a tiny $2.2 million as of mid-1996—the smallest fund in this group. It's a good thing expenses are being capped at 2 percent.

Actually, the story for the United Kingdom today is a good one. After bowing out of the exchange rate mechanism in 1992, Britain was free to let its currency slide. Back then, that was a negative event, but the combination of a lower currency and relatively aggressive restructuring activity has made British companies very competitive in the European region.

Time will tell if manager Samuel Morse can do as well as Europe Fund and Europe Capital Appreciation (both funds are investing heavily in British firms as of mid-1996), but I suspect this fund will be a solid performer over the long run.

Worldwide

Worldwide was started in May 1990, and it seeks growth of capital by investing in securities issued anywhere in the world. The fund invests primarily in common stocks and other equity securities, generally focusing on companies in the three major world markets: North America, Europe, and the Pacific Basin. The fund competes with the Morgan Stanley World Index. Distributions occur in December, and the fund is sold no-load.

Penny Dobkin, the fund's manager since inception, has maintained a highly diversified portfolio and has focused heavily on value stocks. At times, she has taken on large cash positions as well. Although Worldwide invests in U.S. stocks as well as those of other countries, its domestic weighting is usually less than 20 percent. Dobkin's largest stake is typically in European stocks, and occasionally she takes on a small position in emerging markets.

Like International Growth & Income, Worldwide is a very low-risk fund and is a good choice for investors who want to reduce risk through international diversification.

6

Growth and Income Funds

Compared to growth funds, growth and income funds seek growth in moderation. A significant percentage of their portfolios is dedicated to income-producing securities, which are more stable and tend to reduce overall risk. The resulting lower level of volatility means that growth and income funds, on average, do not suffer as much in a down market.

The trade-off is that growth and income funds generally grow at a slower rate than their growth-oriented cousins. Historically, the long-term difference between growth funds and growth and income funds has ranged from one to three percentage points per year.

When choosing a growth and income fund, you don't have to worry as much about being in the right fund. There is less variation in long-term performance in this group because of the greater focus on income-producing securities. Fund manager ability, while still important, is not going to make or break a growth and income fund the way it can for a growth fund.

The way this group achieves income depends on the type of fund. Stock-oriented and equity-income funds generate income by emphasizing dividend stocks. Balanced funds earn income by investing in bonds as well as dividend stocks. Asset allocation funds earn current income by devoting a portion of their portfolios to cash and bond positions.

Most of Fidelity's growth and income funds have quarterly dividend payouts in addition to their annual distributions of capital gains. Investors often set up their accounts to reinvest this income, but some retirees use it to help cover living expenses. Although the yield is not large (2 to 4 percent is typical), the amount of income obtained should increase as long-term capital growth raises the value of the investment. Some investors view a growth and income fund as an income source that grows at a faster rate than inflation when distributions of capital gains are reinvested.

More often, however, investors choose a growth and income fund simply because it's more conservative than a stock fund. With reinvested distributions, the long-term growth rate of most funds in this group is likely to range from 8 to 10 percent per year.

GROWTH AND INCOME FUND CHOICES

Following is a fund-by-fund review of Fidelity's growth and income group. For all funds in this category, Fidelity reserves the right to block additional purchases after four trips in and out of the same fund in a 12-month period. For calendar-year performance, see Appendix A. For suggested portfolios of growth and income funds, please see chapter 10.

Asset Manager

Asset Manager was started at the end of 1988, and it seeks high total return with reduced risk by allocating assets among stocks, bonds, and short-term instruments of U.S. and foreign issuers, including emerging markets. Dividends are paid quarterly in March, June, September, and December. Capital gains are usually distributed in December. The fund is sold no-load.

This fund has a neutral mix of 40 percent stocks, 40 percent bonds, and 20 percent short-term. (Bonds with less than a three-year maturity are considered "short-term," as are cash-type holdings.) Asset Manager has limits for each of these asset classes as well as for foreign holdings: stocks must be in the range of 10 to 60 percent of holdings; bonds must be 20 to 60 percent of assets; and short-term securities may be up to 70 percent of the fund. The fund limits total foreign securities to 50 percent of holdings.

Fidelity implemented a team approach for this fund when it replaced manager Bob Beckwitt. Stockpicking is now the responsibility of George Vanderheiden, a long-time Fidelity veteran who has an excellent 15-year track record at Destiny I (one of Fidelity's long-running broker-sold funds). The asset allocation mix is the job of Dick Habermann, and bonds are selected by Michael Gray. Under this team, Asset Manager resembles a more traditional growth and income fund and is not likely to experience unusually good or bad years, as it did under Bob Beckwitt. Primarily because George Vanderheiden is picking stocks, I think this fund will be a good long term performer. The fund is likely to do at least as well as the S&P 500 in the years ahead, yet risk should only be about 60 percent as great.

Asset Manager: Growth

Introduced on the coattails of Asset Manager's success, Asset Manager: Growth was introduced at the end of 1991. It offers a more aggressive approach to asset allocation. Its objective is maximum total return over the long run by allocating assets among stocks, bonds, and short-term instruments of U.S. and foreign issuers, including emerging markets. Dividends and capital gains are usually paid out once a year, in December. The fund is sold no-load.

Run by the same team that leads Asset Manager, Asset Manager: Growth has a neutral mix of 65 percent stocks, 30 percent bonds, and 5 percent short-term. There are no limits on allocation percentages or foreign holdings, and the fund may invest up to 15 percent of assets in precious metals. Stocks are clearly dominant in this portfolio.

Asset Manager: Growth now looks a lot like the Destiny funds, except that cash and bond levels are a little higher. In effect, this fund lets you maximize the benefit from Vanderheiden's great stockpicking ability. Assuming that Habermann's asset allocation mix doesn't shift around too much, this fund will probably have about 75 percent of the S&P 500's volatility. Over the long run, I think this fund can outperform the S&P 500 by a few percentage points per year.

Asset Manager: Income

Introduced in October 1992, this fund was the last of the Asset Manager trio. Asset Manager: Income seeks a high level of current income by allocating its assets among stocks, bonds, and short-term instruments of U.S. and foreign issuers, including those in emerging markets. Dividends are paid out monthly, but usually January is skipped. Unlike bond funds, however, all income earned is reflected in the share price until the monthly distribution date. The fund pays out capital gains in December. There is no load.

The most conservative fund in Fidelity's growth and income group, this fund has risk on par with that of an intermediate bond fund. Run by the same team that manages the other two versions, Asset Manager: Income has a neutral mix of 20 percent stocks, 30 percent bonds, and 50 percent short-term. Stock holdings can be no more than 35 percent, bonds must range from 20 to 45 percent of assets, and short-term instruments can be 20 to 80 percent of the portfolio. Foreign holdings are kept below 35 percent.

Even with the new management team, this fund should behave similarly. Over the last four years, Asset Manager: Income outperformed most bond funds while maintaining comparable risk. The fund's income stream is not as high as most bond funds, but the difference should be made up in share price appreciation. For investors who are uncomfortable with losses, Asset Manager: Income is a good alternative to a money market fund.

Balanced

Launched in November 1986, Balanced seeks high income with preservation of capital. The fund invests in a broadly diversified portfolio of high-yielding securities, including common stocks, preferred stocks, and bonds. Dividend payouts occur in March, June, September, and December; distribution of capital gains usually takes place in September and December. There is no load.

Stephen Petersen took over at this fund in March 1996 and, compared to prior manager Bob Haber, has cut foreign exposure and increased stock holdings. The fund now looks a lot like Puritan and can be expected to perform better than it has in the past.

I expect Balanced to return about 10 percent per year over the long run. That's similar to how the fund has done historically, and it would represent a relatively attractive return for a fund that has only about 60 percent of the S&P 500's risk.

Convertible Securities

Convertible Securities was started in January 1987. It seeks a high level of total return through a combination of current income and capital appreciation. The fund invests mainly in convertible securities. Dividends occur in March, June, September, and December. Capital gains can occur in January and December. The fund does not carry a load.

The convertible securities market is an area where Fidelity has considerable expertise, which helps explain why this fund has been a good performer under many different managers.

Convertible Securities carries about 60 percent of the S&P 500's risk, and it can be expected to follow when the stock market makes a major move up or down.

Don't expect future returns to match those of the past with this fund. Still, with Fidelity's expertise, it's reasonable to assume that Convertible Securities will compare favorably against other funds with similar risk.

Equity-Income

Equity-Income was started in May 1966. It aims for reasonable income by investing in income-producing stocks. The fund seeks a yield that exceeds that of the S&P 500. Capital appreciation is a secondary objective. Dividends are paid in March, June, September, and December. Capital gains can occur in March and December. The fund is sold no-load.

As evidenced by this fund's 30-year return of 14.3 percent annually, Fidelity's equity-income strategy is one that has stood the test of time. This fund has had a string of successful managers, including Bruce Johnstone, Beth Terrana, and present manager Stephen Petersen (who has run the fund since August 1993).

Equity-Income invests mainly in the higher-yielding stocks of the S&P 500, although the fund also takes on small positions in convertibles and bonds. In recent years it has held 10 to 20 percent in foreign securities.

Equity-Income is a relatively sure bet for the long run because of Fidelity's research and its value-oriented strategy of buying high-yield stocks. I think the fund stands an excellent chance of outperforming the S&P 500 over the long run.

Equity-Income II

Equity-Income II began in August 1990. The fund seeks income that exceeds the S&P 500 yield by investing primarily in income-producing stocks while considering the potential for capital appreciation. Dividends are paid out in March, June, September, and December. Capital gains usually occur in January and December. There is no load.

Brian Posner did a great job with this fund by emphasizing turnaround situations. Rising star Bettina Doulton has done well at a variety of similar assignments and is likely to maintain the fund's attractive returns. Equity-Income II emphasizes capital appreciation a bit more than Equity-Income and usually maintains a slightly lower yield. The fund is similar to Value Fund, except that it has a more conservative bias.

Although Equity-Income II's large size precludes a repeat of its unusually strong historical performance, the fund is likely to be a solid performer in the future. These days, Equity-Income II does not offer any clear-cut advantage over Equity-Income, but it stands an excellent chance of outperforming the S&P 500 in the years ahead.

Fidelity Fund

The original Fidelity Fund got its start back in April 1930. Its current objective is to achieve long-term capital growth with reasonable current income by investing in common stocks and convertibles. Dividends are distributed in March, June, September, and December. Capital gains are typically paid out in August and December. It is sold with no load.

Fidelity Fund has exceeded the S&P 500 over the last 66 years, providing an annual return of 10.7 percent versus 9.9 percent for the index. The good performance seemed to be slipping in the 1980s and early 1990s, but under Beth Terrana, the fund seems to be getting back into the swing of things. Terrana, who proved her ability to beat the S&P 500 while managing Growth & Income and Equity-Income, has remained slightly ahead of the index since taking over in July 1993.

Under Terrana, Fidelity Fund is starting to look like Growth & Income did back when she managed it between December 1985 and October 1990. With a broad base of blue-chip stocks and a balanced industry mix, Fidelity Fund is likely to maintain a risk level similar to that of the S&P 500. With Terrana picking the stocks, there's a good chance Fidelity Fund will stay in front of the S&P 500 in future years as well.

Global Balanced

Global Balanced was started in February 1993. The fund seeks high current income with regard for both preservation of capital and potential for capital growth, and it aims for broad diversification by investing in stocks and bonds issued anywhere in the world. Dividends occur annually in December. Payouts of capital gains can take place in September and December. The fund is sold no-load.

This fund, which is run by foreign fund leader Rick Mace, should be considered an international fund and not a growth and income fund. (I've covered it in this group because Fidelity currently classifies it as a growth and income fund.)

Some of the fund's past volatility under manager Bob Haber came from exposure to emerging-country debt. Mace appears to be taking a lower-risk approach, but it's hard to say how his approach will work in the future. Compared to the other two funds he runs (International Value and Overseas), this one has a lower risk profile.

Global Balanced has the capability for good performance when conditions are favorable in foreign markets, but it can also lag when things go the wrong way. Until the fund has a longer-term track record, Worldwide (see Chapter 5) might be a better choice. Like Global Balanced, Worldwide is measured against the Morgan Stanley World Index. Although the two have similar risk levels, Worldwide may hold up better during difficult market conditions.

Growth & Income

Growth & Income was started at the end of 1985. It seeks high total return through a combination of current income and capital appreciation. The fund invests mainly in stocks of companies that pay current dividends and that offer potential growth of earnings. Dividends are paid in March, June, September, and December. Capital gains can be distributed in September and December. There is no load.

Like Fidelity Fund, this fund is one of the more aggressive in the group; it usually holds at least 80 percent of assets in a diversified mix of domestic stocks. It owes its attractive long-term performance to a string of top management talent, including Beth Terrana and Jeff Vinik. Current manager Steven Kaye has also performed well since January 1993, and his previous record at Blue Chip Growth was also a good one. Despite the fund's title, there has never been much of an income focus with this fund. As of mid-1996, bond holdings are near zero and the dividend yield on the fund's stocks is less than 2 percent.

Owing to its stock-oriented focus, Growth & Income is one of the better long-term performers in Fidelity's growth and income group. Under manager Steven Kaye, I think it will continue to outperform the S&P 500 by several percentage points annually.

Market Index

Market Index started in March 1990, and it seeks investment results corresponding to the total return of the S&P 500 while keeping expenses low. Dividends are paid out in March, June, September, and December. Capital gains can be distributed in June and December, but they are usually small with this type of fund. Market Index is sold with no front-end load, but there is a 0.5 percent redemption fee on shares held for less than 90 days.

The fund has been quite accurate in mimicking the S&P 500. Typically it lags the index by 30 to 60 basis points (0.3 to 0.4 percentage points) over the course of a 12-month period, reflecting the management fee and other costs of operation.

Despite several good years for S&P 500 funds, I think Fidelity investors are better off with actively managed funds for future years. Instead of this fund, consider Equity-Income or Value (see Chapter 4), both of which invest mainly on the value side of the S&P 500 universe.

Puritan

Puritan was started in April 1947, and it seeks high income consistent with preservation of capital. It invests in a broadly diversified portfolio of high-yielding common stocks, preferred stocks, and bonds of any quality. Dividends are paid in March, June, September, and December. Capital gains are usually paid out in September and December. The fund has no load.

Puritan has stayed with the conservative 60-40 mix of stocks and bonds with some variation for over 49 years running, and it has provided a 12.3 percent annualized return during that period. Rich Fentin, who ran the fund for a nine-year period ending in March 1996, returned 11.5 percent per year versus 12.6 percent for the S&P 500.

New manager Bettina Doulton, along with Kevin Grant for fixed income, is likely to continue to do well on a risk-adjusted basis. Doulton has a good eye for value and has been quite successful at other assignments.

Puritan is one of my long-time favorites; over the long run it tends to keep up with the S&P 500 while incurring just 60 percent as much risk. Recent management changes at Asset Manager and Balanced have resulted in both of these funds being positioned similar to Puritan. I suspect that over time all three funds will tend to perform somewhat similarly.

Real Estate

Real Estate's inception was in November 1986. The fund seeks above-average income and long-term capital growth. It invests mainly in equity REITs (Real Estate Investment Trusts), both domestic and foreign. Dividends occur in March, June, September, and December. Capital gains can occur in March and December, but in almost ten years the fund has yet to make any payouts other than dividends. The fund does not carry a front-end load, but there is a 0.75 percent redemption fee in the first 90 days.

Considering the conditions that prevailed in the real estate market, this fund's lifetime return of about 9 percent annually has been pretty good. Clearly it has done better than the millions of worthless limited partnerships sold in the 1980s by stockbrokers caring more about lucrative commissions than their clients' portfolios. When you buy Real Estate Fund, you won't find any misdirected priorities. Barry Greenfield's professional expertise has been at work with this fund since 1986.

This fund is on the aggressive side of the growth and income group because of its narrow focus on a less-liquid investment class, but measured by volatility it is similar to Balanced and Puritan. It has a higher dividend yield than other funds in this group, and it doesn't get hurt as much by higher levels of inflation the way stocks and bonds can.

Because of its low correlation with the stock and bond markets, this fund is a good choice for those wanting to add diversity to their portfolio. Supply and demand are coming into balance in the commercial real estate market, and yields remain attractive. I think this fund stands to do at least as well as the S&P 500 over the long run.

Utilities Fund

Utilities Fund (previously known as Utilities Income) was started in November 1987. The fund seeks high total return through a combination of current income and capital appreciation by investing primarily in stocks of public utility companies. Dividends are paid out in March, June, September, and December. Distributions of capital gains can occur in March and December. There is no load fee.

Utility stocks have a long-time reputation for producing solid investment returns, and they have often been favored by investors in their retirement years. These days, however, there's nothing utilities offer that can't be obtained by a diversified portfolio of high-yielding stocks. Many investors insisting on a portfolio of utility stocks would be better off in an equity-income fund or a conservative balanced fund like Puritan or Balanced.

Manager John Muresianu has been managing Utilities Fund since December 1992. Since taking over, he has increased the fund's stake in telephone companies. Even though their yields are lower, many telecommunications stocks have growth potential and could improve the fund's long-term return. Muresianu has reduced the fund's weighting of electric utilities because many of these firms will lose their monopoly advantage as a free market for electricity is created. The fund also has exposure to utilities that supply oil and natural gas.

Over the long run, this fund can be expected to do about as well as the S&P 500 with slightly less risk. Taking a large position in this fund is not a problem, but investors may want to consider Asset Manager, Balanced, or Puritan as alternatives. Over the long term, these funds should perform at least as well as Utilities Fund, and all three maintain less risk.

7

Bond Funds

Bond funds usually provide little or no capital appreciation over the long run. Instead, they focus on providing a monthly income stream. Over time, their total return is determined primarily by the accumulation of monthly dividends. Bond funds are generally considered to be a conservative investment, but they are far from risk-free. An intermediate-term bond fund has roughly 30 to 40 percent of the volatility inherent in the S&P 500. While a growth fund might fall 25 percent from its peak in a major sell-off for stocks, an intermediate-term bond fund might decline 10 percent in a similarly negative period for bonds.

Whereas corporate earnings are the dominant factor for stock valuations, bond funds are affected mainly by interest rates and inflation expectations. If interest rates are moving down, bond funds will usually rise in value. Conversely, if interest rates are edging up, you can expect a loss in principal.

SHORT-TERM VERSUS LONG-TERM INTEREST RATES

Changes in the yield curve (a plot of interest rates versus maturity) can affect different bond funds in different ways. Short-term interest rates are more or less controlled by the Federal Reserve, whereas long-term rates are set by supply-and-demand forces. When the Fed is trying to promote economic expansion, it will reduce short-term rates, increasing the spread between short-term and long-term rates; when the Fed is trying to fight inflation or slow the economy, it will raise short-term rates, which can cause the yield curve to become flat or even inverted. A short-term fund will be more affected by what the Fed does, but intermediate- and long-term funds are affected more by market forces. Suppose the Fed raises short-term rates to fight inflation. Long-term rates may increase as well if inflation concerns remain, but they can decline if the Fed's actions result in an economic slowdown (when expansion-related credit demand declines, it usually causes long-term rates to fall). In the latter situation, long-term bond funds can actually benefit from a rate hike on the short end.

INTEREST RATE SENSITIVITY

In general, the degree of interest-rate risk in a bond fund increases with the fund's weighted-average maturity (usually referred to as "average maturity"). Thus, a fund with a three-year average maturity will usually fluctuate very little, whereas a 20-year fund can be many times as risky. Most mutual fund companies, including Fidelity, are able to quote a fund's average maturity if you ask.

A more exact measure of a fund's interest rate risk is duration. A fund's duration tells you how much it would gain or lose in value for a one percentage point "across-the-board" change in interest rates, assuming that other factors such as credit risk are unchanged. For example, a fund with a duration of 5.0 would experience a 5 percent increase in principal if interest rates declined one percentage point, or it would lose 5 percent if rates went up one percentage point. Unfortunately, duration figures are not commonly available, and there is a lot of inconsistency in the way that they are calculated. I prefer the figures in *Morningstar Mutual Funds,* which come from an outside firm that makes calculations from each fund's list of securities. Morningstar's figures can be a few months old, but you do get an accurate comparison between funds.

CREDIT RISK AND EXCHANGE-RATE RISK

Credit risk, or risk of default, is another factor that can affect some types of bond funds. In U.S. government bond funds, this risk factor is usually not an issue because the government has the power to raise taxes to meet obligations. Bond funds investing in corporate debt carry some elements of credit risk, but most are diversified enough that a default by a single bond issuer would have only a minor impact on the fund. Once in a while a slowdown in the entire economy will cause investment-grade funds to lag slightly behind government funds, but interest rates are still the dominant risk factor. In the junk bond universe, a diversified fund can be significantly affected by credit risk perceptions. If the economy heads for a recession, the entire junk bond market can experience a significant sell-off as investors anticipate a higher default rate. Conversely, junk bond funds can be good performers when the economy is getting stronger. That's because the negative impact of rising long-term rates is partially offset by a corresponding decline in credit risk. These same effects can occur in emerging-market bond funds, where entire countries can be perceived as an improving or deteriorating credit risk.

Exchange-rate risk, or currency risk, is a third factor that can affect bond funds with foreign holdings. Unhedged positions in foreign bonds will fluctuate with exchange rates, and the resulting volatility can be several times greater than fluctuations caused by interest rates or credit-risk perceptions. For that reason, some bond funds hedge their foreign positions, meaning that they purchase currency-forward contracts to offset the exchange rate fluctuations. The drawback is that hedging is not free; it takes away from the fund's income stream.

YIELD

A bond fund's 30-day yield, which is calculated based on the SEC's definition of yield-to-maturity, is usually a reasonable indicator of what a bond fund is capable of earning when interest rates are flat. The 30-day yield is recalculated each day because it fluctuates with market conditions. Usually it goes up when a fund's net asset value (principal) declines, and it goes down when a fund gains value from falling interest rates. It's important to note that a bond fund's actual income stream may be higher or lower than its 30-day SEC yield. The actual income stream (sometimes called dividend yield) can be higher or lower than the 30-day yield figure if the fund holds bonds that were purchased at premium or discounted prices. A fund's income stream can also be below its stated yield if the fund engages in hedging activity on its foreign holdings. Due to the SEC's requirement that mutual funds calculate their 30-day yield independent of any "yield altering" transactions, hedging expenses are left out of the picture. As such, some foreign bond funds have rosy yields but fail to deliver the goods when the monthly income is posted to the account. New Markets Income has gone through periods when its SEC yield was two to three percentage points higher than the actual dividends paid out.

Fidelity bond funds don't reflect the accumulation of regular income in their share price. Fidelity tracks it separately and posts dividends once a month based on actual income less expenses. The dollar amount of the dividend can be figured by multiplying the fund's monthly mil rate (a figure Fidelity determines) by the number of shares in the account. When buying or selling in mid-month, you receive a partial month of income based on accumulated income at the time you leave the fund. The accumulation of income is based on the daily mil rates, which are figured for every day of the year. The only time you ever lose out on any bond fund income is when you buy a Spartan fund on a Friday. In this particular case, you don't start accruing income until the following Monday.

TAXABLE VERSUS MUNICIPAL

One of the first decisions you should make before buying a bond fund is whether to go with a taxable fund or a municipal fund. The income stream from a taxable fund is usually higher but is taxed along with your other income sources, whereas the income from a municipal fund is lower but is not taxed in most cases (although distributed capital gains and gains or losses from the sale of a muni fund are taxable events).

Generally speaking, taxable bond funds will offer the higher after-tax income stream if your federal tax bracket is below 36 percent. Nobody likes to pay taxes, but from a rational point of view it is best to go with the choice that will maximize your after-tax income.

Municipal funds avoid tax on their income stream, but the gain or loss in share price is taxed just like a regular fund (as are distributions of capital gains). In general, investors with a federal tax bracket of 36 percent or higher will realize a higher after-tax return with a muni fund. If you are subject to Alternative Minimum Tax (AMT), you may owe tax on some of the income stream, depending on how much AMT paper the fund holds. In this situation, you may be better off in a taxable fund—unless you can find a fund that holds very little AMT paper and you can call Fidelity periodically to monitor AMT holdings.

With the exception of Spartan Short-Intermediate Muni, all of Fidelity's municipal funds take on a lot of interest rate risk. Most have a duration of between 5 and 8, meaning that a one percentage point increase in interest rates can wipe out more than a year's worth of income. For that reason, I recommend a minimum investment horizon of three years. Over that period of time, the income stream is usually dominant over fluctuations in principal. If you'll be needing your money in less than three years, play it safe and go with Spartan Short-Intermediate Muni.

If you want to make an apples-to-apples yield comparison between a taxable fund and a municipal fund, first pick two funds with similar maturities. If you are considering Spartan Short-Intermediate Muni, compare it to Spartan Short-Term Bond or Spartan Limited Maturity Government. If you are looking at an intermediate- or limited-term muni fund, benchmark it to Investment Grade Bond.

Next, compare the yield of the muni fund to the taxable fund by computing a "taxable equivalent yield." The equation is:

$$\text{Tax-Free Yield} \div [(1 - \text{Fed Bracket}) \times (1 - \text{State Bracket})] = \text{Taxable Equivalent Yield}$$

Fed Bracket is your federal tax bracket in decimal form, and State Bracket is your state tax bracket in decimal form. (Use 0 for State Bracket if you are not evaluating a state-specific fund.) The formula takes into account the fact that state taxes are deductible at the federal level; that's why the federal and state brackets aren't simply added together. Two examples follow.

Mary

Mary lives in Connecticut. Her federal bracket is 36 percent, and her state tax rate is 4.5 percent. Using yield figures from mid-1996, Mary's taxable equivalent yield for Spartan Connecticut Municipal Income is

$$4.71\% \div [(1 - 0.36) \times (1 - 0.045)] = 7.71\%$$

Doing the same calculation for Spartan Aggressive (using 0 for the state bracket because Spartan Aggressive is a national fund), Mary comes up with

$$5.53\% \div [(1 - 0.36) \times (1 - 0)] = 8.64\%$$

Spartan Aggressive will generate the highest income for Mary. Although the fund has slightly more credit risk than Spartan Connecticut Municipal Income, the benefit of national diversification and a higher after-tax yield make it a reasonable choice.

Frank

Frank has a federal tax rate of 28 percent and is trying to decide between Spartan Short-Term Bond (a taxable fund) and Spartan Short-Intermediate Muni. His taxable equivalent yield for Spartan Short-Intermediate Muni is

$$4.06\% \div [(1 - 0.28) \times (1 - 0)] = 5.64\%$$

Because Spartan Short-Term Bond is yielding 5.94 percent, Frank will probably realize more after-tax income by staying on the taxable side.

Because of diversification, going the insured municipal route is probably overkill unless you are purchasing a state-specific fund. Although insured muni funds are a notch higher in credit quality, they fluctuate more with interest rate changes. In the end, overall volatility is higher, not lower, than that of an uninsured fund.

The possibility exists that a change in the tax code may some day grant taxable bonds the same tax-free status that municipal bonds now enjoy. If the playing field is ever leveled, most municipal funds would face a one-time lag of 10 to 15 percentage points relative to taxable funds. It would be like losing two years of tax-free income.

SPARTAN VERSUS NON-SPARTAN

Spartan bond funds generally have a small advantage in yield but carry higher minimums ($10,000 is required to open an account, versus $2,500 for most non-Spartan funds; additional contributions must be at least $1,000, versus $250 for most other funds). Unless your balance is $50,000 or more, your account fees will run $5 for exchanges and $2 per check. The fees can easily erase the yield advantage of a Spartan fund if you make frequent transactions. Only if you expect to maintain a balance of $50,000 or more (in which case Fidelity waives all fees) are the Spartan funds the clear choice.

TAXABLE BOND FUND CHOICES

As of early 1995 domestic funds in this group have gone "back to basics" by eliminating foreign holdings and maintaining a stable duration. As a result, these funds are unlikely to see a repeat of the poor performance that occurred in 1994.

Following is a recap of Fidelity's taxable bond fund choices. Except where noted, dividends are declared daily and paid out monthly. All of these funds are sold no-load. Those that have redemption fees are noted in the discussion. For all funds in this group, Fidelity reserves the right to block additional purchases after four trips in and out of the same fund over a 12-month period. Calendar-year performance is listed in Appendix A. For suggested bond fund portfolios, see Chapter 10.

Capital & Income

Started in November 1977, Capital & Income seeks to provide a combination of income and capital growth, focusing on low-quality debt and securities of distressed companies. Capital gains and excise dividend distributions can occur in June and December. The fund carries a 1.5 percent redemption fee on shares held for less than 365 days.

Originally known as High Income Fund, the fund changed its name and its objective on December 30, 1990. Today, as always, it continues to focus mainly on the junk bond universe, but after a five-year "experiment" with high-profile deal making, the fund is now settling on a strategy it can live with under manager David Glancy.

At least 75 percent of Capital & Income is run like a traditional junk bond fund, and Fidelity draws on more than 18 years of experience in the junk bond universe. Its analysts often figure out which companies are getting healthier before the bond-rating agencies, and the fund then profits from the rating agency upgrades. Here's one of many examples: In

1992, Capital & Income and Spartan High Income loaded up on Chrysler debt when it was still classified as junk, because Fidelity analysts were confident from discussions with Chrysler execs that the company was going to survive the recession. Both funds benefited from the high yield on Chrysler bonds and also realized a nice capital gain when the rating agencies upgraded Chrysler many months later. Time and again this game has been played, almost always to the benefit of Capital & Income shareholders.

Up to 25 percent of Capital & Income can invest in the stocks or bonds of distressed firms, usually companies with a heavy debt load. For about five years Fidelity had an entire "vulture investing" team that would buy up a majority stake in a distressed bond issue, then meet with the company's management to do a deal. It worked well for three years, but after some unexpected complications with two deals (Macy's and El Paso Electric), Fidelity decided to abandon the vulture investing approach. As of this writing, manager David Glancy is focusing on high-yield stocks for the distressed portion of the fund. Glancy doesn't think there's much potential for distressed bonds in today's market.

In both the traditional selection and distressed company plays, Fidelity's ability to assess risk has made its junk bond funds the industry's best performers over the last five years. Nevertheless, the opportunities in the junk bond market are somewhat sensitive to the economic cycle. Although junk bonds hold up reasonably well when economic growth is pushing up interest rates, these securities can perform poorly when the Federal Reserve goes too far in fighting inflation. In normal times, the yield premium on junk bonds (compared to government bonds) is about three to four percentage points, but at the onset of a recession it can go significantly higher as junk bonds decline in value.

Since inception, Capital & Income has returned 12 percent per year with about half of the S&P 500's risk. I expect future years will be almost as good, making this fund an attractive long-term performer. Investors with a larger balance may want to consider Spartan High Income because of its slightly lower redemption fee.

Ginnie Mae

Ginnie Mae seeks high current income and invests primarily in mortgage-related securities issued by the Government National Mortgage Association. The fund began in November 1985; distribution of capital gains can occur in September and December.

Like other funds that deal in mortgage securities, this fund typically earns a higher yield than a broad-based government securities fund. However, mortgage funds usually lag traditional bond funds when interest rates are declining—an effect that occurs because borrowers can pay off their old mortgages early and refinance at lower rates. With stable or rising interest rates, however, these types of funds tend to perform relatively well. Nevertheless, I think Mortgage Securities is a slightly better bet because manager Kevin Grant (who manages both funds) can pick and choose from a wider variety of securities.

Global Bond

Global Bond seeks high total return by investing principally in debt securities issued anywhere in the world. The fund was started at the end of 1986. Capital gains are distributed in February or December.

Being subject to both currency risk and credit risk in developing and mature markets, this fund has been one of Fidelity's most volatile bond funds. Manager Christine Thompson stands to bring some consistency to its investment approach, which has been on the wrong side of too many strategy changes by prior managers. Still, I don't think this fund offers any long-term advantage compared with domestic bond funds.

Government Securities

Government Securities seeks high current income free from state and local taxes; it invests only in U.S. government securities and agencies whose income is exempt from state and local income tax. Capital gains are usually paid in December. Most states allow you to avoid state and local income tax on the portion of income generated from U.S. Treasury holdings, but you still have to pay federal income tax on the full income stream.

Manager Robert Ives took over the fund in February 1995. Ives is sticking to a straightforward approach as opposed to the short-term trading techniques that prior manager Curt Hollingsworth used to boost returns.

Government Securities has essentially no credit risk, but it is one of Fidelity's more interest rate–sensitive funds. With a duration that is usually close to 5, the fund can gain or lose 5 percent with a one percentage point change in interest rates. Over the long run, this fund is likely to provide a total return that's higher than short-maturity funds but less than Investment Grade Bond.

Intermediate Bond

Intermediate Bond was started in May 1975; before 1988 it was known as Thrift Trust. It seeks high current income by investing mainly in bonds rated BBB or better with a weighted average maturity of between three and ten years. Payouts of capital gains can occur in June and December.

Manager Christine Thompson took over this fund in October 1995, and she is running it slightly more conservatively than prior manager Michael Gray. Overall, Intermediate Bond carries slightly more credit risk than government funds but less than Fidelity's investment-grade funds. Interest rate risk is average with a duration of around four.

The fund is a good choice for bond investors who don't want any fancy footwork—just good solid performance that won't create any surprises when times get tough.

Investment Grade Bond

Investment Grade Bond seeks high current income consistent with reasonable risk. It invests in a broad range of investment-grade fixed-income securities. The fund was started in August 1971; before 1992, it was known as Flexible Bond. Capital gains can be paid out in June and December.

Michael Gray has been at the helm since September 1987. This fund has more latitude than others to vary credit quality and duration. While Gray has benefited from this freedom in the past, he has been less willing to go out on a limb in recent years.

Over its life this fund has returned about 8.5 percent per year on an annualized basis. I expect future years to bring slightly lower returns.

Mortgage Securities

Mortgage Securities was started at the end of 1984. It seeks high current income and invests in mortgage-related securities of all types. Capital gains can be paid in September and December.

Compared to Ginnie Mae, this fund has more flexibility to seek out opportunities in the mortgage arena. Manager Kevin Grant has run the fund since July 1993, and he was one of the few bond managers who performed well in 1994's bear market.

The fund usually has a higher yield than investment-grade funds, and it tends to perform well when interest rates are stable or rising modestly. When rates are falling, however, it won't benefit as much as traditional bond funds. That's because borrowers can pay off their old mortgages early and refinance at lower rates. Over the long run I anticipate returns to range 7 to 8 percent annually.

New Markets Income

New Markets Income was started in May 1993, and it seeks high current income with capital appreciation as a secondary objective. The fund invests at least 65 percent of its assets in debt securities issued in emerging countries. The fund pays particular attention to countries with relatively low GDP per capita, as these have the potential for rapid economic growth. There is a 1 percent redemption fee on shares held less than 180 days.

With its focus on emerging-country debt, New Markets Income is by far the most risky fund in this group; it's even more risky than many stock funds. Since inception, the fund has invested primarily in Latin America, where political uncertainty and dramatic capital flows have resulted in a roller coaster ride for investors. Mexico's financial crisis caused a large sell-off for the fund, but it recovered in 1996. If Fidelity can add value with this fund the way it did with its junk funds, New Markets Income may end up with strong performance to go along with its high risk level. If you invest, don't bet the farm. Limit New Markets Income to no more than 15 percent of your income-oriented holdings and be willing to see results over the long term.

Short-Intermediate Government

Started in September 1991, Short-Intermediate Government seeks a high level of current income consistent with preservation of capital by investing mainly in U.S. government securities. Before 1992, the fund was known as Limited Maturity Government; at that time it maintained a longer average maturity. Payouts of capital gains can occur in November and December.

With a duration of around 2.5 and a focus on securities backed directly by the U.S. government, this fund has the least credit risk and very low interest rate risk relative to Fidelity's other bond funds. Unfortunately, it also has the lowest yields most of the time.

Short-Intermediate Government is a good choice for the investor who would otherwise remain in a money market fund. Depending on the shape of the yield curve, the fund usually has an income stream that's 50 to 200 basis points higher than a government money market fund.

Short-Term Bond

Short-Term Bond was started in September 1986 and seeks high current income consistent with preservation of principal. It invests primarily in a broad range of investment-grade fixed-income securities; the fund maintains a weighted average maturity of three years or less. Capital gains are usually small if they occur at all; they can be distributed in June and December.

Short-Term Bond is essentially a short-maturity version of Investment Grade Bond. The fund has always kept interest rate risk low but in the past has ventured out on the credit risk side. Its small position in Latin American debt was largely responsible for its 4 percent loss in 1994.

Current manager Charles Morrison has sold all of the fund's foreign debt and is now maintaining a high-quality domestic-only portfolio. As such, Short-Term Bond remains one of my favorite alternatives for investors who would otherwise keep their dollars in a money market fund. It has averaged a lifetime return of 6.6 percent per year and is likely to provide similar returns in the future.

Spartan Ginnie Mae

Spartan Ginnie Mae started at the end of 1990. It seeks a high level of current income by investing mainly in mortgage-related securities issued by the Government National Mortgage Association. Capital gain payouts can occur in October and December.

Spartan Ginnie Mae usually has a slightly higher yield and a slightly lower expense ratio than Ginnie Mae. In a typical year, you can expect it to outperform Ginnie Mae by about 10 to 20 basis points (0.1 percent to 0.2 percent). As such, it's a better choice than Ginnie Mae if you can meet the minimums and you don't expect a lot of transaction fees for checks and redemptions.

Manager Kevin Grant took over this fund and its non-Spartan twin in February 1995. He also manages Mortgage Securities, where he has performed quite well.

This fund's universe is somewhat restricted in comparison with Mortgage Securities, which can invest in a wider variety of securities. Assuming Grant continues to run both funds, Mortgage Securities would seem to have a slight edge over the long run.

Spartan Government Income

Spartan Government Income began in December 1988 and seeks a high level of current income by investing in U.S. government securities and related issues. Capital gains can be distributed in June and December.

This fund was the first of the Spartan series. As government funds go, its portfolio is relatively broad-based. Typically, the fund keeps a modest position in mortgage-related securities with the balance in Treasuries and other agency obligations. As you might expect, it has very low credit risk.

With a duration of around 5, however, the fund can gain or lose about 5 percent for each percentage point change in interest rates. This makes it one of the more interest rate–sensitive choices in the taxable bond group.

There isn't much difference between this fund and Government Securities. As such, I prefer Government Securities for its lower minimums.

Spartan High Income

Spartan High Income started in August 1990, and it seeks high current yields available from high-yielding lower-quality, fixed-income securities. Growth of capital may also be considered when it's consistent with seeking high current income. Capital gains and any excise distributions can occur in June and December. There is a 1 percent redemption fee on shares held less than 270 days.

Spartan High Income is more of a pure play on junk bonds than Capital & Income. Recently, however, manager Thomas Soviero has put a small portion of the fund in distressed dividend stocks. Like Capital & Income, this fund should benefit from Fidelity's expertise in the junk bond universe (see the earlier section on Capital & Income).

Soviero seems to be using Fidelity's high-yield research to his advantage since taking over Spartan High Income in January 1996. Even so, don't expect the fund to repeat its winning record in 1991, 1992, and 1993. Those years were a rare opportunity for junk bond investors. In the long term, I expect Spartan High Income to perform about as well as Capital & Income, perhaps around 10 percent per year over the long run. That's a good return for a fund with less than half the risk of the S&P 500, but keep in mind that performance can be poor at the onset of a recession.

Spartan Investment Grade Bond

Spartan Investment Grade Bond was introduced in October 1992, and it seeks high current income. The fund invests in a broad range of fixed-income securities and holds at least 65 percent of total assets in corporate debt securities of investment-grade quality. Capital gains can be paid in June and December.

Manager Michael Gray also runs Investment Grade Bond, which tends to perform similar to this fund but is usually 10 to 20 basis points lower in its 30-day yield.

As a medium-maturity corporate bond fund, Spartan Investment Grade Bond is likely to be one of Fidelity's better long-term performers. I suspect the fund will perform at least as well as Investment Grade Bond over the long run, providing long-term returns in the range of 7 to 8 percent per year.

Spartan Limited Maturity Government

This fund was started in May 1988, and it seeks as high a level of current income as is consistent with preservation of capital; it invests primarily in U.S. government and agency obligations, including repurchase agreements secured by U.S. government obligations. Capital gains can be paid out in September and December.

This fund is a tiny bit higher in credit risk than Short-Intermediate Government and Spartan Short-Intermediate Government. In the real world, however, it will probably never make a difference.

I favor Short-Term Bond or Spartan Short-Term Bond for obtaining the best yields without much interest rate risk. If you want to avoid credit risk too, this fund probably is the best choice among short-maturity funds. Over the long term, it will probably exceed the return on a money market fund by 1.0 to 2.5 percentage points per year.

Spartan Short-Intermediate Government

Started at the end of 1992, Spartan Short-Intermediate Government seeks as high a level of current income as is consistent with preservation of capital. It invests primarily in securities backed by the full faith and credit of the U.S. government as well as repurchase agreements secured by those obligations. The fund can also purchase options and futures contracts. Capital gains are paid out in June and December.

This fund is similar to Short-Intermediate Government, but it carries a yield that's 10 to 20 basis points higher.

Although the difference is not likely to be great, I have a slight preference for Spartan Limited Maturity Government for those looking for a short-term fund without much credit risk. If you can tolerate an investment-grade portfolio, consider Short-Term Bond or Spartan Short-Term Bond, both of which should provide an even higher yield while keeping interest rate risk low.

Spartan Short-Term Bond

This fund was established in October 1992. Spartan Short-Term Bond is a Spartan clone of Short-Term Bond; it has an identical objective and is also run by manager Charles Morrison. Capital gains can be paid out in June or December; usually the payouts are small if they occur at all.

Like Short-Term Bond, this fund also performed poorly in 1994 due to its small Latin American bond position. Under its revised strategy of holding high-quality domestic-only bonds, performance should be more consistent in future years. The fund's yield is usually about 10 to 20 basis points better than Short-Term Bond, but unless you are over the $50,000 fee waiver threshold, Short-Term Bond is probably the better bet.

Target Timeline 1999

Target Timeline 1999 seeks an annual total return within 0.5 percent of the fund's quoted yield at the time of purchase—assuming the fund is held to maturity and all distributions are reinvested. The fund's focus since inception has been investment-grade corporate bonds. Capital gains are distributed in September and December. At the end of the investment period (September 1999 for this fund), you can have your shares redeemed or you can "roll over" your capital into another fund. There is a 0.5 percent fee if you redeem shares in the first 90 days.

Fidelity introduced the Timeline funds for investors who would normally buy an individual bond instead of a bond fund. There's no guarantee you'll get the quoted yield as your total return if you hold the fund to maturity, but odds are you'll be quite close. Managing a fund like this isn't any harder than running an index fund. Over time the duration (and the interest rate risk) of this fund will decline as it nears its "maturity" date of September 1999.

Although this fund is designed to be held to maturity, there is no requirement to do so. Timeline 1999 is essentially an investment-grade bond fund with an average maturity that becomes shorter as time goes on.

Target Timeline 2001

Like Timeline 1999, this fund also aims for a lifetime annual total return within 0.5 percent of quoted yield at the time of purchase with reinvested distributions. Capital gains payouts can occur in September and December. When September 2001 arrives, your capital can be placed in another fund. A 0.5 percent fee applies if you redeem shares in the first 90 days.

Like Timeline 1999, this fund invests primarily in investment-grade corporate bonds. As of mid-1996, its interest rate sensitivity is similar to Investment Grade Bond, but over time it will become less interest-rate sensitive.

Target Timeline 2003

Like the other two in this series, Timeline 2003 seeks a lifetime annual total return within 0.5 percent of the fund's quoted yield at the time of purchase, assuming all distributions are reinvested. Like the other two Timeline funds, it invests mainly in investment-grade corporate bonds. Capital gains payouts can occur in September and December. At the end of the investment period (September 2003), you can redeem or move into another fund. A 0.5 percent redemption fee applies for the first 90 days.

This fund can be used for a "protected" bet on a decline in long-term interest rates (if any new Timeline funds are available, you'll want to use the one with the longest horizon). Here's how it works: First, invest a sum of money you won't need until the maturity date. If interest rates move down and you realize a large gain in share price, you can sell and take the profits. On the other hand, if interest rates rise and the share price goes down, you simply hold the fund until maturity and obtain an annual return similar to what the 30-day yield was at purchase. There's no guarantee that you'll do better than the fund's lifetime return if you sell early, but this approach is one way to bet on lower interest while knowing you can still earn a decent return if you're wrong.

MUNICIPAL BOND FUND CHOICES

Following is a recap of Fidelity's municipal bond fund choices. Except where noted, dividends are declared daily and paid out monthly. All of these funds are sold with no front-end load. Some have redemption fees, which are noted in their respective section. For all funds in this group, Fidelity reserves the right to block additional purchases after four trips in and out of the same fund in a 12-month period. Calendar-year performance is listed in Appendix A. For suggested bond fund portfolios, see Chapter 10. Many funds in this group were renamed in 1996, replacing the phrase "Tax-Free" with "Municipal Income".

Aggressive Municipal

This fund started in September 1985. It seeks high current income that is free from federal tax by investing primarily in medium- and lower-quality municipal bonds with typical maturities of 20 years or more. Distribution of capital gains can occur in February and December. There is a 1 percent redemption fee on shares held for less than 180 days.

Aggressive has some resemblance to a high-yield (junk) fund, with two important distinctions. First, the fund usually keeps about 50 percent of its portfolio in higher-quality issues. Second, nonrated municipal bonds tend to have a much lower default rate than corporate junk bonds. That's because the issuers usually aren't liquidated; they usually stay around and work out a way to pay their debt.

Therefore, while Aggressive Municipal may seem like a risky fund, the truth is that its volatility isn't usually any worse than higher-quality municipal funds.

In some states, Aggressive's yield premium over a state-specific fund will be high enough to more than make up for the state income tax you'll pay on the fund's income stream. (This is often true for Spartan Aggressive as well.) In effect, you can get the benefit of national diversification without any performance penalty.

This fund is one of my favorites for maximum tax-free income. Keep in mind that its interest rate risk, while slightly lower than other long-term muni bond funds, is still significant.

California Insured

Started in September 1986, California Insured seeks high current income exempt from federal and California state personal income tax. The fund invests primarily in municipal securities that are covered by issuer or portfolio insurance, guaranteeing the timely payment of principal and interest. Distributions of capital gains can occur in April and December. The fact that this fund holds insured bonds does not prevent it realizing a loss if interest rates go up.

Despite the fact that insured municipal bonds yield slightly less than investment-grade issues, California Insured has performed as well as California Municipal Income. Unlike other insured funds in the industry, California Insured is allowed to put some of its portfolio into noninsured bonds, and the flexibility helps to boost returns. Historically, the fund has kept about 25 percent in noninsured issues, but it is allowed to hold up to 35 percent.

California Municipal Income

This fund was introduced in July 1984. It seeks high current income exempt from federal and California state personal income tax. The fund invests primarily in investment-grade municipal securities. Payouts of capital gains can occur in April and December.

Jonathan Short took over this fund in early 1995, and he also manages California Insured, Spartan California Municipal Income, and Spartan California Intermediate.

Although the yield from this fund is a hair less than Spartan California Municipal Income, it boasts a solid long-term record and has no redemption fee.

Insured Municipal Income

Insured seeks high current income free from federal income tax and consistent with preserving principal. It invests primarily in municipal securities covered by issuer or portfolio insurance, guaranteeing the timely payment of principal and interest. The fund began in November 1985. Distributions of capital gains can occur in February and December. The fact that this fund holds insured bonds does not prevent losses due to higher interest rates.

Credit quality is top-notch in this fund because insured obligations must make up at least 65 percent of the fund's portfolio. (The fund has typically held 80 percent.) Still, Insured has slightly greater volatility than do other muni funds, owing to its higher interest rate sensitivity. Unlike lower-grade funds, Insured does not benefit from the improvement in credit risk that can slightly offset the negative impact of rising interest rates. A one percentage point increase in long-term interest rates can result in an 8 to 10 percent decline in share price. Although the income stream on this fund is usually lower than its uninsured counterparts, it still has a good long-term return.

Insurance can make sense when buying an individual muni bond or a state-specific fund. In a national muni fund, however, the risk of default is already reduced by diversification; you might as well enjoy the higher income stream of a lower-grade portfolio. On the other hand, if it is risk in general you want to avoid, the best municipal choice is Spartan Short-Intermediate Muni.

Limited Term Municipal Income

Limited Term was started in April 1977, and it seeks the highest level of current income that is free of federal income tax and consistent with preserving principal. The fund invests primarily in high- and upper-medium-quality municipal obligations. It maintains an average dollar-weighted portfolio maturity of 12 years or less. Payouts of capital gains can occur in February and December.

One has to question how "limited" a portfolio is when it carries a duration that seldom dips below 5. Limited Term's risk level is a bit lower than that of the long-term funds, but the difference is not that great.

Still, the fund has a good long-term track record, with an annualized return of 6.6 percent over the last 17 years. Future returns may be about a percentage point lower because interest rates are likely to remain below the unusually high levels of the 1980s.

Massachusetts Municipal Income

This fund started in 1983. It seeks high current income exempt from federal and Massachusetts state personal income tax. It invests primarily in investment-grade municipal bonds. Capital gains can be paid out in March and December.

This is an excellent long-term performer that can provide relief from Massachusetts's relatively high maximum tax bracket. The fund's portfolio is basically investment-grade, but it often includes 15 to 20 percent lower-grade issues.

Michigan Municipal Income

Michigan Municipal Income started in November 1985. The fund seeks high current income exempt from federal and Michigan state personal income tax. It also seeks to distribute income exempt from certain business or corporate taxes. It invests primarily in investment-grade municipal bonds. Capital gains can be paid in February and December.

Like most of Fidelity's other state funds, this fund has a solid record. Its investment-grade portfolio often includes 15 to 20 percent lower-grade issues.

Minnesota Municipal Income

Minnesota Municipal Income started in December 1985. It seeks high current income exempt from federal and Minnesota state personal income tax. The fund invests primarily in investment-grade municipal bonds. Capital gains can be distributed in February and December.

Minnesota Municipal Income has less latitude than other state funds, partly because the state's muni bonds tend to be high-quality issues and partly because the state allows only a 5 percent stake in issues from other states. As such, the fund's total return tends to be slightly less than Fidelity's other state-specific funds.

Municipal Income

Formerly called High Yield, this fund was started in December 1977 and seeks high current income that is free of federal income tax. The fund focuses primarily on investment-grade municipal bonds. Payouts of capital gains can occur in January and December.

With a restriction that limits lower-grade issues to 25 percent or less of the portfolio, the result is a mainstream investment-grade muni fund. Municipal Income has a respectable long-term track record with an annualized return of 7.5 percent since inception 19 years ago. I suspect that future returns will be slightly lower.

New York Insured

New York Insured began in October 1985. The fund seeks high current income, exempt from federal, New York state, and New York City personal income tax. It invests primarily in municipal securities covered by insurance that guarantees the timely payment of principal or interest. Distributions of capital gains can occur in March and December. The fact that this fund holds insured bonds does not prevent losses due to higher interest rates.

With about one-quarter of the fund devoted to uninsured issues (the fund can hold up to 35 percent in investment-grade munis), this fund keeps up pretty well with New York Municipal Income. A good choice for hedging against any potential state-related credit problems.

New York Municipal Income

New York Municipal Income began in July 1984. It seeks high current income exempt from federal, New York state, and New York City personal income tax. The fund invests primarily in investment-grade municipal securities. Distributions of capital gains can occur in March and December. Although the yield from this fund is a bit less than Spartan New York Municipal Income, it boasts a solid long-term record and has no redemption fee.

Ohio Municipal Income

Started in November 1985, Ohio Municipal Income seeks high current income exempt from federal and Ohio state personal income tax. The fund also seeks to distribute income exempt from certain business or corporate taxes. The fund invests primarily in investment-grade municipal bonds. Capital gains distributions can occur in February and December.

Like Fidelity's other single-state muni funds, Ohio Municipal Income has a very respectable long-term record. Its investment-grade portfolio often includes 15 to 20 percent lower-grade issues.

Spartan Aggressive

Spartan Aggressive was introduced in April 1993, and it seeks a high current yield free of federal income tax. The fund invests in municipal securities of any quality, with an emphasis on lower-quality securities. Distributions of capital gains can take place in October and December. There is a 1 percent redemption fee on shares held for less than 180 days.

Spartan Aggressive is the Spartan version of Aggressive Municipal. Like Aggressive Municipal, this fund keeps about one-half of its portfolio in lower-grade muni bonds. One advantage is a slight reduction in interest rate sensitivity, because lower-grade bonds suffer slightly less when rates go up (that's because their credit quality often improves at the same time). Keep in mind, of course, that Spartan Aggressive still has significant exposure to long-term interest rates. An increase of one percentage point in long-term interest rates can wipe out a year's worth of income in the short run.

Compared to Aggressive Municipal, Spartan Aggressive has provided a slightly higher long-term return. Its only drawbacks are a higher minimum investment and the redemption fees that apply on balances of less than $50,000.

Spartan Arizona Municipal Income

This fund began in October 1994, and it seeks high current income exempt from federal income tax and Arizona state personal income tax. Capital gains can be distributed in October and December. There is a redemption fee of 0.5 percent on shares held less than 180 days.

Spartan Arizona doesn't have much of a track record yet, but it appears likely to perform on par with other state-specific funds.

Spartan California Intermediate

Spartan California Intermediate, started at the end of 1993, seeks high current income exempt from federal and California state personal income tax. The fund invests primarily in investment-grade municipal securities. Capital gains can be paid in April and December.

This fund has slightly less interest rate risk than Fidelity's other three California funds, owing to its slightly lower duration. Nevertheless, its interest-rate risk is still significant, and it can be vulnerable to credit quality concerns that affect the state of California. If you are looking for a low-risk muni fund, the only choice that reduces volatility by a significant amount is Spartan Short-Intermediate Muni.

Spartan California Municipal Income

Started in November 1989, Spartan California Municipal Income seeks high current income exempt from federal and California state personal income tax. The fund invests primarily in investment-grade municipal securities. Capital gains can be paid in April and December. A 0.5 percent redemption fee is charged on shares held less than 180 days.

This fund is a Spartan version of California Municipal Income and can be expected to perform 10 to 20 basis points better on an annual basis. With one of the better records in the California muni fund universe, Spartan California is a good choice for high-bracket California taxpayers who won't incur too many fees.

Spartan Connecticut Municipal Income

Spartan Connecticut was started in October 1987. It seeks high current income exempt from federal and Connecticut state personal income tax. The fund invests primarily in investment-grade municipal bonds. Payouts of capital gains may occur in January and December. There is a 0.5 percent redemption fee on shares held for less than 180 days.

Like Fidelity's other state-specific funds, this fund has a good long-term track record and is a solid choice for high-bracket Connecticut investors.

Spartan Florida Municipal Income

This fund was started in March 1992. It seeks high current income exempt from federal income tax and the Florida state intangible tax. The fund invests primarily in investment-grade municipal bonds. Capital gains payouts can occur in January and December. There is a 0.5 percent redemption fee on shares held less than 180 days.

This fund has a good record among Florida muni funds, and it has outperformed many of Fidelity's national funds. This fund is a good long-term choice for high-bracket Florida investors.

Spartan Intermediate

Spartan Intermediate seeks high current income free from federal income tax by investing in municipal obligations. The fund was started in April 1993. Its investments are typically high-grade or upper-medium-grade municipal securities. It will normally maintain a dollar-weighted portfolio maturity of between three and ten years.

This fund sounds lower-risk than it really is. While it does have slightly less interest rate risk than the long-term funds, it can still decline the equivalent of a year's income if long-term interest rates go up by one percentage point. Investors looking for a low-risk muni fund should go with Spartan Short-Intermediate Muni. In the long term, Spartan Intermediate can be expected to return slightly less than Spartan Municipal Income.

Spartan Maryland Municipal Income

Spartan Maryland started in April 1993, and it seeks a high level of current income that is free of federal income tax and Maryland state and county income tax. The fund invests primarily in investment-grade municipal bonds. It usually maintains an average maturity of 8 to 18 years. Capital gains distributions may occur in October and December. There is a 0.5 percent redemption fee on shares held less than 180 days.

Spartan Maryland has performed on par with Fidelity's other single-state funds, and it is a viable long-term choice for high-bracket Maryland investors.

Spartan Municipal Income

This fund was started in June 1990, and it seeks high current income free from federal tax by investing primarily in investment-grade municipal securities. Capital gains distributions can occur in October and December. There is a 0.5 percent redemption fee on shares held less than 180 days.

Among Fidelity's national muni funds, Spartan Municipal Income produces one of the higher income streams, usually lagging behind only Aggressive Municipal and Spartan Aggressive. However, it maintains one of the group's higher duration figures, meaning that it can be hit hard when long-term interest rates move up.

Spartan New Jersey Municipal Income

Spartan New Jersey was started in January 1988, and it seeks high current income exempt from federal and New Jersey gross income tax. The fund invests primarily in investment-grade municipal bonds. Payouts of capital gains may occur in January and December. There is a 0.5 percent redemption fee on shares held less than 180 days.

This fund has a solid long-term record. Its portfolio often includes 15 to 20 percent in lower-grade issues.

Spartan New York Intermediate

This fund was started at the end of 1993. It seeks high current income exempt from federal, New York state, and New York City income taxes. The fund invests primarily in long-term, investment-grade municipal securities. Capital gains distributions can occur in March and December.

This fund has slightly less interest rate risk than Fidelity's other three New York funds because of its moderate duration and above-average portfolio quality. However, it is far from being low-risk. If you want a relatively safe fund, the best alternative is Spartan Short-Intermediate Muni. In the long term, Spartan New York Intermediate should provide a slightly lower return than Spartan New York Municipal Income.

Spartan New York Municipal Income

Started in February 1990, Spartan New York Municipal Income seeks a high level of current income exempt from federal, New York state, and New York City income taxes. The fund invests primarily in long-term, investment-grade municipal securities. Capital gains distributions can occur in March and December. There is a 0.5 percent redemption fee on shares held less than 180 days.

This fund is a Spartan version of New York Municipal Income and can be expected to perform 10 to 20 basis points better on an annual basis. This is a good long-term choice for high-bracket New York investors, particularly those in New York City. Keep in mind that the yield advantage with this fund can be offset by redemption fees if you maintain a balance of less than $50,000.

Spartan Pennsylvania Municipal Income

This fund began in August 1986, and it seeks a high level of current income exempt from federal and Pennsylvania state personal income taxes. The fund invests primarily in longer-term, investment-grade municipal bonds. Capital gains distributions can occur in February and December. A 0.5 percent redemption fee is charged on shares held less than 180 days.

This fund is one of the better performing state-specific choices. Spartan Pennsylvania's advantage comes from an investment-grade portfolio with up to 30 percent in higher-yielding lower-grade issues. This fund is a good long-term choice for high-bracket Pennsylvania investors.

Spartan Short-Intermediate Muni

Spartan Short-Intermediate Muni was started in December 1986, and it seeks as high a level of current income exempt from federal income tax, as is consistent with preservation of capital. It invests primarily in high- and upper-medium-quality short-term municipal obligations, maintaining an average maturity of two to five years. Although capital gains are rare (one cent in 1993 is the only distribution on record), it is possible for the fund to make payouts in October and December.

This fund is Fidelity's only municipal choice that I would characterize as low-risk. With a duration that's typically about three years, the fund has less than half of the interest rate exposure of Fidelity's other muni bond funds. As such, it is not likely to suffer a loss over a 12-month period.

The disadvantage, of course, is a lower yield. Spartan Short-Intermediate Muni usually doesn't offer an after-tax advantage when compared to taxable funds like Short-Term Bond and Spartan Short-Term Income—unless you are in one of the highest federal tax brackets.

Money Market Funds

Money market funds have been around since the 1970s, and Fidelity was the first company to offer checkwriting as an option. Competitors followed suit, and in the 1980s money market funds were a very popular alternative to keeping money in the bank. Back then, of course, short-term interest rates were abnormally high while the Fed wrestled to get inflation under control.

A money market fund is essentially a bond fund with a high-quality portfolio and a very short average maturity, typically less than 90 days. The fund is managed to hold the share price stable at one dollar, resulting in the number of shares in the account being equal to the dollar value of the account.

Money market funds operate with a different structure than other cash-type investments such as bank CDs (certificates of deposit) and Treasury bills:

- A money market fund is not insured by the FDIC. This bothers some investors, but you have to remember that money market funds are managed for a high degree of safety. Many invest in government notes, which have near-zero credit risk, and the ones that invest in corporate debt are broadly diversified. Although a default by a single institution or a rapid increase in short-term interest rates could cause the one dollar share price to drop by a penny or two, this is an unlikely event. (Even if it happened, you wouldn't lose your dividend income the way many CD owners lost their interest when their banks failed.) In a Fidelity money market fund, you have the skills of Fidelity analysts working in your favor. With top-notch risk-assessment abilities, chances of a Fidelity money market fund ever "breaking the buck" are pretty minimal.

- Your rate is not locked in. A money market fund's seven-day yield varies based on market conditions and is only an estimate of the dividend income you will earn in the coming 12 months. The actual amount of income you receive may be higher or lower, depending on whether short-term interest rates move up or down.
- There are no penalties or loads. Except for Select Money Market, Fidelity's money market funds have no front-end or back-end charges, and there is no minimum amount of time you must invest. Dividend income you earn is computed daily and credited to your account on a monthly basis. It doesn't matter when you take the money out of your account; you still earn a prorated amount of income for the time your money was held.

A MONEY MARKET FUND AS HOME BASE

Unless you plan to establish a Fidelity brokerage account, a money market fund can be a good way to get started with Fidelity. Once your account is set up with a money market fund, you can exchange into other funds over the phone (although you will have to order and read the prospectus for each fund before you call in any switches). With checkwriting or Fidelity's Moneyline service in place, a money market fund provides a fast and easy way to redeem shares. Suppose you want to sell $15,000 of your Puritan shares to purchase a vehicle. Just call in a switch from Puritan to your money market fund, wait until the close of the next business day, and then write a check after verifying that the funds are in your money market account.

If you do have a Fidelity brokerage account, a money market fund can boost the return on the money that would otherwise remain in your core account (money market funds usually pay 0.25 to 0.5 percent more than the core account rate).

A money market fund is suitable as a place to keep money you need for near-term living expenses or to maintain an emergency reserve for unexpected events. In either case, the rate you earn will probably be better than what you can obtain from a bank.

TAXABLE VERSUS MUNICIPAL

Unless your federal tax bracket is 36 percent or higher, a taxable money market fund is probably the best bet. You can verify this by comparing taxable equivalent yields (detailed in Chapter 7). To avoid getting a distorted comparison, you should compare taxable and tax-free yields at different times over a three-month period. Also avoid taking the municipal yield figures too seriously around the end of December and early January, when year-end liquidity demands tend to raise the yield on municipal money market funds.

A state-specific money fund can often be a better bet than a national fund. While there is some exposure to state-related credit problems, Fidelity's state-specific money market funds have relatively high credit quality and the risk is pretty minimal.

SPARTAN VERSUS NON-SPARTAN

Most Spartan money funds provide 10 to 20 basis points more income than their non-Spartan counterparts. In a money market fund, however, the Spartan advantage can be easily erased by checkwriting and exchange redemptions. In a Spartan fund, checks cost $2 and redemptions run $5 unless your balance is above $50,000 (in which case both are free). Below $50,000, two checks per month or one exchange redemption per month will more than wipe out the typical yield advantage of a Spartan money market fund.

Even if your transaction frequency is low, Spartan money market funds are less attractive because of their minimums. The checkwriting minimum is $1,000 versus $500 for most non-Spartan funds, and to open an account it takes a significant sum ($20,000 for Spartan taxable money markets and $25,000 for Spartan Municipal money markets). All things considered, a regular non-Spartan money market is probably your best bet unless you expect your balance to stay above $50,000 and you aren't concerned about a higher checkwriting minimum.

TAXABLE MONEY MARKET FUND CHOICES

Even here Fidelity offers many choices, but for most funds the results are pretty similar. Cash Reserves is probably as good as any other fund, and it usually carries a competitive yield. If your account balance will be over $50,000, Spartan Money Market is a viable option. When trading the Selects, keep your loaded Select money in Select Money Market and keep your no-load money in a no-load money fund to avoid paying extra fees (more on this in Chapter 12). A fund-by-fund recap follows; calendar-year performance is listed in Appendix A.

Cash Reserves

Fidelity's most popular money market fund seeks as high a level of current income as is consistent with preservation of capital and liquidity; the fund invests in high-quality U.S. dollar-denominated money market instruments of U.S. and foreign issuers. The fund's yield will fluctuate.

It takes $2,500 to open a Cash Reserves account, and a $1,000 balance is required to maintain it. (IRA accounts can be opened with just $500.) There is no charge for writing checks, although they must be made out for $500 or more.

Cash Reserves provides a good combination of yield, features, and investment minimums. It is my favorite money market fund except for investors who expect to maintain a balance over $50,000. In that case, Spartan Money Market could be a better choice for investors who don't mind a higher checkwriting minimum.

Fidelity Daily Income Trust

Fidelity Daily Income Trust (FDIT) seeks current income consistent with preservation of capital and liquidity; the fund invests in a broad range of high-quality U.S. money market instruments. The fund's yield will fluctuate.

FDIT differs from Cash Reserves in investing in domestic-only notes and in requiring twice as much to open an account ($5,000 for regular accounts). Yield is not significantly different from that of Cash Reserves.

Writing checks for less than $500 is permitted with this fund, but there is a $1 charge in each case.

Select Money Market

Seeking high current income consistent with preservation of capital and liquidity, Select Money Market invests in a broad range of high-quality money market instruments. The fund is managed as a diversified portfolio with at least 80 percent of the portfolio's assets in money market instruments.

Intended only as a cash option for money invested in Fidelity's Select family (see Chapter 9), this fund carries a 3 percent load if the money being invested hasn't already paid a 3 percent load at some point in the past. Checkwriting is not available.

Investors trading the Selects can choose other money market funds when they want to get out of the market, but this can sometimes result in unintended load fees. Suppose you just invested $10,000 in Spartan Money Market and then you sell $10,000 of Select Automotive and add the proceeds to the same account. A few months later you purchase $10,000 in Asset Manager shares, not realizing that you just used up your loaded Spartan Money Market shares. Later you move $10,000 back into Select Biotechnology. Surprise! You'll pay $300 in load fees. (See Chapter 12 for more on avoiding load fees.)

Using Select Money Market to "quarantine" your loaded shares prevents such a situation from occurring. Granted, Select Money Market yields about 20 to 50 basis points less than Spartan Money Market, but in the preceding example you would have had to stay in Select Money Market for many years to lose $300 from a yield standpoint.

Spartan Money Market

Spartan Money Market seeks as high a level of current income as is consistent with the preservation of capital and liquidity by investing principally in money market instruments of domestic and foreign issuers. The fund's yield will fluctuate.

This fund is typically Fidelity's highest-yielding money market, and it is my recommended choice for investors who expect to maintain a balance of $50,000 or more. (Fidelity waives all fees if the account balance is above that threshold.) For an account between $20,000 and $50,000, it can sometimes make sense to hold the fund, but only if your check-writing and redemption activity is low. Otherwise, go with Cash Reserves instead.

Additional investments and checks drawn on the account are both subject to a $1,000 minimum.

Spartan U.S. Government Money Market

This fund seeks as high a level of current income as is consistent with the preservation of capital and liquidity. The fund invests at least 65 percent in obligations issued or guaranteed as to principal and interest by the U.S. government or its agencies and instrumentalities and in repurchase agreements secured by these obligations. The fund's yield will fluctuate.

Spartan U.S. Government has the same structure as Spartan Money Market, except that it runs a slightly higher-quality portfolio and produces a lower yield. I think it amounts to splitting hairs. Spartan Money Market's portfolio is also high in quality and risk is minimal. You might as well enjoy the extra yield that Spartan Money Market provides. If you want maximum safety, go with Spartan U.S. Treasury Money Market, where you might be able to offset the lower yield by avoiding state income taxes on a portion of the income stream.

Spartan U.S. Treasury Money Market

This fund seeks as high a level of current income as is consistent with the security of principal and liquidity. It invests primarily in money market instruments guaranteed as to the payment of principal and interest by the U.S. government. Interest dividends may be exempt from state and local taxes in qualifying states; yield will fluctuate.

This fund offers portfolio quality that's about as safe as you can get, but a large jump in interest rates could still threaten the $1 share price in an extreme situation. The yield from this fund is usually a bit lower than others in the group.

Most states allow some or all of the income from this fund to be exempted from state and local income taxes (although you still have to pay federal taxes).

The features and minimums for this fund are the same as for Spartan Money Market.

U.S. Government Reserves

U.S. Government Reserves seeks a high level of current income as is consistent with the security of principal and liquidity; the fund invests only in obligations issued or guaranteed as to principal and interest by the U. S. government or its agencies and instrumentalities, in repurchase agreements secured by these obligations, and in reverse repurchase agreements. The fund's yield will fluctuate.

Basically, this fund is similar to Cash Reserves, except for a slightly higher-quality portfolio and a yield that's a bit lower. I prefer Cash Reserves—it provides a higher yield with about the same amount of interest rate risk that higher-quality funds are exposed to.

MUNICIPAL MONEY MARKET FUND CHOICES

For investors subject to Alternative Minimum Tax (AMT) on their federal taxes, Municipal Money Market usually doesn't have much AMT paper in its portfolio. You can invest in Municipal Money Market and periodically call Fidelity to verify that this is still the case, or you can go with a taxable fund and pay the going rate.

Following is a breakdown of the Fidelity choices available. The non-Spartan funds require $5,000 to open an account; Spartan funds have a $25,000 minimum. Calendar-year performance is listed in Appendix A. Fidelity renamed most of these funds in 1996, replacing the phrases "Tax-Free" and "Tax-Exempt" with "Municipal".

California Municipal Money Market

California Municipal Money Market seeks current income exempt from federal and California state personal income tax; the fund invests in high-quality, short-term municipal securities. Yield will fluctuate.

Connecticut Municipal Money Market

Connecticut Municipal Money Market seeks a high level of current income exempt from federal income tax and, to the extent possible, Connecticut taxes on dividends and interest income taxes. The fund invests primarily in high-quality, short-term Connecticut municipal obligations. Yield will fluctuate.

Massachusetts Municipal Money Market

Seeking as high a level of current income as is consistent with preservation of capital and liquidity, Massachusetts Municipal Money Market invests in high-quality, short-term municipal obligations exempt from federal and Massachusetts state personal income tax. Yield will fluctuate.

Michigan Municipal Money Market

Michigan Municipal Money Market seeks as high a level of current income as is consistent with preservation of capital and liquidity exempt from federal and Michigan state personal income tax and the Michigan intangible tax. It invests in high-quality, short-term Michigan municipal obligations. Yield will fluctuate.

Municipal Money Market

Municipal Money Market (formerly Tax-Exempt Money Market Trust) seeks current interest income exempt from federal income taxes. It invests in high-quality, short-term municipal obligations, and its yield will fluctuate. Like others, there are no restrictions on holding AMT paper, but AMT holdings are often less than 20 percent.

Among the non-Spartan money market funds, Municipal Money Market holds its own reasonably well. Its minimum initial investment is $5,000, and its yield is sometimes high enough to beat the after-tax return of non-Spartan state-specific funds.

New Jersey Municipal Money Market

New Jersey Municipal Money Market seeks as high a level of current income exempt from federal income tax and New Jersey gross income tax as is consistent with the preservation of capital. The fund invests in high-quality, short-term municipal obligations. Yield will fluctuate.

New York Municipal Money Market

This fund seeks current income exempt from federal, New York state, and New York City income taxes. It invests in high-quality, short-term municipal obligations. Yield will fluctuate.

Ohio Municipal Money Market

Ohio Municipal Money Market seeks a high level of current income exempt from federal and Ohio state personal income tax, a school district tax, and the net income base of the Ohio corporation franchise tax. The fund invests in high-quality, short-term Ohio municipal obligations. Yield will fluctuate.

Spartan Arizona Municipal Money Market

This fund seeks high current income exempt from federal income tax and Arizona state personal income tax. It invests in high-quality, short-term municipal money market securities of all types. Yield will fluctuate.

Spartan California Municipal Money Market

This fund seeks a high level of current income exempt from federal and California state personal income tax. The fund invests in high-quality, short-term California municipal obligations. Yield will fluctuate.

Spartan Connecticut Municipal Money Market

Consistent with capital preservation, this fund seeks a high level of current income exempt from federal income tax and, to the extent possible, Connecticut taxes on dividends and interest income. The fund invests primarily in high-quality, short-term Connecticut municipal obligations. Yield will fluctuate.

Spartan Florida Municipal Money Market

This fund seeks as high a level of current income as is consistent with the preservation of capital and liquidity exempt from federal income tax and Florida's intangible personal property tax. The fund invests in high-quality, short-term Florida municipal obligations. Yield will fluctuate.

Spartan Massachusetts Municipal Money Market

This fund seeks as high a level of current income exempt from federal income tax and, to the extent possible, the Massachusetts state personal income tax as is consistent with capital preservation and liquidity. The fund invests primarily in high-quality, short-term Massachusetts municipal obligations of all types. Yield will fluctuate.

Spartan Municipal Money Market

Spartan Municipal Money Market seeks a high level of current income exempt from federal income tax by investing in high-quality, short-term municipal obligations with an average maturity of 90 days or less. As with other funds in this group, the fund seeks to maintain a $1 share price.

This fund has the benefit of national diversification, and it is one of Fidelity's best-yielding municipal money funds. At times it even exceeds the after-tax return of state-specific funds. However, if your balance is less than $50,000 and you expect to do more than one transaction per month or if you expect to pay AMT, you should consider Municipal Money Market instead.

Spartan New Jersey Municipal Money Market

This fund seeks a high level of current income exempt from federal income tax and, to the extent possible, New Jersey gross income tax. The fund invests in high-quality, short-term New Jersey municipal obligations. Yield will fluctuate.

Spartan New York Municipal Money Market

This fund seeks current income exempt from federal, New York state, and New York City personal income tax. It invests in high-quality, short-term municipal obligations. Yield will fluctuate.

Spartan Pennsylvania Municipal Money Market

This fund seeks a high level of current income exempt from federal and Pennsylvania state personal income taxes. The fund invests in high-quality, short-term municipal obligations. Yield will fluctuate.

9

Select Funds

Fidelity's family of Select funds is intended for venturesome mutual fund investors. Each portfolio concentrates on stocks in a particular industry group, casting away the concept of diversification and concentrating instead on providing opportunities. Not surprisingly, many Selects have price volatility that more closely resembles individual stocks than diversified mutual funds.

Studies have shown that industry trends account for roughly 30 percent of the price movement in individual stocks, with broad market and company-specific factors accounting for the rest. Stocks in similar industry groups tend to move together because economic factors that affect a particular stock are likely to have a similar impact on others in the same industry.

The Selects are an attractive way to trade industry trends. In addition to having Fidelity's research skills working in your favor, trading expenses are much lower than if you were covering the stock commissions and price spreads yourself. Checking hourly prices during market hours is made easy by Fidelity's phone quote system, and there are no limits on the number of trades you can make (although trading inside of 30 days is not cheap because of the 0.75 percent redemption fee).

SELECT HISTORY

Fidelity started its Select family in July 1981 with Energy, Health Care, Precious Metals, and Technology. Financial Services and Utilities were added in December 1981. Investor interest in the Selects was slow to catch on in the beginning, but after Select Technology's 50 percent plus gains in 1982 and 1983, investors took notice. Fidelity responded by adding additional portfolios for other industries. By 1987 there were 35 sectors and a money market option and Fidelity had introduced hourly pricing to allow investors to buy and sell throughout the day instead of waiting for close of the market for their transactions to take place.

In 1988, however, investor interest stalled. Selects generally hold smaller stocks, and the 1987 crash hit them harder than it hit diversified funds (which hold a higher percentage of blue chips). Mutual fund investors also became wary of program trading (computerized stock selling and buying by large institutions) which was blamed for creating such a large one-day decline.

Fidelity also faced tough times. Congress had eliminated the IRA deduction for many investors, and this took away a lot of Fidelity's business. Facing staff cuts, Fidelity killed plans to introduce additional Selects. About the same time, existing sectors became more difficult to manage because large investors, aided by hourly pricing, were increasingly trading for the short term. Technology funds were the worst; there were times when $50 million would leave in a matter of hours. In late 1989, Fidelity imposed a 0.75 percent redemption fee on trades of 29 days or less to restore order to its internal trading operation. The fee did the trick, but it alienated many of the more active traders.

Things began to come together in 1991. A rally in small stocks breathed new life into the Select funds. A large boost in research spending helped Fidelity's Selects to begin delivering performance that outstripped their rivals at other fund companies. Nevertheless, the majority of assets in the Select family remained heavily concentrated in just a few sectors.

At the end of 1991, about 50 percent of the $4.2 billion in Select assets was in just two sectors: Select Biotechnology and Select Health Care.

Good performance has kept the group alive and well since then. As of mid-1996, about 60 percent of the 35 equity Selects have exceeded the S&P 500 over a trailing five-year period. Select assets are over $10 billion and are now more evenly distributed throughout various sectors. In a mutual fund universe where attractive small-cap funds don't always stay that way, the Selects continue to offer a wide range of attractive small-cap opportunities.

Fidelity tends to rotate managers frequently in the Select family. This helps to broaden skill levels and to identify candidates who have the right set of skills for managing one of Fidelity's larger diversified stock funds. In my experience this practice has had relatively little effect on the group's long-term performance.

INVESTING IN SELECTS

Picking the winning Selects is tougher than it looks. As with any aggressive growth strategy, it's a balancing act between taking on enough risk to be rewarded but not going so far that it's difficult to recover from losses. When trading Selects, you should avoid margin and short selling. These strategies involve too much risk. Sooner or later, you'll be in the wrong place at the wrong time, and you can erase over a year's worth of gains in no time at all.

Some Select investors set their expectations too high. To give an example, my Select System model in *Fidelity Monitor* has returned about 18 percent annually during the last five years, but throughout that period I received letters from subscribers asking why my model hadn't done better. When I lagged the S&P 500, I could always count on hearing all about how a dartboard strategy would have done better.

If you decide to get involved in the Selects, you need to be realistic. Over a five-year period you may score a few home runs, but you won't be in the top fund every year. (The odds of doing that well are about the same as winning the state lottery.) You won't be able to avoid declines because they come with the territory. Even if you are good, you'll probably still do worse than the S&P 500 about 25 percent of the time.

Basic Strategies

Following are three different strategies that can be used to invest in the Selects. I've used all three methods at different times over the years, and my thoughts about each approach are included.

Industry Analysis   If you can identify the industries best positioned for long-term growth, it would seem relatively easy to exceed the market's return. This approach can work, but only if you are aware of something the market has not already factored in. Good news industries usually mean higher-priced stocks, and these can decline if future news is less favorable than expected. Similarly, bad news sectors are usually cheap and can rally if events turn out to be less gloomy than expected. (In early 1992, automotive stocks jumped 30 percent as the big three announced losses in the billions.) If you go with industry analysis, what works best is to try to identify sectors that are benefiting from unforeseen long-term change in the economy. It also helps if you are analyzing a sector you are familiar with, such as the one you work in (that way, you are likely to notice if business is improving or deteriorating before it shows up in the stock prices). In any case, it helps to have a long-term investment horizon and to have some background on the choices that are available. My discussion of each Select portfolio (following this section) should be helpful in this respect.

Short-Term Price Momentum   This is currently one of the more popular Select strategies, partly because it has worked well since 1990 and partly because of the increasing use of investment software and computerized technical systems. When using this approach with the Selects, care must be taken to minimize the number of 0.75 percent redemption fees paid on trades made inside of 30 days. It's also important to be faster than the "herd," or else you can end up selling on dips and buying on peaks. As market efficiency improves in the coming years, I think it will become more difficult to beat the market with momentum techniques.

Undervalued Sectors   My current Select System model is based on a valuation model that compares each sector's current price-to-book ratio to historical averages. Selects with the largest discount are then ranked based on risk-adjusted performance over a trailing one-year period. My back-testing suggests this approach can consistently outperform the S&P 500 with far less turnover than is typical for momentum systems.

Regardless of the approach you use, you'll probably do better if you avoid timing the market or holding gold sectors (Select American Gold and Select Precious Metals & Minerals) and focus only on the equity sectors. Also be aware that some technology sectors (Computers, Electronics, Software, and Technology) are relatively unpredictable and carry high volatility; gains and losses of 10 to 15 percent in a matter of days are par for the course with these industries.

THE SELECT PORTFOLIOS

Following is a review of each Select portfolio. These funds are sold with a 3 percent load, but the load is paid only once when you first buy in and not on subsequent switches. The minimum investment is $2,500 per fund or $500 in retirement accounts. There is no limit on exchanges, but there is an exchange fee of $7.50 and a redemption fee of $7.50 for trades of 30 days or more (0.75 percent of assets is charged for short-term trades of 29 days or less). The fees do not apply when switching out of Select Money Market. As of 1996, Fidelity is waiving the $7.50 exchange fee if you use an automated approach to execute your trades. All of the following portfolios seek capital appreciation by investing primarily in the equity securities of the specific industry sector they are named for. Distributions can occur in April and December.

Select Air Transportation

A classic cyclical sector, Air Transportation tends to perform well during periods of economic growth and not so well when the economy is sliding into a recession. It is also negatively affected by rising oil prices, since fuel is a key cost component of the industry. The fund invests mainly in equity securities of companies engaged in the regional, national, and international movement of passengers, mail, and freight via aircraft.

Competition in the airline industry has made it tough for many carriers to make money over the last five years, but stocks in this group are relatively cheap, as of mid-1996. The industry will remain highly competitive for years to come, making for price volatility that rivals the technology sectors. Air Transportation can also invest in freight companies like Federal Express and aircraft manufacturers such as Boeing, but these types of companies are also sensitive to economic growth and the price of fuel.

Select American Gold

A classic gold fund, Select American Gold invests mainly in equity securities of companies engaged in exploration, mining, processing, or dealing in gold, or—to a lesser degree—in silver, platinum, diamonds, or other precious metals and minerals. The fund may also invest directly in the metal itself, although traditionally its bullion position has been small. In recent years the fund's primary holdings have been Canadian gold-mining companies.

Increasing worldwide jewelry demand is a positive for gold, but gold stocks remain high priced as of mid-1996. As such, this fund can experience substantial short-term declines even if it does post reasonable returns over the long run (I cover gold in more detail in Chapter 3).

Gold stocks don't usually follow the stock market because mining company profits are tied directly to the price of the metal. Because of the fixed cost of getting gold out of the ground, mining profits (and so mining stocks) tend to fluctuate about twice as much as does the metal itself. Despite their low beta, which is due to a lack of correlation with the general market, gold stocks are among the most risky equity securities around.

If you buy into American Gold, you should limit your overall gold position to less than 10 percent of your portfolio. Plan to ride the ups and downs for the long haul, because this sector is virtually impossible to predict in the short run.

Select Automotive

This fund invests mainly in the equity securities of companies engaged in the manufacture, marketing, or sale of automobiles, trucks, specialty vehicles, parts, tires, and related services.

Select Automotive tends to be an "early" cyclical because auto sales are one of the first things to pick up when the economy recovers from a down cycle and consumer confidence comes back. It is one of the more predictable cyclical sectors because once it starts to outperform the market, it tends to keep doing so for a number of months. It also tends to be one of the better long-term performers in the Select group because Fidelity researchers have a good understanding of the industry and are able to spot turnaround situations in the making.

Select Biotechnology

Biotechnology invests mainly in equity securities of companies engaged in the research, development, scale-up, and manufacture of various biotechnological products, services, and processes.

Many of the companies in this fund have the potential to be acquired by pharmaceutical companies in the future, but right now most of them are spending heavily on research and development and may not have income-producing products for several years. Many firms may never get off the ground. Others that come up with winning products may be worth 10 or 20 times their current valuation a few years down the road.

The industry as a whole is risky but is likely to be one of the faster-growing areas of the economy over the next 10 to 15 years. Investor outlook for this group tends to swing between wild optimism and sobering reality, and the prevailing sentiment can last two or three years. Although biotech stocks are considered part of the health care group, genetically engineered products have broad-based potential. Some food and agricultural products have already gained approval and are generating revenue—a trend that is likely to continue.

Select Brokerage & Investment

Select Brokerage & Investment invests mainly in equity securities of companies engaged in stock brokerage, commodity brokerage, investment banking, tax-advantaged investment or investment sales, investment management, or related advisory services.

The sector has a sketchy history, but things are looking up. Many of the brokerage houses that lost accounts to the mutual fund companies are cleaning up their act and finding new business opportunities overseas. Money management companies are benefiting from the aging baby boom population, which stands to inherit a large sum from the prior generation and is increasingly saving for retirement. Nevertheless, the brokerage industry remains somewhat unpredictable and can magnify the swings in the stock market.

Select Chemicals

Select Chemicals invests mainly in equity securities of companies engaged in the research, development, manufacture, or marketing of products or services related to the chemical process industries.

This industry is another broad-based cyclical sector like the automotive group. Many of these companies supply raw materials and are often the last to see a pickup in demand during an economic recovery cycle. (Product and factory inventories are consumed first before chemical commodities such as plastic make the turn upward.) Compared with other "late cyclical" sectors, chemical companies tend to be among the more predictable industry groups. Their profit margins are often higher than those of other commodity producers, which helps explain why Select Chemicals is one of the better long-term performers.

Select Computers

Investing mainly in the computer industry, Select Computers looks for equity securities of companies engaged in research, design, development, manufacture, or distribution of products, processes, or services that relate to currently available or experimental hardware technology.

As a technology sector, Select Computers is one of the most risky and least predictable sectors in the Select family. Technology stocks often move to the beat of a different drummer, and it is not uncommon to see this sector gain or lose 10 to 15 percent in a matter of a days. A correction of 20 percent or more often occurs at least once during the course of a typical year.

After a seven-year bearish period, this industry has been in a bull phase since late 1990. Some of this is because competitive pressures are prompting many companies in the general economy to invest more in computers and to automate their operations. Foreign demand also plays a major role.

Fidelity does a good job of researching computer companies, but because of the volatility in this sector you may want to consider a more broadly based fund like Select Technology.

Select Construction & Housing

Formerly named Housing, Select Construction & Housing invests mainly in equity securities of companies engaged in the design and construction of residential, commercial, industrial, and public works facilities as well as of companies engaged in the manufacture, supply, distribution, or sale of products or services to those construction industries.

As a cyclical sector, this fund has characteristics similar to those of the automotive group, except that it is more sensitive to long-term interest rates. Select Construction & Housing has a respectable record but lagged Select Automotive in the early 1990s because real estate was overbuilt.

The future for this sector appears a bit more positive than in the past, but it might look even better over the long term if some of the portfolio were invested in stocks of developing countries. Emerging markets are home to the world's biggest construction boom, but so far the fund has only held a tiny position in this area.

Select Consumer Industries

Formerly known as Consumer Products, Consumer Industries invests mainly in equity securities of companies engaged in the manufacture and distribution of goods to consumers, both domestically and internationally. That covers a lot of ground. The fund owns stocks in sectors such as automobiles, telecommunications, food, household products, retailers, broadcasters, and casino resorts.

Having a broad-based charter has not helped this fund. As of mid-1996, Select Automotive, Select Leisure, Select Multimedia, and Select Telecommunications have been better performers over the last five years. Furthermore, the stocks in Consumer Industries' portfolio continue to be somewhat overvalued.

Select Defense & Aerospace

This fund invests mainly in equity securities of companies engaged in the research, manufacture, or sale of products or services related to the defense or aerospace industries.

The fall of Communism and the resulting heavy cuts in the defense budget kept this fund in the doldrums until 1993. But thanks to consolidation, downsizing, and growth in the aerospace industry, performance has now picked up. The aerospace industry has been spurred on by strong demand in Asia, and this trend could continue.

Select Developing Communications

This fund invests in equity securities of companies engaged in the development, manufacture, or sale of emerging communications services or equipment. Most of the fund's assets are invested in technology firms and cellular telephone companies. Being a technology sector, Developing Communications is subject to the same roller coaster valuation changes that occur with related sectors like Select Computers. However, Developing Communications doesn't have quite as much volatility.

The fund has a good track record, and the long-term outlook seems favorable. Not only is the United States investing heavily in wireless communications, but emerging nations are skipping the wiring and starting out with cellular-based telephone systems. U.S. companies in this industry group have domestic opportunities as well as export business potential. On the negative side, however, stock valuations remain very high in this group.

Select Electronics

Select Electronics invests in equity securities of companies engaged in the design, manufacture, or sale of electronic components as well as of companies that sell electronic components, electronic component distributors, and vendors of electronic instruments and electronic system vendors.

The fund's primary emphasis is on chipmakers, otherwise known as integrated circuit manufacturers. Chips provide the brains and memory for products such as computers, consumer electronics, cellular phones, and automobiles.

After losing market share in the 1980s, this industry was revitalized by a lower U.S. dollar, restructuring, and the ongoing growth of computers and communications. A seven-year bear cycle ended in 1990 when the industry started to gain back market share that had previously been lost to the Japanese.

Although 20 percent corrections are more or less routine in this sector, the industry as a whole has a good chance of increasing its earnings at a faster rate than the market over the long run. The only concern is that a rising dollar could put pressure on foreign revenue.

Select Energy

Investing mainly in equity securities of companies in the energy field, Select Energy's portfolio includes the conventional areas of oil, gas, electricity, and coal as well as newer energy sources such as nuclear, geothermal, oil shale, and solar power.

This sector lagged through the early 1990s because oil prices were kept in check by increasing worldwide supplies. Aggressive restructuring and expanding demand from developing countries has improved performance in recent years. As of mid-1996, energy stocks remain undervalued relative to other industry sectors.

Select Energy Services

A more aggressive portfolio than Select Energy, Select Energy Services invests mainly in equity securities of companies in the energy service field, including those that provide services and equipment to the conventional areas of oil, gas, electricity, and coal as well as to newer areas such as nuclear, geothermal, oil shale, and solar power.

These types of firms help oil and gas producers to locate new reserves and to handle the drilling of new wells. After a long restructuring period, many of these companies are facing a prosperous future driven by expanding demand for services and new technology for improving the output of existing wells.

Keep in mind that Energy Services is a relatively volatile fund. Go with Select Energy if you want a less risky bet on oil prices.

Select Environmental Services

Introduced in June 1989, Select Environmental Services invests mainly in equity securities of companies engaged in the research, development, manufacture, or distribution of products, processes, or services related to waste management or pollution control.

When Fidelity initiated this fund, it was widely expected that increasingly strict environmental laws would create a boom for such types of companies. However, the boom went bust when local recycling programs caught on and companies drew upon their own internal resources to comply with federal regulations.

After a long shakeout that ended in 1995, this sector is now looking better. However, it's too early to tell how it might perform over the long run.

Select Financial Services

Concentrating on banks, S&Ls, insurance, credit cards, mortgage lenders, and brokerages, Select Financial Services invests mainly in equity securities of companies providing financial services to consumers and industry.

This portfolio benefited from a strong run in financial stocks between 1990 and 1995. Because of its broad-based charter, however, the fund did not perform as well as the more narrowly defined Select Home Finance and Select Regional Banks portfolios.

After five strong years, the financial sector seems fully valued and could be entering a long-term cooling off period. Still, Fidelity is adept at analyzing financial stocks and could remain ahead of the S&P 500 with this fund.

Select Food & Agriculture

This portfolio invests mainly in equity securities of companies engaged in the manufacture, sale or distribution of food and beverage products, agricultural products, and products related to the development of new food technologies.

Select Food & Agriculture has the characteristics of a growth and income fund, mainly because the food and beverage business changes very little under varying economic conditions. Select Food & Agriculture is one of my favorite low-risk sectors because it tends to beat the S&P 500 over the long run.

The fund also makes for a good defensive play when the market outlook is bleak. It rarely does worse than the S&P 500 in a correction or bear market, yet it can participate if market conditions turn bullish.

Select Health Care

Select Health Care invests mainly in equity securities of companies engaged in the design, manufacture, or sale of products or services used for or in connection with health care or medicine. Throughout its history, the fund has focused mainly on pharmaceutical stocks.

I suspect long-term performance for this fund will continue to exceed the S&P 500, although the valuation on this sector is considerably higher than the market. Favorable long-term factors include a more responsive FDA and new technology for developing more effective drugs. On the negative side, competition from biotech companies could dampen the long-term outlook for profit growth.

Select Home Finance

Originally known as Select Savings & Loan, Select Home Finance invests mainly in the equity securities of companies that provide mortgages and other consumer-related loans.

Former Manager David Ellison ran this fund for ten years and made it one of the best performing mutual funds in the industry—not that the fund didn't see tough times. At one point, in 1990, it was down 42 percent over a one-year period as savings and loan problems escalated. The group finally recovered when the Fed pushed down short-term interest rates in 1991, creating a profitable spread for the industry in the nick of time. Resolution Trust Corporation (the federal liquidation company Congress created) also helped the survivors by eliminating a lot of competition from the industry.

New manager Bill Rubin will have his work cut out. After five years of recovering equity values, the rally in this group has probably run its course. Fidelity research should help him to perform better than the financial group in general, but a repeat of the 1991 through 1995 years is very unlikely.

Select Industrial Equipment

Formerly known as Industrial Technology (and before that as Capital Goods), Select Industrial Equipment invests mainly in equity securities of companies engaged in the manufacture, distribution, or service of products and equipment for the industrial sector. These companies include integrated producers of capital equipment, parts suppliers, and subcontractors.

Select Industrial Equipment is a cyclical sector investing in an industry that struggled to survive against heavy foreign competition in the 1980s. Helped by years of downsizing and a lower U.S. dollar, the industry started to pick up in 1993 as the economy began to recover. Future growth is likely to be better than in the past eight years, but this sector can still decline in an economic slowdown.

Select Industrial Materials

Select Industrial Materials invests mainly in equity securities of companies engaged in the manufacture, mining, processing, or distribution of raw materials and intermediate goods used in the industrial sector.

This portfolio concentrates on deep cyclical stocks—producers of plastics, chemicals, paper, mining, energy, and steel. These types of companies usually pick up when an economic recovery is far enough along that inventories have been depleted and factories need raw materials to produce new goods. Industrial Materials can benefit when the market worries about inflation, because inflation usually means rising prices for industrial commodities. Keep in mind that if inflation is due to rising energy prices, Select Energy may be a better choice.

In any event, this portfolio is one of the more difficult to predict. Surprise moves up or down can be triggered by seemingly minor economic events. Imbalances in the commodity markets can appear suddenly, and this fund can make equally quick adjustments.

Select Insurance

Previously known as Select Property & Casualty Insurance, Select Insurance invests mainly in equity securities of companies engaged in underwriting, reinsuring, selling, distributing, or placing of property and casualty, life, or health insurance.

A string of natural disasters, a trend toward more government regulations, and an oversupply of insurers had put a damper on this portfolio in recent years. On the plus side, many players in the industry are starting to focus more on cost cutting. Also, some companies are looking to reduce risk with a new class of securities that allow the investing public to earn above-average returns if disaster claims stay below a certain threshold.

Select Leisure

Select Leisure invests mainly in equity securities of companies engaged in the design, production, or distribution of goods or services in the leisure industries. Typical investments include broadcasters, cable TV operators, beverages, publishing, hotels and motels, casinos, and other entertainment companies.

This fund has a good track record, and the long-term outlook appears positive. An aging population in the United States points toward increasing demand for leisure activities a few years down the road. In developing countries, the trend could be similar as productivity rises and work weeks grow shorter. On the negative side, many of the companies in this sector tend to be overvalued relative to the market.

Select Medical Delivery

Known as Health Care Delivery before 1987, Medical Delivery invests mainly in equity securities of companies engaged in the ownership of hospitals, nursing homes, and health maintenance organizations as well as in other companies specializing in the delivery of health care services. The fund usually maintains a position in medical equipment suppliers as well.

This industry group tends to be relatively risky, but long-term performance seems likely to outperform the S&P 500.

Because of the aging U.S. population, this group of stocks represents a long-term growth opportunity—particularly for HMOs and medical equipment makers. Remember, however, that short-term surprises can take a big toll on this portfolio.

Select Multimedia

Formerly known as Broadcast & Media, Select Multimedia invests mainly in equity securities of companies engaged in the development, production, sale, and distribution of goods or services used in the broadcast and media industries. Typical groups include cable TV, broadcast TV, cellular communications, electronic equipment, book publishers, newspapers, and magazine companies.

With the exception of a bad year in 1990 (brought on by the re-regulation of the cable industry), this sector has outperformed the market on a relatively consistent basis.

In the future, many of the companies in this group will be the ones providing the actual content for new technology. Whether the source is an on-demand movie from your cable company, a digital video disk, or an electronic magazine transmitted over the World Wide Web, the companies in this fund are likely to benefit from new forms of distribution. The only drawback is that deregulation and new technology stand to make this industry more competitive than it has been in the past.

Select Natural Gas

Select Natural Gas invests mainly in equity securities of companies engaged in the production, transmission, and distribution of natural gas and involved in the exploration of potential natural gas sources as well as of those companies that provide services and equipment to natural gas producers, refineries, cogeneration facilities, converters, and distributors.

Even though natural gas has its own supply and demand factors, it experiences price trends similar to Select Energy and Select Energy Services. Part of the reason is that many companies produce both oil and gas, and their equity values tend to move as a group. The other reason is that some businesses and electric utilities can use either oil or gas and will choose the one that is less expensive. If oil prices fall, for example, some users may switch to oil, and the resulting decline in natural gas demand will bring down natural gas prices too.

Natural gas does have one key advantage that may become more important over time: it burns clean compared to other fossil fuels, making it a practical alternative for meeting stricter air pollution standards. In the United States, its use could become more widespread not only among electric power producers but also in heavy industry and in vehicles. (A few city bus systems use natural gas to reduce pollutants without having to resort to the less convenient option of overhead electric lines.) In developing countries, where air pollution is far worse, natural gas may be the only viable option for meeting the growing demand for electricity.

All things considered, this portfolio seems to have more opportunity for growth than Select Energy does, but like Select Energy Services it also carries a higher risk level.

Select Paper & Forest Products

Select Paper & Forest Products invests mainly in equity securities of companies engaged in the manufacture, research, sale, or distribution of paper products, packaging products, building materials, and other products related to the paper and forest products industry.

Select Paper & Forest Products focuses mostly on paper and lumber companies, which have deep cyclical characteristics similar to those of Select Industrial Materials and Select Chemicals. Historically, it has been the least predictable of the three sectors.

A few of these companies have vast timber resources that may become more valuable over time, but this portfolio is not likely to produce the kind of returns available from growth-oriented sectors. Paper companies are part of a mature market in which competition exists worldwide. The primary strategy here is in keeping costs in line, delivering quality products, and being able to respond as the economy fluctuates.

Although this portfolio makes a good inflation hedge, it is not as broad-based as Select Industrial Materials.

Select Precious Metals & Minerals

The group's longest-running gold fund, Select Precious Metals & Minerals invests mainly in equity securities of companies engaged in exploration, mining, processing, or dealing with gold, silver, platinum, diamonds, or other precious metals and minerals; it may also invest directly in precious metals. (See my discussion of gold characteristics in Chapter 3.)

Select Precious Metals differs from Select American Gold in that it invests on a global basis, usually with South Africa as the dominant region. Under normal conditions, the two gold funds tend to move in tandem, with Precious Metals usually having the greater sensitivity to the price of gold.

Like Select American Gold, this fund is at least twice as volatile as the underlying metal, making it one of the most risky and least predictable Selects. The road to long-term gains in this fund will probably include many substantial short-term corrections as the price of gold edges higher over the long run. I don't recommend putting more than 10 percent of your overall portfolio into gold funds because of their excessive short-term risk.

Select Regional Banks

This fund invests mainly in the equity securities of companies engaged in accepting deposits and making commercial and principally nonmortgage consumer loans.

Although this sector has an excellent long-term record, it has not performed quite as well as Select Home Finance, a similar fund that competes in the same industry group with some variations.

After five years of strong performance, the rally in bank stocks would seem to have run its course. Many of these firms were undervalued in 1990 because of the industry's poor profitability and major problems with bad loans. Recovery was strong when the Fed created a profitable spread between long-term and short-term interest rates in 1991, but this unusually steep yield curve is less attractive now that the Fed has turned its attention to inflation.

Fidelity's research is a positive for the sector, but even so it's unlikely that this fund will repeat the strong performance it delivered between 1990 and 1995.

Select Retailing

Select Retailing invests mainly in equity securities of companies engaged in merchandising finished goods and services primarily to individual customers.

Following a significant slowdown in consumer spending from 1993 to 1995, this sector now appears to be back on track for the long run.

Fidelity research on retail companies tends to be good. Even though the industry itself is mature, there are many new entrants to the field every year as well as shifting consumer tastes. Fidelity analysts and managers seem to have a knack for identifying the up-and-coming companies as well as the larger firms that are poised for a turnaround. I expect this fund to be a good long-term performer.

Select Software & Computer Services

This fund invests mainly in equity securities of companies engaged in research, design, production, or distribution of products or processes that relate to software or information-based services.

This fund is a subsector of the volatile technology group. Software companies tend to have characteristics different from those of electronics manufacturers and computer makers, but their stocks are still quite volatile because small mistakes can quickly become big problems in the high-tech universe. During one year, a particular company can "own the market" with a successful software application, but the next year it can face serious problems if a competitor comes out with a better product and customers switch over. Software companies can copyright their current application programs, but there is relatively little protection for general concepts or user interfaces. Companies frequently take their competitor's good ideas, add a few of their own, and come up with a better product. In this kind of environment, the only way to insure long-term success is to be innovative and to constantly reinvent one's own products.

This fund has compiled one of the better long-term records within the technology group. Fidelity does a good job of analyzing software companies, but new methods of obtaining and using information could slow the growth of the software industry as it currently exists. You may want to consider Select Technology for greater diversification.

Select Technology

Select Technology invests in equity securities of companies that Fidelity believes have developed (or will develop) products, processes, or services that will provide or will benefit significantly from technological advances and improvements.

In practice, this portfolio invests in a broad-based group of technology firms, including computer makers, software developers, electronic producers, and communications equipment manufacturers.

Despite the fact that it branches out in the high-tech universe, it is still one of the more risky choices in the Select group. Like other technology-oriented sectors, Select Technology can gain or lose 20 percent in a matter of weeks. Price trends can abruptly change direction as a result of a seemingly minor hiccup relating to earnings or the economy.

Fidelity has been sharpening its skills in the analysis of high-tech companies and stands to do well with this type of fund. If you have the patience to ride out the big short-term swings, this fund is likely to be a good long-term performer.

Select Telecommunications

This fund invests mainly in equity securities of companies engaged in the development, manufacture, or sale of communications services or communications equipment.

Select Telecommunications has traditionally invested most of its assets in telephone companies, both the regional Bells and the long-distance carriers. In recent years, cellular companies and communications equipment manufacturers have been commanding a larger share of the portfolio.

Telecommunications has been a good performer, delivering a nice combination of growth and stability. The fund's price trend is unique, but it exhibits characteristics of both the utilities and technology groups.

On the negative side, new technology and increasing competition could take its toll. Fidelity analysts should do a good job picking the winners from the losers, but stock valuations in this group are on the high side as of mid-1996.

Select Transportation

A more broadly based portfolio than Select Air Transportation, Select Transportation invests mainly in equity securities of companies that provide transportation services or companies that design, manufacture, distribute, or sell transportation equipment.

Select Transportation typically invests in truck carriers, railroads, and air transportation companies. To a small degree, the fund also invests in auto and truck part suppliers.

This group is a classic cyclical sector, and it tends to move in concert with the economy and the Dow Transportation Index (although Select Transportation has outperformed the index by a wide margin over the last five years). Fuel represents a key cost component for many companies in this group; when oil prices move up, it puts pressure on the sector's earnings, and when oil prices fall, the group tends to get a lift.

As a long-term performer, this portfolio has a good record. As with other cyclical sectors, however, it usually performs poorly when the economy is heading toward a slowdown.

Select Utilities Growth

Formerly known just as Select Utilities, Select Utilities Growth invests mainly in equity securities of companies in the public utilities industry and companies deriving a majority of their revenues from their public utility operations.

It generally holds a mix of telephone companies, electric utilities, electric power producers, and gas utilities. Compared with the non-Select Utilities Fund, Select Utilities Growth places more emphasis on capital appreciation and less emphasis on dividends. (The fund does not provide quarterly payouts.)

Because most utilities borrow heavily to finance their capital costs, interest rates play a key role in the cost of debt service and thus the bottom line. As a result, utility stocks tend to be interest rate–sensitive, like bonds.

Compared with the long-term opportunities offered by other Select portfolios, Select Utilities Growth doesn't exactly jump off the page. Still, it can perform quite well during times when other sectors are doing poorly. Many investors who time the market with a money market fund would be better off if they moved into this fund every time they became nervous. That way, they wouldn't be left behind in the majority of instances when stocks perform better than a cash position.

10

Designing a
Suitable Portfolio

Portfolio management seems to be one of the bigger challenges for many mutual fund investors. In this chapter, I describe a relatively straightforward approach that is flexible enough for a wide variety of situations.

Some investors may already be familiar with Fidelity's workbook approach to portfolio allocation, which involves filling out a questionnaire about your investment experience, risk tolerance, investment horizon, age, and financial situation. A point scoring system identifies the most suitable mix of assets from a choice of five portfolios. Once a suitable mix is identified, you can pick funds to match the suggested stock/bond/short-term mix or you can go with one of the three Asset Manager funds if your suggested allocation mix is in the middle range.

I think the workbook and point scoring system are straightforward, and the survey asks good questions. However, the program seems to consider too many variables, and in some cases investors in retirement may have trouble defining their investment horizon accurately.

My approach, while not perfect either, tends to emphasize the investment horizon as the major factor. I also consider personal risk tolerance, but unless you are highly risk-tolerant or very risk-averse I prefer to let the investment horizon be the key driver. What follows is an approach used successfully by many *Fidelity Monitor* subscribers. I have made some refinements over the years, but the basic four-step process is unchanged.

PUTTING TOGETHER YOUR FIDELITY PORTFOLIO: A BASIC FOUR-STEP PROCESS

I'll start with an overview of the process and then go into detail.

1. First, you decide whether your risk tolerance is low, medium, or high, based on how you feel about investment losses and your preference for income versus growth.
2. Second, you make reasonable estimates of when you will need to spend the principal. These estimates are based on your income sources, living expenses, and the timing of major financial expenditures. You then break up your spending needs into three time periods. (This step can be skipped if all your investments are long-term and you don't expect to spend the money for eight years or more.)
3. Third, you apply the suggested fund categories to the dollar amounts in each time period and come up with a suggested overall mix. More details and a chart to help you can be found later in this chapter under "Determining an Appropriate Mix."
4. Fourth, if you have existing investments you review them to see how your current portfolio stacks up. Adjustments can then be made to move your portfolio closer to the suggested mix. If you are a first-time investor or if all of your current holdings are in a cash position, you can purchase funds to fit the suggested mix. (In this situation, the merits of a dollar cost averaging approach for purchases of growth-oriented funds are discussed later in this chapter.

Determining Your Risk Tolerance

Try not to let any preconceived notions get in the way when deciding whether your risk tolerance is low, medium, or high. Unless your feelings about risk are very strong one way or the other (or if you have a strong preference for conservative or aggressive holdings), you should consider your risk tolerance to be medium. The idea here is to simply decide on an appropriate category for your general disposition.

Consider your risk tolerance low if you are very uncomfortable with sustaining losses, or if you are the type who has a strong preference for a predictable income stream. Suppose you knew that bank CD rates would be 5 percent and inflation would be 3 percent for the rest of your life. Would you be tempted to cash in all your investments for this "worry no more" investment strategy? If the answer is yes, you're definitely in the low category.

Consider your risk tolerance high if you are willing to ride through the ups and downs of the market in order to build your nest egg at a faster rate. Suppose you just added a large sum of money to a successful domestic growth fund you've been in for ten years, and the fund declines 25 percent along with the overall market. If you would be disappointed but not worried, you probably have a high tolerance for risk. Investors who can "roll with the punches" would not lose much sleep in such a situation and would probably make only minor changes in their portfolio.

If neither of these two examples describes your situation, you're probably in the medium group, as are the majority of investors. Investors with medium risk tolerance don't like losses but are willing to live with them to build wealth over the long run. They understand that some exposure to growth-oriented investments is necessary to grow a portfolio faster than inflation, but they don't want to take unnecessary risk.

You may want to consider your spouse in selecting a risk level, particularly if there's a big difference in the way the two of you look at risk. Even when dealing with combined assets, it can often be less stressful to run a split portfolio with each half tailored to the individual's own level of risk tolerance.

If you're picking investments for friends or relatives, it's a good idea to use their threshold for risk tolerance, especially if it's lower than your own. You may understand long-term investing, but those who trust you might tend to view any significant short-term loss as an error in judgment on your part.

The Trade-Offs of Time

Figure 4 illustrates why the length of time you plan to invest is so important in determining how to structure your portfolio. This chart, which is based on 50 years of market behavior, shows how $1,000 grows with different classes of assets over various periods of time. These figures are adjusted for inflation to give a clear picture of real growth. Inside each box, the figure at the top shows what $1,000 would be worth after the best-case gain for the period indicated. The middle figure is the typical value of an initial $1,000 investment, based on the average return for the period. The bottom figure is the worst-case result over the time frame indicated.

As you might expect, investment returns increase as you take on more risk. This is evident for all time periods and is consistent in both the averages (the middle figures) and the best-case figures (shown at the top). A cash strategy represented by 30-day T-bills was about even with inflation (0.3 percent per year real return) for the 50-year test period. An income approach, represented by a portfolio of 70 percent bonds (50 percent intermediate-term government bonds and 20 percent long-term corporate bonds) and 30 percent stocks (S&P 500 index), provided a real 50-year return of 3.1 percent annually. A growth and income approach using 60 percent stocks (S&P 500) and 40 percent bonds (intermediate-term government bonds) delivered an

Asset Allocation Class		1 Year	3 Years	5 Years	8 Years	12 Years	Real Growth
Aggressive Growth: 100% Small Stocks	Best Case	$ 1927	$ 4759	$ 6894	$10281	$13424	9.5% Real Growth
	Average	$ 1095	$ 1313	$ 1574	$ 2067	$ 2972	
	Worse Case	$ 504	$ 458	$ 390	$ 529	$ 1080	
Growth: 100% S&P 500	Best Case	$ 1570	$ 2300	$ 3150	$ 4591	$ 6749	7.2% Real Growth
	Average	$ 1072	$ 1233	$ 1417	$ 1747	$ 2308	
	Worse Case	$ 545	$ 575	$ 593	$ 697	$ 748	
Growth & Income: 60% S&P 500, 40% Int. Gov't Bonds	Best Case	$ 1430	$ 1837	$ 2487	$ 2773	$ 3662	5.0% Real Growth
	Average	$ 1050	$ 1158	$ 1277	$ 1479	$ 1798	
	Worse Case	$ 674	$ 702	$ 752	$ 732	$ 819	
Income-Oriented: 50% Int. Gov't Bond, 20% Corp LT Bond, 30% S&P 500	Best Case	$ 1362	$ 1673	$ 2187	$ 2619	$ 3544	3.1% Real Growth
	Average	$ 1031	$ 1097	$ 1166	$ 1279	$ 1447	
	Worse Case	$ 762	$ 771	$ 738	$ 701	$ 782	
Money Market Equivalent: 100% 30-Day T-Bills	Best Case	$ 1070	$ 1182	$ 1310	$ 1392	$ 1516	0.3% Real Growth
	Average	$ 1003	$ 1010	$ 1016	$ 1026	$ 1039	
	Worse Case	$ 836	$ 749	$ 722	$ 587	$ 564	

Legend:
Best Case
Average
Worse Case

Figure 4   After-inflation growth of $1000 for five asset allocation classes; tested over 50 years.
Source: Ibbotson Associates, Inc.

after-inflation growth rate of 5.0 percent. A growth strategy with 100 percent stocks (S&P 500) averaged a real return of 7.2 percent. Finally, an aggressive growth strategy holding 100 percent in small stocks grew 9.5 percent after inflation.

More interesting, however, is how the worst-case numbers vary. For an investment horizon of more than a year, taking on additional risk actually reduces the odds of a loss (indicated by increasing worst-case numbers). At some point, however, your risk of loss jumps up significantly. This is why the investment horizon is key for deciding on the appropriate asset class. For a given investment horizon, there exists an investment strategy that represents the best overall trade-off in terms of risk and total return. (This is indicated by shaded boxes in Figure 4.)

For a one-year investment period, the risk of loss goes up with any strategy involving more risk than cash. While higher average returns are available, you're taking more of a chance with such a short time period.

For a three-year horizon, an income-oriented approach is the best bet. Notice how the bottom number is actually worse with cash—that's because the higher income stream stands up to inflation better than a cash investment can.

Over five years, a growth and income strategy is the best fit. Notice how the bottom number goes up when moving from cash up to growth and income. Once you take on more risk than a growth and income mix, the potential of bear market losses begins to offset the benefit of taking on more risk.

For an eight-year horizon, the worst-case numbers tend to suggest growth and income again. Looking closely, however, the risk of loss between growth and income and growth is only slightly higher, whereas the after-inflation average return is better by more than two full percentage points. Stocks win out here when you weigh the odds.

For very long-term investments it pays to be aggressive. In the 50-year test period small stocks never lagged inflation or cash investments over a horizon of 12 years or more. If you can stand the year-to-year fluctuations, the long-term risk of holding small stocks is very low.

Cash, on the other hand, is actually more "risky" than stocks over long periods of time. The worst-case figure shows how a cash approach lagged inflation in the 1970s. A portfolio in 30-day T-bills would have lost almost half of its purchasing power during the 12 most inflationary years of the last half century.

Your Investment Horizon

Most investors do not invest for a certain period of time and then spend their savings all at once. Putting a son or daughter through college may come close to this scenario, but even then you spend the money over a period of several years. To do a good job of designing a suitable portfolio, you need to characterize your investment horizon.

Unless your investment portfolio is large relative to your annual living expenses, you should consider setting aside three to six months' living expenses as an emergency reserve. A higher amount could be appropriate if your job security is low or if the chance of unexpected medical expenses is high. The emergency fund should be kept in a liquid cash investment such as a money market fund or a savings account.

Now, let's determine the investment horizon for the balance of your investment savings. You don't have to be precise; just try to make some rough estimates based on a likely scenario with no surprise events.

For each of the following periods, estimate your gross income from sources other than your investment holdings. Then figure approximate living expenses, including all major expenses such as housing, food, utilities, insurance, travel, cash outlays for vehicles or property, college expenses, taxes, and medical costs.

The amount by which total expenses exceed income sources is the amount of your investment principal needed in the specified period.

The Next Three Years   If you are employed and no major expenses are anticipated, this figure will probably be $0. If you expect major expenditures, such as a home, car, or college expenses, include any outlays that will exceed your regular income sources. If you are in retirement or if you expect to retire in the next few years, include the amount of your living expenses that will exceed income sources such as social security, pensions, rental income, etc.

A Period Starting Three and Ending Eight Years from Now
As with the previous step, figure the amount by which your expenses will exceed noninvestment income sources. Investors expecting to work during this period may end up with $0 in this period as well. Investors in retirement should make allowances for higher costs. Assuming inflation averages 3 percent per year, living expenses that aren't fixed are likely to be about 20 percent higher in this five-year period.

A Period of Eight Years in the Future and Beyond   This is the easiest amount to figure, because you simply take your total investment holdings and subtract the previous two figures. Those age 50 or less may find that most or all of their investment holdings are in this category. Retirement investors with a substantial asset base may also end up with a high percentage of their assets in this group. This category is also appropriate for investment holdings you don't ever expect to draw on, although these may eventually be passed on to heirs or donated to charitable causes.

You may be retired and find that your portfolio will not cover eight years of living expenses. This may be okay depending on your age and health, but you should meet with a fee-based financial planner to review the situation.

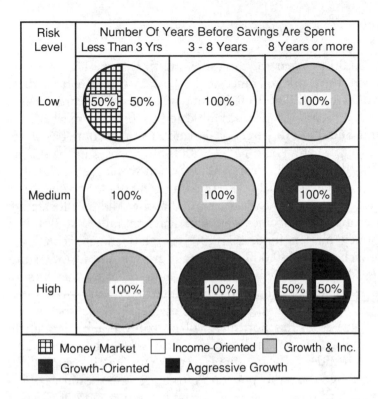

Risk Level	Number Of Years Before Savings Are Spent		
	Less Than 3 Yrs	3 - 8 Years	8 Years or more
Low	50% / 50%	100%	100%
Medium	100%	100%	100%
High	100%	100%	50% / 50%

⊞ Money Market   ☐ Income-Oriented   ▨ Growth & Inc.
■ Growth-Oriented   ■ Aggressive Growth

Figure 5   Recommended allocation strategy.

Determining an Appropriate Mix

At this point, you are ready to apply the allocation chart shown in Figure 5. This matrix takes into account your risk tolerance and your investment horizon.

Find the row that matches your risk tolerance and apply the amounts for each spending period to the suggested mix. Then add up the dollar amounts dedicated to each investment approach for a final allocation mix. Some examples follow.

Ron and Cathy   A retired couple, Ron and Cathy have investment holdings of $800,000. Living expenses that are not covered by social security and pension income are expected to average about $40,000 per year over the next three years and

$50,000 per year for the following five years. The two considers their risk tolerance to be low. In this situation, there would be $120,000 in the first box (less than three years), with $60,000 (50 percent) allocated to a money market fund and $60,000 (50 percent) allocated to an income-based approach. There would be $250,000 of expenses in the second box (three to eight years), all of which would be allocated to an income approach. The remaining $430,000 would be in the third box (eight years or more) and would be allocated to a growth and income approach. The final tally: $60,000 in a money market fund, $310,000 in an income-oriented approach, and $430,000 following a growth and income strategy. When invested in Fidelity mutual funds, this mix of investments should produce a long-term growth rate of about 8 to 9 percent per year. Although dividends alone (the income stream) from this portfolio will probably not be enough to meet living expenses, Ron and Cathy should be comfortable with the idea of selling shares to make up the difference. Over the long term, the portfolio's total return should be high enough to meet living expenses with some growth of capital.

Tom   At age 35, Tom considers himself to have medium risk tolerance. His only significant investment is $30,000 in a Fidelity 401(k) retirement plan that his employer offers. Tom figures his salary will cover all of his expenditures until retirement. In this situation, all $30,000 would be in the medium risk box (eight years or more). Tom should pursue a growth-oriented strategy.

Mike and Lori   A couple with young children, Mike and Lori have saved $16,000 for their children's college expenses, and they will start needing the money in about 12 years. The couple has an adequate emergency fund but has not saved much for retirement. Both have good jobs that should provide for all expenditures in the next eight years, and the two consider their risk tolerance to be high. In this situation, Mike and Lori should follow the box in the lower right and invest 50 percent of the money in a growth strategy and dedicate 50 percent to aggressive growth. The couple should also try to save 10 percent of their combined gross salaries for their retirement.

Cynthia   At age 27, Cynthia is saving to purchase a home and expects to have enough for a down payment in about two years. She considers herself to have medium risk tolerance. Cynthia should go with a 100 percent income-oriented approach. Given the short-term need for capital, it doesn't make sense for Cynthia to have much exposure to the stock market.

Bill and Debbie   As they near retirement with investment savings of $600,000, Bill and Debbie consider themselves to have medium risk tolerance. Bill will quit next year; Debbie has three years left to work. The couple won't need to draw on investments until Debbie retires because Bill's pension is a good one and should provide enough to live on while Debbie works. Upon Debbie's retirement they plan to travel and figure they'll draw an average of $50,000 per year for the following five years. In this situation, $250,000 of expenses are in the medium risk box (three to eight years), where a growth and income strategy is recommended. The remaining $350,000 would go to the eight years or more box and be invested for growth.

Keep in mind that in all of these examples the suggested mix may not be appropriate if the financial situation is complex or if there are unusual circumstances. If you have any doubts, you should meet with a fee-based financial planner to obtain some unbiased personal advice.

CATEGORIZING YOUR EXISTING HOLDINGS

If you have existing investments, the next step is to group them to see how your existing mix of investments compares to the suggested allocation mix. Here are some grouping guidelines that should provide a reasonable estimate of your current position:

- Any investment with stable principal can be considered a *cash investment*. This includes bank accounts, credit union accounts, CDs, short-term T-bills (less than a year), guaranteed investment contracts, and money market funds.
- The *income-oriented* group includes domestic corporate bonds (except junk bonds), U.S. government bonds, municipal bonds, treasuries maturing in one year or more, and any mutual funds that invest in these types of securities.
- *Growth and income* includes all growth and income funds, junk bonds (and junk bond funds), foreign bonds (and foreign bond funds), and dividend stocks.
- Diversified stock funds, index funds, foreign stock funds (except emerging-market funds), and any individual blue-chip stocks belong in the *growth-oriented* category.
- Other stock positions go in the *aggressive growth* group, as do sector funds, emerging market funds, gold funds, small-cap growth funds, and any other aggressive growth stock funds.

To figure your current mix, divide the total assets in each group by the total value of all your investments. Then compare your current mix to the suggested allocation to see how well you match up.

WORKING TOWARD YOUR SUGGESTED MIX

The next step is to work toward your suggested allocation mix by purchasing the Fidelity funds that I recommend (later in this section) in each of the asset groups. Depending on your situation, however, you may not want to move out of your current holdings right away.

Unless you are dealing with assets in a retirement account, selling securities that have increased in value since their purchase could trigger unnecessary capital gains tax on your 1040. If this is the case, you may want to sell selectively and increase your Fidelity holdings gradually. For example, if your overall position is more aggressive than the recommended mix, sell the aggressive positions that have appreciated the least and buy conservative Fidelity funds to obtain a better balance. If possible, you may want to sell losing positions along with profitable ones to offset capital gains. It could even make sense to sell over several years to minimize taxes. For investments that continue to perform well, you may not want to sell at all until you actually need the money.

If you are starting from cash or from a relatively conservative mix of investments, you may still want to dollar cost average if you plan to go with a growth-oriented strategy. Dollar cost averaging over two years provides some protection against a market decline and is discussed later in this chapter.

If possible, it may be to your advantage to use retirement accounts to fulfill your growth-oriented or aggressive growth allocation. The benefit of tax-deferred compounding is particularly valuable at higher growth rates (see Chapter 11 for more details).

ANNUAL REBALANCING

Keep in mind that maintaining your allocation mix is a continuing process, not something you do once and forget. I recommend that investors go through the exercise at least once a year. The reallocation that results from this process has two benefits. First, it takes into account any changes that have occurred in your financial situation and adjusts accordingly. Second, it rebalances the asset classes. Suppose stocks have a strong year, whereas bonds are weak. Selling some of your stock holdings and adding to bond funds may not seem like the right thing to do at the time, but it actually reduces your exposure to a higher-priced group of securities and increases your position in a group that is more attractively valued.

SELLING TO MEET LIVING EXPENSES

If you are living off your investments, the annual rebalancing of your portfolio is a good time to raise the cash you'll need for the coming year's living expenses. Estimate what you think you'll need over the next 12 months, and then sell assets from the group you are the most overweighted in.

For example, let's say you need $40,000 for the coming year's expenses. Based on earlier steps your target mix is $120,000 income, $200,000 growth and income, and $300,000 growth. Now suppose your actual holdings are $60,000 income, $200,000 growth and income, and $360,000 growth. In this case you would liquidate $60,000 of your growth-oriented holdings, putting $40,000 in a money market fund for living expenses, and $20,000 into additional income investments.

Over the course of the year you can then draw down the balance in the money market fund as you need the cash. If it turns out that the $40,000 gets used up in less than a year, you can always go through another rebalancing cycle at that time.

Two other tips. If you do the rebalancing around tax time, you can sell to raise cash for taxes at the same time you sell to raise money for living expenses. It's more convenient that way, and the capital gains you generate won't show up until the following tax year. Also, when estimating the amount needed for living expenses, be sure to reduce it by the appropriate amount if you have other income sources coming in throughout the year—including any bond or money market income that isn't being automatically reinvested.

FORCED RETIREMENT ACCOUNT DISTRIBUTIONS

Once you reach the age where you are forced to take withdrawals from your retirement account (usually above age

70), you have no choice but to pay taxes on the "income" from the distribution. As such, you should use this money for living expenses before selling other securities. If the distribution exceeds your cash needs, the excess should be invested in a regular taxable account according to the steps described.

INVESTING IN THE SUGGESTED ALLOCATION

Following is a discussion of the Fidelity funds that are appropriate for each of the five asset groups shown in the allocation chart (Figure 5).

Money Market Choices

Over the long run, I expect money markets to deliver an average return of around 4 to 5 percent, slightly more than inflation. From a performance standpoint, Fidelity's money market funds are pretty similar, and the taxable group usually offers the best returns for all but the highest-bracket investors. Go with Cash Reserves for low minimums and free conveniences such as checkwriting and Moneyline. If you expect to maintain a balance of $50,000 or more, go with Spartan Money Market for slightly higher yields.

Income-Oriented Fidelity Portfolios

For an income-oriented approach using Fidelity funds, you can follow the Income model published in *Fidelity Monitor,* or you can go with one of the model portfolios shown in Figure 6.

Portfolio A is 50 percent Investment Grade Bond, 25 percent Short-Term Bond, and 25 percent Capital & Income. Over a ten-year period, I estimate that this mix will generate a total return of about 8 percent annually, with 6 to 7 percent from the regular monthly income and 1 to 2 percent from capital appreciation. This mix of funds could lose 5 percent or more in a bond market sell-off, but the chances of a down year for this portfolio are low. The portfolio includes a variety

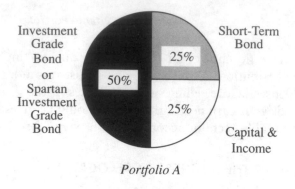

Investment
Grade
Bond
or
Spartan
Investment
Grade
Bond

Short-Term
Bond

50%

25%

25%

Capital &
Income

Portfolio A

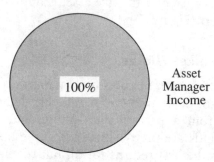

100%

Asset
Manager
Income

Portfolio B: Conservative Total Return

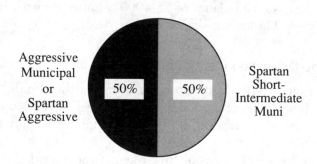

Aggressive
Municipal
or
Spartan
Aggressive

Spartan
Short-
Intermediate
Muni

50%

50%

Portfolio C: Tax-Free Income

Figure 6   Income-oriented portfolios.

of corporate and government bonds and a modest stake in conservative stocks and junk bonds (via Capital & Income). This mix tends to provide some stability because of the differences among the three funds; during most periods in the economic cycle at least two of these three holdings should perform well.

Portfolio B is the single-fund solution—Asset Manager: Income. Backed with a balanced mix of conservative securities, this fund has about the same long-term performance potential as Portfolio A, but its income stream is likely to be a bit lower. Risk of loss in a bear market is about the same.

Portfolio C seeks tax-free income with 50 percent in Aggressive Municipal and 50 percent in Spartan Short-Intermediate Muni. For investors in the top brackets, its long-term after-tax return of about 5 percent per year will probably be slightly better than for Portfolios A or B. The drawback is greater interest rate risk; in a bond market sell-off, Portfolio C could lose a little more than Portfolios A or B.

Growth and Income Fidelity Portfolios

For a Fidelity growth and income approach, you can follow the Growth and Income model published in *Fidelity Monitor,* or you can choose a model portfolio from Figure 7.

Portfolio A is 50 percent Puritan, 25 percent Equity-Income II, and 25 percent Asset Manager: Income. Over a ten-year period, I project a total return averaging 10 percent per year for this mix of funds, with 3 to 4 percent coming from reinvested dividends and 6 to 7 percent from capital appreciation. This portfolio could decline 15 percent or more in a bear market.

Portfolio B is 50 percent Puritan and 50 percent Asset Manager. This approach has the advantage of being simple, yet

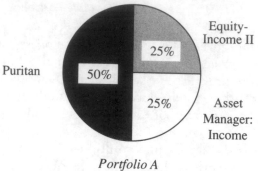

Portfolio A

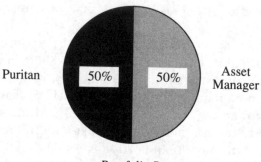

Portfolio B

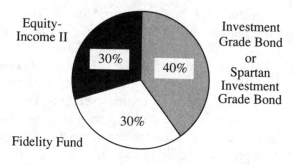

Portfolio C

Figure 7   Growth and Income portfolios

it avoids complete dependency on a single fund. The characteristics of this portfolio should be similar to those of Portfolio A.

Portfolio C is 40 percent Investment Grade Bond, 30 percent Fidelity Fund, and 30 percent Equity-Income II. This approach uses the classic 60 percent stock and 40 percent bond mix that has proven out over time. Again, risk and return should be a close match to Portfolio A.

Growth-Oriented Fidelity Portfolios

The Growth model published in *Fidelity Monitor* is my preferred approach for investing in growth-oriented Fidelity funds, but the portfolios in Figure 8 should also provide an attractive long-term return.

Portfolio A is 40 percent Low-Priced Stock, 30 percent Dividend Growth, and 30 percent Contrafund. My ten-year total return estimate for this group is 13 percent per year. This mix of funds could decline 25 percent or more in a bear market. Contrafund and Dividend Growth tend to be growth-oriented, whereas Low-Priced Stock is more value-oriented and focuses on small-cap stocks. Together these funds cover a broad spectrum of markets, which adds an element of stability to the portfolio.

Portfolio B offers a no-load approach for all accounts (Portfolio A is no-load only for retirement accounts). It holds 40 percent Value, 30 percent Dividend Growth, and 30 percent Large Cap Stock. This approach should provide a growth rate close to that of Portfolio A. Large Cap Stock is substituted for Contrafund. Value is substituted for Low-Priced, which reduces the overall weighting in small-cap issues. Bear market risk should be similar to that of Portfolio A.

Portfolio C provides more international exposure. With a mix of 40 percent Stock Selector, 30 percent Asset Manager: Growth, and 30 percent Diversified International, this portfolio is likely to have a 30 to 40 percent position in foreign

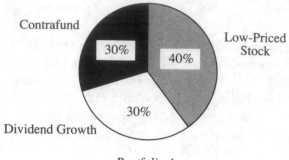

Portfolio A

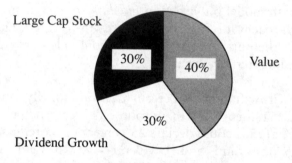

Portfolio B: No-Load

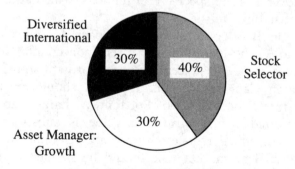

Portfolio C: Global

Figure 8   Growth-oriented portfolios.

markets most of the time. Stock Selector and Asset Manager: Growth usually maintain 10 to 30 percent in foreign holdings. Diversified International focuses mainly on European and Japanese stocks. The long-term growth rate of Portfolio C could be slightly less than the other two choices, but it should not suffer as much in a domestic bear market.

Aggressive Growth Fidelity Portfolios

The Select System model in *Fidelity Monitor* provides a sector-based approach for aggressive growth. In this portfolio I use a quantitative model to choose Selects based on valuation measures and risk-adjusted performance over a trailing one-year period. I've come to prefer the numbers-driven approach for the aggressive side because it's unbiased by emotion and it reacts consistently to changing market conditions. The fixed portfolios in Figure 9 aren't able to move around as new trends emerge, but I've tried to choose funds that have a high probability of long-term success.

Portfolio A uses a sector-oriented approach. With 25 percent each in Select Energy, Select Technology, Select Multimedia, and Select Health Care, this portfolio is capable of a ten-year growth rate of 15 percent per year. In a bear market it could decline 30 percent or more. My thoughts about these choices:

Health Care is a play on the aging population of the United States and other developed countries. That may be an old theme, but it still holds true for pharmaceutical firms. The other thing I like about Select Health Care is that the manager can invest heavily in biotech companies if opportunities exist. Although the profits have been slow to materialize, companies in the biotech sector seem to be where technology companies were in the 1950s. There will be many opportunities.

Select Multimedia is in this portfolio because companies stand to benefit from the growth that deregulation will bring. Also, U.S. companies stand a good chance of dominating

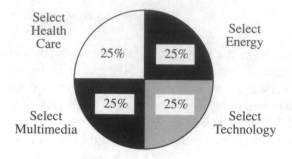

Portfolio A: Selects Only

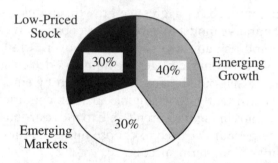

Portfolio B: Non-Select

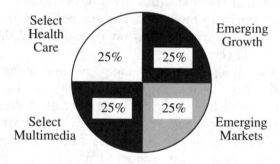

Portfolio C: All Groups

Figure 9   Aggressive growth portfolios.

many of the new types of media that will be made possible by technology.

An investment in Select Technology takes advantage of a sector with above-average long-term growth. Fidelity seems to do a good job of analyzing these firms, and clearly the growth rate is high in this sector.

Last but not least, we have Select Energy. The energy sector often performs well during bear markets, and Select Energy should add some long-term stability to the portfolio. Furthermore, energy companies stand to benefit as emerging markets increase their demand for oil and natural gas.

Portfolio B uses diversified funds rather than sectors, and it includes exposure to emerging markets. With 40 percent in Emerging Growth, 30 percent in Emerging Markets, and 30 percent in Low-Priced Stock, this portfolio should do about as well as Portfolio A in terms of total return and downside risk. Low-Priced Stock manager Joel Tillinghast looks for undervalued stocks in the small-cap realm, the asset class that provides the best long-term opportunities. Emerging Growth focuses on larger companies with strong growth opportunities, typically those in the technology sector. Emerging Markets is a developing-country fund that concentrates on Latin America and Southeast Asia (excluding Japan), the two major emerging world markets.

Portfolio C includes both sector funds and diversified funds. Each of the four funds accounts for a 25 percent position: Emerging Growth, Emerging Markets, Select Multimedia, and Select Health Care. This mix does not have the exposure to small-caps that you get with Portfolio B, but it is more globally oriented than Portfolio A. Growth potential and bear market risk should be similar to that of Portfolio A.

HOW MANY FUNDS SHOULD YOU OWN?

Depending on where you are in the allocation chart and on which portfolios you follow, you can end up having to purchase as few as three or as many as ten different mutual funds for your investment holdings. (Conservative strategies generally involve fewer funds, whereas aggressive strategies involve more.)

Investors who previously owned individual stocks and bonds sometimes feel that this number is too low. If you feel this way, remember that the average fund invests in more than 100 securities, and broadly diversified funds such as Asset Manager often own more than 500 different issues. Owning more than ten funds really isn't necessary to achieve broad diversification, and if you are investing conservatively you don't even need that many.

Along that line of thinking, the number of funds you own does not need to change for a large investment portfolio. Investment bankers rarely put their wealthy clients into more than 500 different securities, a level of diversification that can easily be obtained with just two to three broad-based mutual funds. The mix of funds I've recommended in each set of model portfolios is appropriate whether the amount being invested is $10,000 or $10,000,000.

In some cases it can make sense to *reduce* the number of funds you hold. Fidelity waives its annual account fee of $12 per fund (currently capped at $60 maximum) if you maintain a balance of $2,500 or more in each fund or a total of $50,000 or more in all of your accounts. Consolidating to eliminate fees may improve your performance by a small amount if you have a number of funds with small balances.

DOLLAR COST AVERAGING

Dollar cost averaging is an excellent way to move from cash into a growth-oriented or aggressive growth strategy because it disciplines you to buy more shares when prices are lower and to buy fewer when prices are higher. This advantage is significant because most investors will do exactly the opposite when making decisions in an unstructured fashion.

When you dollar cost average, you invest at regular intervals of time (usually monthly or quarterly) with a fixed dollar commitment at each interval. You become a value investor without even trying because your fixed commitment in dollars will automatically buy a larger position after a market decline or a smaller position following a rally. To better understand the benefit, consider this simple example involving a technology stock: Initially, the stock has a price of $10 per share and a purchase of $1,000 (100 shares) is made. Three months later the price has plummeted to $5 per share, and another $1,000 is invested (200 shares are purchased). Another quarter later, and the price has rebounded to $7.50 per share. A final purchase is made (133.3 shares).

What are the results? At first glance many investors would say the investor either broke even or lost money. In reality, a gain of 8.3 percent has been realized because of the effects of averaging down. Because more shares were purchased when the price was low, the average cost per share was $6.92 versus an average purchase price of $7.50. The final investment value is $3,250 versus $3,000 paid.

Generally speaking, there are two ways to use dollar cost averaging to your advantage:

- The first and most widely used method is to invest a percentage of your salary into a growth-oriented portfolio during your working years. Often the goal is to build a nest egg for future college expenses or for retirement. Many 401(k) investors are doing this with the added benefits of using pretax money and realizing tax-deferred compounding. Over the long run, this kind of program can be a very powerful tool for building wealth.
- The second approach is useful for reducing the risk of going from cash to a growth-oriented position. The benefit of dollar cost averaging in this situation is that you buy in at a progressively lower price if a market sell-off takes place (as opposed to experiencing the full impact of the decline right after you invest a large sum). When recovery eventually comes, it seldom takes long before your portfolio is worth more than you paid in.

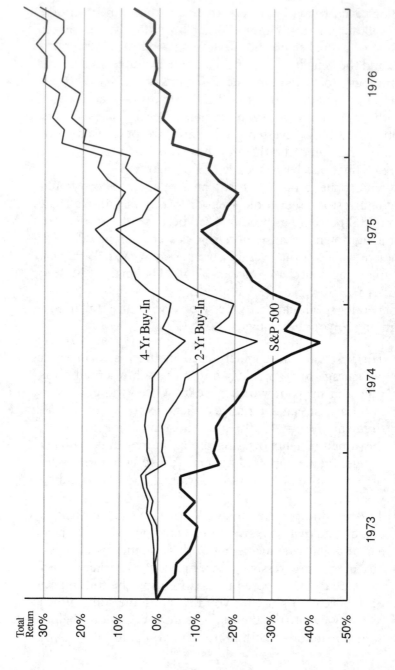

Figure 10 Impact of dollar cost averaging during worst bear market in modern history.

I recommend a buy-in period of two years when dollar cost averaging from a cash position. Take the amount you want to invest, divide by 8, and make purchases once a quarter for eight quarters. Don't wait for a good time to start; it isn't necessary to worry about what the market will do next because dollar cost averaging takes advantage of whatever comes along.

Figure 10 shows the benefit of dollar cost averaging during the worst bear market in modern history. In this example, the initial balance is in a money market fund (represented by short-term T-bills), and quarterly purchases of an S&P 500 index fund are made (both two-year and four-year buy-ins are shown). In both of these examples, the dollar-cost average portfolios decline less and recover faster than the market as a whole.

Of course, dollar cost averaging won't help you during bullish times. If stocks move up continuously, you'll lag the market because you'll have a heavy cash position while you are joining up with the market. As a practical matter, I favor the two-year buy-in period because it protects reasonably well against a downturn but isn't so long that you sacrifice gains in the more probable scenario of a rising market. Quarterly purchases are the most practical when you consider fund minimums, although a monthly approach could improve performance by a few percentage points during sideways or rising market conditions.

Dollar cost averaging works best with a growth-oriented or aggressive growth strategy. It can be used with the portfolios outlined earlier in this chapter or with the growth-oriented models in *Fidelity Monitor.* In the latter case, each portfolio switch requires that you change the invested portion and any new purchases to reflect the new mix.

The benefit of dollar cost averaging is diminished when investing for growth and income or when pursuing an income-oriented strategy. There simply isn't enough equity risk to reduce; you might as well invest everything in one step. Still, if you are after a very low-risk approach, averaging into a growth and income fund over three years is one way to nearly eliminate risk of loss during the buy-in period.

11

Taxes and Retirement Accounts

If a mutual fund has a long term return of 12 percent per year, is that the rate of growth you will achieve in your own account? The answer is yes if your investments are held in a tax-deferred account such as an IRA, Keogh, 401(k) plan, or a 403(b) plan. Such retirement plans do not incur any tax on investment gains (although you do pay tax at full income rates when you make withdrawals in your retirement years).

In a regular account, however, the long-term return is typically a few percentage points less after you pay the taxes due on fund distributions each year. In order to avoid tax penalties, mutual funds must distribute most of the income and capital gains they realize each year. Even if you reinvest a fund's distributions, you still have to pay tax on the payout unless the fund is held in a retirement account. Your after-tax return, which takes into account the income tax you pay on the reinvested distributions, is the actual rate of return on your holdings.

After-tax return varies depending on your own personal tax bracket, but Figure 11 can give you an idea of the impact. For this chart, I computed the after-tax returns for all of Fidelity's diversified growth funds in existence since the beginning of 1987 (except for Retirement Growth, which isn't

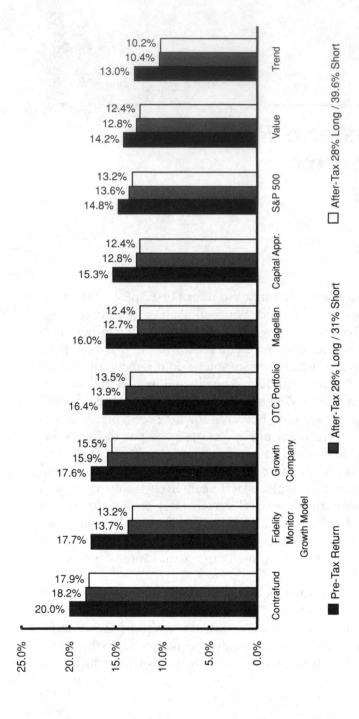

Figure 11 Annualized return of Fidelity growth funds for 9.5 years ending June 30, 1996.

available for taxable accounts). Two after-tax situations are shown for the 9.5-year period that covers through mid-1996. The first assumes the 28 percent maximum federal rate for long-term capital gains distributions and a 31 percent rate for dividends and short-term capital gains distributions. The second scenario also assumes the 28 percent bracket for long-term payouts, but it uses the maximum federal rate of 39.6 percent for dividends and short-term capital gains. In both cases, the chart shows the annualized return that would exist prior to selling the entire fund position and paying tax on the unrealized capital gain.

Not surprisingly, funds that did well on a pretax basis generally performed well after taxes. Quite a few funds outperformed the S&P 500 on an after-tax basis, which counters the argument that index funds are the best way to go in a taxable account. (Proponents of indexing claim an advantage over regular funds because of their low payouts of capital gains.) Fidelity's growth funds have been good performers for both taxable and retirement accounts.

The leader of the pack, Contrafund, did unusually well after taxes because of unique circumstances that are unlikely to be repeated. Because of steady inflows of new money throughout the period, this fund provided its managers plenty of new capital for buying attractive stocks. Accordingly, the fund didn't have to sell much of its portfolio for many years. This made for relatively low payouts of capital gains and relatively high after-tax returns. However, situations like this don't last forever. With assets of more than $20 billion, Contrafund is now relatively mature. Future years are now likely to bring payouts that are similar to other growth funds.

TAX IMPLICATIONS OF EXCHANGES

In a tax-deferred retirement account, you can switch all you want with no tax implications. In a regular account, however, each exchange you make produces a capital gain or capital loss, depending on whether the price at which you sell is higher or lower than the price at which you bought. If the shares you are selling have been held for less than one year, your capital gain is short term. Losses in a period of less than a year are short term to the extent that they are not offset by long-term gains. These rules also apply to municipal funds, which are generally tax-free on dividends but not on capital gains.

The capital gain you incur when selling a fund is usually not the full gain you have obtained in owning the fund. Rather, it is the gain that hasn't been already been taxed as a result of the fund's distributions. Prior to selling a fund, the difference between the current share price (NAV) and the purchased price (plus any transaction fees) is called the un-realized capital gain.

DOES SWITCHING HELP OR HURT LONG-TERM RETURNS?

Some advisors claim an actively managed portfolio will per-form worse than a buy and hold portfolio after taxes are fig-ured in. However, as Figure 11 shows, this has not been the case for my *Fidelity Monitor* Growth model. In computing an after-tax return for the Growth model, I included not only the tax impact of the fund distributions but also the capital gains taxes that were paid after making switches. Even though the Growth model has paid more taxes along the way (and will owe less taxes when sold), it compares well to the alternative of buying and holding a single position.

When it comes to after-tax returns, an actively managed growth portfolio can outperform one that stays put as long as its pretax return is better by about two percentage points per year. Moving around between funds might trigger more capital gains taxes, but if you are making the right choices you'll be better off in the long run. When you finally sell your holdings, you won't be facing a huge capital gains tax as you would from holding a single fund for many years.

MINIMIZING THE TAX BITE

Over the long term, there is little you can do to prevent distributions from reducing your return in a taxable account, but there are some techniques you can use for a tax-advantaged portfolio.

Retirement Accounts

If you have the option, keep your growth-oriented and aggressive-growth funds in retirement accounts. Tax-deferred accounts provide the most benefit at higher long-term growth rates (more on this later in the chapter). You can balance your growth-oriented retirement holdings with conservative holdings in your taxable accounts—where the money will be available without penalty if you need it. I realize this strategy may be the opposite of what many investors practice, but the benefits are significant, especially if you are under age 50 (at this age you still have at least 20 years available before you are required to take money out of your tax-deferred accounts).

Timely Purchases

Avoid purchasing a stock fund in a taxable account if it is close to making a distribution. Many large payouts of capital gains occur in December, so try to purchase the fund after the payout has occurred.

Hold Positions

If your federal tax bracket is higher than 28 percent, try to hold profitable positions for at least one year. That way, you'll receive the more favorable 28 percent maximum rate on long-term capital gains. This doesn't mean you should hang on to a fund with deteriorating performance; but other factors being equal, you should strive for a one-year holding period. Likewise, try to take losses short-term if your long-term gains are small. (I use both of these techniques with the *Fidelity Monitor* Growth model.)

First Few Years of Ownership

In the following, you will find some suggestions that might hold down taxes during the first few years you own a fund. Unfortunately, these techniques aren't always a sure bet, and they only delay the impact of taxes. Ultimately, you still end up paying taxes on gains. Still, if your intent is to hold a fund for a long time, it is possible to get a head start in building up unrealized capital gains.

Newer, Small Funds   For domestic growth, consider one of Fidelity's newer funds if it is small (less than $250 million) and has outperformed the S&P 500 for at least a year. These funds tend to be above-average performers, and the typical inflow of new money allows the manager to buy attractive stocks without needing to sell many of the existing holdings. This makes for relatively small distributions. Keep in mind that this approach can backfire if performance falls out of favor and redemptions increase.

Carryforward Losses   Consider a small position in a fund that has carryforward losses. The best bet here is a hard-hit Select with potential for a turnaround. Look for one with several negative years combined with no payouts of capital gains.

FILING YOUR INCOME TAXES

Except for retirement account holdings, Fidelity will send you and the IRS a 1099-DIV form after the end of each year. This statement lists all of the mutual fund distributions that must be reported on your federal 1040 form. All taxable dividend income, including the regular monthly income from bond and money market funds, will be listed on this form and must be reported on Schedule B, Interest and Dividend Income. (For IRS purposes, a fund's ordinary dividends include both distribution of income and short-term capital gains.) Long-term capital gains must be reported on Schedule D, Capital Gains and Losses. Note that it does not matter how long you owned the fund. A long-term distribution of capital gains must be reported as such even if it was paid out a few days after you bought the fund. Finally, be sure to check Fidelity's state-by-state list of municipal income dividends if you owned a national muni fund. You can avoid state taxes on the percentage of income earned from bonds specific to your state.

If you owned any municipal bond funds or municipal money market funds, Fidelity will send you a statement of tax-exempt income that lists the amount of tax-free dividends you earned and any income subject to Alternative Minimum Tax (AMT). Your total for tax-free dividends must be listed on Schedule B, but it gets totaled into the nontaxable section where you don't incur any taxes on it (unless you have to pay under AMT rules).

If you held any limited partnerships (some of Fidelity's funds are structured this way), you'll receive a schedule K-1 listing dividends and capital gains. Like regular funds, these are reported on Schedules B and D, respectively.

Unless you've confined your switching activity to a retirement account or money market fund, all mutual fund redemptions must be reported on Schedule D of your federal 1040 return. Fidelity will send you and the IRS a 1099-B form showing all of the Fidelity transactions you must report. However, it's up to you to do the hard part, figuring out cost basis. (Fidelity sends year-end cost basis information for accounts opened in 1987 or later; it may be a great time-saver if you fit the requirements for using it.)

Cost Basis

There are four options for determining cost basis, and when you select a method you should state it on your tax form or on an attachment. Once you start using a method for a particular fund, you must get permission from the IRS if you want to change methods before selling all shares owned in that fund. (The only exception is that you are allowed to switch without permission once from either FIFO or specific shares to average cost per share.)

First In, First Out (FIFO) This method is relatively simple and easy, and it requires the least record keeping if you are doing your own taxes. It assumes the first shares purchased are the first to be sold. Suppose your first purchase of Magellan was 50 shares at $50 per share and your second was 75 shares at $60 per share. Later you sell 100 shares at $70 per share. Your cost basis for the first 50 shares sold would be $2,500 (50 shares at $50 per share), and your cost basis on the second 50 shares would be $3,000 (50 shares at $60 per share). Together you would have paid $5,500 on the shares you sold. Your gain on the sale would be $1,500, and if both were held for a year or more it would be considered a long-term capital gain.

Specific Shares With this approach, you identify specific blocks of shares to sell (usually those that produce the smallest gain or largest loss). Write a letter and let Fidelity know you are selling specific shares, and then identify the specific block of shares by account, quantity, and date purchased. Save a copy of the letter and Fidelity's acknowledgment for your tax records.

Average Cost per Share, Single Category With this method, a weighted average of all purchase prices is computed, and the average price is used for the cost basis on all shares you've sold. If the selling activity is spread out over more than one year, the average is updated each year.

If you have not started with a different method, you can use the average cost per share figures Fidelity now provides on accounts opened after 1986. If you have used a different method in the past, Fidelity's figures will not be valid even if you switch over to this method, because the average cost figure would no longer be accurate after the first sale.

Average Cost per Share, Double Category   This is similar to the single category method, except that your short-term holdings (positions held less than a year) and long-term holdings are grouped separately, and a weighted average cost per share is computed for each.

Other Schedule D Considerations

Regardless of which cost basis method you choose, there are some other things to be aware of when filling out your Schedule D (all of which are included in Fidelity's cost basis figures if you are able to use them).

For reinvested dividends and capital gains distributions, each is considered a separate purchase. In the case of a bond fund, for example, you make at least 12 purchases every year, each at a different price. When you sell a long-term position, you may have reinvestment purchases that represent short-term capital gains.

A sale involving a capital loss can be deemed a wash sale (a sale intended solely for creating a tax loss) if the same fund is repurchased within 30 days (or if it is purchased up to 30 days ahead of the sale). Losses are disallowed for wash sales, but the loss can be added to your cost basis on your repurchase of the fund. Wash sale rules can be tripped accidentally, so be sure to consider your situation before you sell at a loss. Also be aware that Fidelity's cost basis statement may not properly detect and adjust for a wash sale if more than one account is involved. (Wash sale rules do not apply to retirement accounts because their transactions are not reported on Schedule D.)

If you sell shares at a loss in a fund you've held for less than six months, you may have to treat part or all of your loss as long-term if you received a distribution of long-term capital gains during the period. For each share sold, the amount that must be treated as a long-term capital loss is equal to the amount of the long-term distribution of capital gains on that share.

TAX-DEFERRED ACCOUNTS

Many investors who have money in an IRA, Keogh, 401(k), or 403(b) account fail to take advantage of the unique opportunity these tax-deferred vehicles provide. Some put their money into cash-type investments because they don't want to "take a chance" on something as important as retirement. Others don't comprehend the advantage they have with tax deferral, and as a result they don't contribute the maximum amount to their plans.

Figure 12 shows how the combination of pretax compounding and a growth-oriented strategy can produce powerful results. You've probably seen this type of graph before, but note that these results are adjusted for inflation (at an assumed rate of 3 percent per year). The results show real increases in purchasing power on an initial $1,000 investment. Although there are no guarantees for the growth rates that are shown, I think the total returns shown are achievable with the model portfolios outlined in Chapter 10.

At lower growth rates, such as those available from money markets, CDs, T-bills, or bond funds, a tax-deferred account offers little advantage over a taxable account (other than the benefit of being able to contribute pretax money). Keeping long-term retirement account assets in cash is like owning a Ferrari and using it only for low-speed trips to the grocery store. A tax-deferred account that's being used for long-term savings can realize its potential only if it includes growth-oriented investments. It should be used for building wealth, not staying even with inflation.

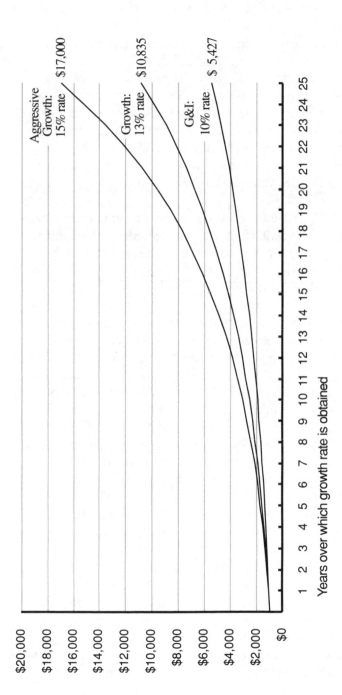

Figure 12 After-inflation growth of a $1000 investment in a tax-deferred account.

Investors in their working years should use a retirement account only for long-term savings. That's because once you make a contribution you'll pay a 10 percent penalty on any withdrawals you take before age 59½ (unless you become disabled or you annuitize with an IRS-approved method). Even if you are older than 59½, investing in a retirement account for just a few years may put you at a slight disadvantage, because you are taxed at income rates that can be higher than the 28 percent long-term capital gains rate for taxable accounts.

You should be aware that taxes can be significant when you make withdrawals from your retirement account during your later years. Current tax code requires that you begin taking withdrawals in the year following the year in which you reach age 70½. At that age, you have no choice but to take out money based on IRS life expectancy tables. (If you don't, you can face a 50 percent excise tax on the amount you should have taken out each year.) Each withdrawal is taxed at your regular income tax rate, which can be as high as 39.6 percent under today's tax code. If you take out more than $155,000 in any one year (over time this amount goes up with inflation), you must pay 15 percent of the amount over $155,000 as an excess distribution penalty. Note: This excess distribution penalty may be temporarily waived or increased in the future; check with your tax advisor for details.

At first glance, higher taxes on retirement account withdrawals might seem to offset some of the compounding advantage of these types of accounts. Over the long run, however, you're usually better off with a retirement account when pursuing a growth-oriented approach. Suppose at age 40 you leave your employer and transfer a 401(k) account worth $100,000 into a rollover IRA at Fidelity. After obtaining a 12 percent return for 25 years, your account is now worth $1.7 million. Suppose you move it to a money market fund and take it out over six years to avoid the excess distribution tax (3 percent inflation over 25 years would raise the current $155,000 limit to about $300,000) and pay income taxes at a rate of

39.6 percent. You end up with about $1.0 million after taxes, not counting the money market income during the withdrawal period. That's equivalent to an after-tax growth rate of about 10 percent for the first 25 years. The same investments in a regular taxable account with a 28 percent tax rate would compound at an after-tax rate of 8 to 9 percent and result in a portfolio worth roughly $800 thousand when all taxes are paid. Even when taxed at the maximum rate of 39.6 percent, the benefit of tax-deferred compounding is worth around $200 thousand. Note: If the tax rate on long-term capital gains is ever reduced to 20 percent or less, retirement accounts would lose some of their advantage over regular taxable accounts.

401(K) PLANS

Almost insignificant a decade ago, 401(k) plans today are enjoying unprecedented popularity. More than 95 percent of large corporations now offer these unique retirement plans to their employees, and smaller firms are setting up their own plans at a rapid clip (new legislation allowing SIMPLE accounts may accelerate this trend). The amount of 401(k) money in Fidelity funds now accounts for perhaps 35 to 40 percent of total Fidelity fund assets, and new contributions from Fidelity 401(k) plans have grown to the point that some funds experience net inflows of capital even during market declines. In the long run, 401(k) money could reshape the entire mutual fund industry and even have a stabilizing effect on the entire domestic stock market.

Companies favor 401(k) plans because they are classified as "defined contribution plans" rather than "defined benefit plans" like traditional pensions. 401(k) programs do not carry the promise of guaranteed retirement benefits, a financial liability that has become increasingly difficult to shoulder with recent accounting changes and increasing government regulations. Many firms want their 401(k) programs to be successful because over the next few decades they would like to phase out their traditional pensions.

Employees also like 401(k) plans because they have control. They decide how much to contribute, and they decide how it should be invested (within the range of choices offered). Unlike a big pension fund, the money is in a designated account and is less likely to be misappropriated if the company gets bought out or falls on hard times. When leaving the company, the money can be transferred tax-free to a rollover IRA account at an institution of the employee's choice.

Financial Advantages of a 401(k)

What many employees may not realize is that 401(k) programs are an excellent opportunity for accumulating wealth. In addition to tax-deferred compounding, a 401(k) account has several other significant financial advantages.

Pretax Contributions   The money contributed to your 401(k) account comes out of your paycheck before federal and state taxes are deducted. Suppose your federal tax bracket is 31 percent. To equal the power of a 401(k) plan you would have to save 45 percent more if you were saving on your own. ($145 per month saved on a pretax basis only reduces your take-home pay by about $100, so you can be saving 45 percent more money just by doing it on a pretax basis.)

Matching Funds   Many employers provide significant matching funds, which give you an immediate large return on your contributions. If your employer makes one for three matching contributions in the preceding example, your 401(k) plan has almost twice the accumulating power of a do-it-yourself approach using after-tax money.

Dollar Cost Averaging   A 401(k) plan sets aside money from each paycheck and makes predetermined purchases at regular intervals, so dollar cost averaging is working in your favor. In a growth fund, the rate of return you obtain on the invested money can be slightly higher than the fund itself because you'll be purchasing more shares whenever the price is lower.

Avoiding Load Fees Mutual fund companies, including Fidelity, generally waive load fees in their 401(k) plans. This allows 100 percent of the money to go to work for you in your chosen fund(s).

Maximizing 401(k) Contributions

With so many factors working in your favor, it makes strong financial sense to maximize your 401(k) contributions. Consider an example where contributions to a Fidelity growth fund are made for 15 years with an employer match of one for three. With an assumed salary of $30,000 and a 10 percent contribution rate, the balance in the 401(k) account would be at $180,000 at the end of the period (I assumed portfolio growth of 12 percent per year and annual salary growth of 3 percent).

Even if your fund choices are mediocre, you can still do well. One of my relatives was in this situation. His 401(k) choices weren't the best, but he contributed the maximum percentage of his salary for the better part of a decade. Because of pretax savings and matching contributions from his employer, he did well despite the lack of a good fund. Ultimately, he was able move a portfolio worth $105,000 into a rollover IRA account at Fidelity.

That's one drawback with most 401(k) plans. Companies tend to hold down administrative expenses by providing only three to six investment offerings, and many do not offer good mutual fund choices. Even if you are one of the lucky ones with access to a Fidelity growth fund, it may not be the one you want. More companies should follow the lead of Unisys and General Motors, which allow their employees to choose from over 40 different Fidelity funds.

If your company's 401(k) is too restrictive, you may be able to get it changed. Companies add funds to their 401(k) programs all the time; you may be able to convince your company to expand the range of options. Tell your benefits manager that you need more choices to pursue an appropriate investment strategy, and name the funds you would like to see included. Don't expect changes overnight, however; it may take a year or more before program changes can be made.

Picking Funds in a 401(k) Account

Finally, here are some tips on the best choices for your 401(k) account:

Retirement Eight or More Years Away Go with a growth-oriented fund. Fidelity 401(k) plans usually include at least one of the following good choices: Contrafund, Growth & Income, Growth Company, and Magellan. If your 401(k) doesn't include any Fidelity funds, consider an equity-income fund. These tend to be consistent long-term performers.

Within Eight Years of Retirement Go with a growth and income strategy if you are within eight years of retiring. Choose Asset Manager or Puritan if available, or invest 70 percent in a conservative stock fund such as Growth & Income or Equity-Income and 30 percent in a bond fund such as Intermediate Bond. In a non-Fidelity 401(k), consider 60 percent in an equity-income fund and 40 percent in a bond fund.

Avoid Guaranteed Investment Contracts (GICs) Many of these are not protected from insolvency the way a mutual fund is, and if the insurer is unable to meet its obligations you could lose some of your principal. Besides, in the long run, a higher level of risk will likely provide a higher rate of return.

Avoid Taking Out a Loan against Your 401(k) Account
These result in the liquidation of current assets, so you don't
see any investment gains until the money is paid back. That
may not matter if you are planning to hold cash anyway, but
if you liquidate an attractive growth fund you can significantly reduce your long-term returns. Borrowing from the
bank can actually be a better choice unless you are close to
retirement; 15 years down the road the benefit of maintaining your 401(k) in a growth-oriented fund could dwarf the
loan interest involved.

Changing Employers   If you leave your employer, take
full possession of your 401(k) holdings for maximum flexibility. Arrange for a direct transfer between your company's
administrator and the financial institution you choose for the
rollover IRA. That way, you don't take the chance of incurring a huge tax bill on your holdings, an event that can occur
if you take possession of the money yourself and don't reinvest the full amount (including the 20 percent federal
withholding) in 60 days.

How and When to Avoid Load Fees

As of mid 1996, Fidelity charges a 3 percent front-end load on 10 domestic growth funds, 14 foreign funds, and 36 Selects. This money goes to Fidelity and can be used to pay for advertising, mailings, investor centers, and other selling-related activities. Fidelity seems to charge loads on funds that investors perceive as offering a unique advantage, either in the form of attractive performance or because they provide an investment vehicle that's not available elsewhere (as in the case of the Selects).

When you purchase a Fidelity fund with a 3 percent load, it is reflected in the offering price, which is 3.1 percent higher than the actual net asset value (NAV). The offering price is calculated so that 97 percent of your original investment goes to work in the fund you purchase.

When you pay the load, Fidelity's computers tag your shares with a 3 percent load credit so that those shares won't be charged again on future trades. (I'll go into more detail on Fidelity's load tracking system later in this chapter.)

IS A THREE PERCENT FUND WORTH THE PRICE?

When you consider that a Fidelity 3 percent load is paid only once on the money invested, the long-term impact on performance is not large. Over a ten-year period, the annual impact to performance is less than 0.3 percent annually. Most of Fidelity's domestic stock funds (including the Selects) stand a good chance of outperforming the indexes over the long run, which means there is a reasonably good chance that you'll make up for the load through improved performance.

Still, the decision to pay a front-end load should be based on what the alternatives are. Here are my thoughts for each fund group.

Growth Funds

Figure 13 compares the performance of load funds and no-load funds over a ten-year period covering through mid-1996. For each month in this study, I computed separate averages for load funds and no-load funds, based on whether the fund was charging a load during a particular month. Unlike many of the industry-wide studies I've seen, Fidelity load funds did actually have a small advantage over Fidelity no-loads. But this advantage has gone away in recent years as many newer funds have been introduced without loads.

Given this situation, I think the appropriate stance to take is to pay the load if the fund's investment approach isn't available in a no-load version. For example, Low-Priced Stock is the only Fidelity fund that invests in small-cap value stocks, and it would seem to be worth its load because of its low risk and attractive performance. On the other hand, Blue Chip Growth is probably not worth its load because Large Cap Stock has a very similar objective and is available no-load.

International Funds

Fidelity's broadly diversified international funds are no-load, whereas funds that are specific to a particular country or

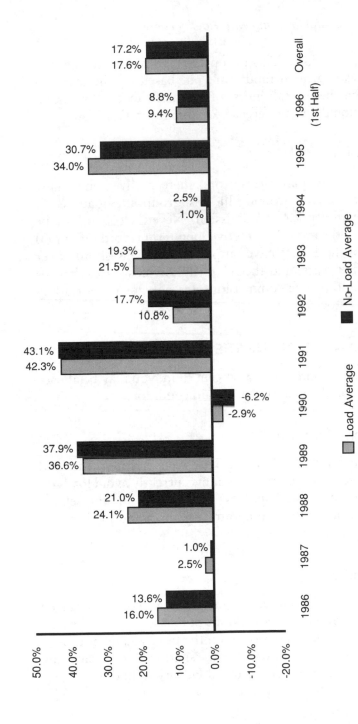

Figure 13 Fidelity domestic growth fund performance: load funds versus no-loads.

region carry a load. This group can't be compared the way the domestic growth funds can, but based on the fact that Fidelity has been weak in its foreign performance I think investors should give preference to no-loads in this group.

Select Funds

If you want to play the sectors, there really aren't many other alternatives around. In this group the load fee is essentially the price of admission. Nevertheless, it can be justified by the group's attractive long-term record (about 60 percent of the Selects have outperformed the S&P 500 over the last five years) and the relatively low cost of exchanges compared to paying commissions and spreads when trading individual stocks.

WAYS TO AVOID PAYING THE LOAD

If you want to purchase a 3 percent fund, you may be able to avoid paying the load under certain conditions.

Retirement Accounts

If you purchase the fund in a retirement account, the load may be waived. Retirement accounts currently avoid loads on all funds except Magellan, New Millennium, and the Selects. The 401(k) and 403(b) programs usually avoid loads on all funds in the program.

Load Credits

If you purchased the fund using shares that have been tagged with a load credit from a previous purchase, you will be able to avoid or reduce the load fee on the fund you want to buy. If you're not sure about whether the shares you own have any load credits on them, you can call Fidelity to find out.

Gifts

If the load fund is obtained as a gift from someone else, the load is not charged a second time. Suppose your son or daughter could benefit from shares of a load fund that you own. As long as the amount involved isn't large enough to trip the gift tax, the transaction is load-free and tax-free (be sure to check with your tax advisor first).

Breakpoint Pricing Program

If you have a large portfolio (or if you are managing a combined pool of assets), you may be able to avoid load fees under Fidelity's breakpoint pricing program. Under this system, large purchases can earn permanent load credits that will apply on future trades. This program is available for all funds except Select Money Market (Fidelity excludes Select Money Market so that shareholders won't try to earn permanent load credits without taking on equity risk). Purchases of more than $250,000 but less than $500,000 get a 1 percent load credit, reducing the load paid to 2 percent or less, depending on whether there is a prior load credit on existing shares. Purchases above $500,000 but below $1,000,000 get a 2 percent load credit, which reduces the load fee to 1 percent or less. If you can pull together $1,000,000 or more for a single fund, you'll earn a permanent 3 percent credit without paying any load at all.

Note that your current balance in the fund also factors into the equation. If you have $500,000 in a 3 percent fund and you add another $500,000, you won't pay a load on the second $500,000.

Interestingly enough, this program doesn't carry any switching restrictions. For example, you could put $1,000,000 in Contrafund to earn the load credit. If you then sell and split the money up into other funds a few weeks later, the credit still applies, allowing you to avoid all future loads. Fidelity must figure that investors won't take on equity risk with a large account unless they are serious about buying the fund in the first place.

USING FIDELITY'S LOAD TRACKING SYSTEM TO YOUR ADVANTAGE

Although you can't eliminate Fidelity loads, you can take steps to minimize them. By understanding Fidelity's computerized load tracking system, you may be able to structure fund switches to your advantage.

All of the money you hold in various Fidelity funds is tagged so that you don't pay a load more than once, provided the money remains in a Fidelity fund. These rules apply also to Fidelity funds held in a Fidelity brokerage account. Depending on which funds your money used to be in, Fidelity's computers may have it tagged for a load credit of 0 percent, 1 percent, 2 percent, or 3 percent. For example, shares of Magellan are tagged with a 3 percent credit. If you bought Equity-Income in a regular account before December 1, 1993, the shares are tagged 2 percent. If you owned International Growth & Income before October 11, 1990, you may have some 1 percent shares. If your money has never been in a load fund, it is tagged 0 percent. The tracking system also knows if you owe any redemption fees on funds purchased before October 12, 1990 (Fidelity charges a 1 percent redemption fee on Selects and a few other funds if they were purchased before that date).

If you are reinvesting capital gains and regular income distributions, the reinvested money will retain the load credit of the shares that generate the payouts. For example, you buy Magellan and pay a 3 percent load. Any reinvested distributions that occur while you are in Magellan will be tagged 3 percent. Then you move to Short-Term Bond. The reinvested income from Short-Term Bond will still be tagged 3 percent, because the load credit of the shares generating the income is 3 percent.

If you buy a fund with a load that's higher than the current status of your shares, you pay the difference and your shares are tagged at the new level. For example, if you purchase Magellan with 0 percent money, you pay a 3 percent load. If you purchase Magellan with shares loaded at 2 percent, you'll pay a 1 percent load on the transaction.

Once your shares are tagged with a 3 percent credit, you never pay a front-end load again on those shares, provided the money stays in a Fidelity fund. Suppose you sell Magellan and buy Cash Reserves, then you purchase New Millennium. There are no charges.

There are only two ways you can lose your load credits:

- From a Fidelity mutual fund account, you lose your load credits if you redeem the shares out of Fidelity. Whether by checkwriting, doing a transfer to a bank, or by having Fidelity send a redemption check, the load credit is lost once the money no longer resides in a Fidelity fund.
- In a Fidelity Brokerage account, load credits are lost when the money is moved into a non-Fidelity fund or any other security such as an individual stock. However, load credits are retained if the money is kept in the core account.

Things start to get more complicated when you combine money with different load credits into a single fund. This is where you need to be careful to avoid paying loads on no-load money when you have loaded shares available. Here's how Fidelity's computers handle the transactions:

- When redeeming shares out of Fidelity, the computer will move the shares with the smallest load credit first. For example, suppose you have $4,000 in Cash Reserves, half of which is no-load money and half of which is tagged with a 3 percent load credit. Then you use Moneyline to transfer $2,500 from Cash Reserves to your bank account. The computer will redeem all of the no-load money and $500 of the 3 percent shares when processing the transaction. This algorithm works to your best interest, but there is no warning mechanism to let you know when you are redeeming loaded shares.

- When making an exchange between Fidelity funds, the computer will move the shares that are tagged with the largest load credit first. Suppose you have $10,000 in Cash Reserves, half of which is tagged 3 percent and half of which is no-load money. You then purchase $5,000 in Magellan, and a few days later you move the remaining $5,000 to Short-Term Bond. In this situation, you pay no load fees because the algorithm worked in your best interest.

- Now suppose you had reversed the transactions. Your 3 percent shares would have been "wasted" on Short-Term Bond, and you would have incurred $150 in new load fees when your no-load money was moved into Magellan. This time, the computer rules worked against you.

Fortunately, there is a simple way to eliminate the problem of combined load credits in a money market fund. Keep a separate money market fund as a holding place for loaded shares, and use your regular money market account or core account for your no-load money. If all of your loaded shares have a 3 percent load credit, Select Money Market is a good place for loaded money, although it may not always have the best yield.

For non–money market exchanges, there is no easy safeguard. You just have to ask about the load status of your shares and do your trades in the best possible order, waiting a day between each if necessary. The only way to avoid mixing load credits in the first place is to try to always keep your 3 percent money invested in load funds.

One last tip: If you discover after the fact that your 3 percent money was inadvertently sent off to a no-load fund, it is possible to recover if the no-load fund does not carry a redemption fee. Take an equivalent amount of no-load money and double your stake in the fund where your 3 percent money is located. Then wait one day and sell half of the doubled position, and your 3 percent money will come out and go where you want it. This technique is not without some risk. The risk is not large if your 3 percent money is stuck in a bond fund, but if you are doubled up in a stock fund you may lose more than you gain if the market sells off sharply. The other problem is that unless this is done in a retirement account, you can create a taxable transaction costing more than you save if you realize a capital gain on the 3 percent shares. Another issue is that selling the 3 percent shares at a loss can trigger wash sale rules, although in this situation it doesn't cost anything other than the accounting work.

ANNUAL ACCOUNT FEES

Fidelity investors with total Fidelity assets of less than $50,000 should also pay attention to the annual account fee that is assessed on fund positions of less than $2,500. While the opportunity for saving on fees isn't as great in comparison to front-end loads, it is possible to save up to $60 per year by structuring your accounts differently.

Here's how the current program (which was introduced at the beginning of 1995) works. Once a year in the fourth quarter, Fidelity adds up all of the investment dollars held under your social security number. If the total is less than $50,000, each fund position with a balance of less than $2,500 is charged a fee of $12. If you have a total of more than five such fund positions, the total annual fee is capped at $60 (Fidelity brokerage core accounts are not subject to the fee).

There are several ways to reduce these charges. First, Fidelity will waive the $12 fee on any account structured to receive regular additional investments under Account Builder or similar plans. Second, if you don't mind consolidating to a fewer number of funds, you can avoid the charge by maintaining at least $2,500 in all fund positions. Third, you can call Fidelity when the fourth quarter draws near and have them tell you when the valuation date will occur. Then you can temporarily consolidate to beat the fees (zero balance fund positions are not charged), and, if you wish, return to your previous position after the valuation date. (Fidelity allows the latter option because they must figure most investors won't bother to split their portfolio back apart after going to the trouble to consolidate.) Finally, you can transfer some assets from another financial institution to bring the balance of your Fidelity holdings above $50,000.

13

Ten Fidelity Managers to Watch

Choosing a Fidelity fund based solely on a particular manager helps to build confidence, but it can also lead to frustration. There's always the possibility that your favorite manager might move on to something else, and you'll be left wondering what to do.

At Fidelity, manager changes can be relatively frequent. Chairman Ned Johnson has never had any reservations about "shuffling the deck" when the opportunity comes up. There is even some evidence that he prefers to move managers around from time to time. It's not that Johnson or any other Fidelity executives are trying to frustrate shareholders. It's just that Fidelity would like investors to view all of its funds in a favorable light and not worry too much about the person at the helm. To some degree, this is a valid goal. Fidelity has a huge group of analysts, and from the standpoint of basic research all managers are set up for success.

However, there are still performance differences among managers. The company is quick to remove any manager who has been significantly lagging for more than two to three years, but among winning funds you can find many successful strategies that have been uniquely shaped by a particular manager. Fidelity's top performing funds often take very different paths to achieve what looks like similar results. Emphasizing the differences in style, I've listed some of my thoughts and observations on 10 managers worth watching. They are listed alphabetically.

WILLIAM DANOFF

Before joining Fidelity in 1986 as a securities analyst, Will Danoff was a research analyst with Furman Selz in New York, where he followed advertising stocks. He began his career in 1985 as a research analyst with Clabir International in London and Steinhardt Partners in New York. Danoff received a bachelor of arts degree in history from Harvard College in 1982 and an MBA from the Wharton School of the University of Pennsylvania in 1986.

After managing Select Retailing between 1986 and 1989, Danoff assisted at Magellan during Morris Smith's tenure. He became manager of Contrafund, his current assignment, in October 1990. At Contrafund he has returned an impressive 24.9 percent per year through mid-1996, well ahead of the S&P 500's 17.7 percent return for the same period.

Backed by Fidelity's research team, Danoff achieved his excellent track record with good stockpicking skills and by overweighting the right industry groups throughout his tenure. During most of his years at Contrafund, Danoff has run the fund as a mainstream growth fund. Starting late in 1995, however, he has been emphasizing the fund's contrarian charter a bit more in the wake of Fidelity's reevaluation of fund objectives and manager styles.

One of Danoff's two big challenges will be to pick out-of-favor contrarian stocks as well as he has picked growth stocks. The other is to manage Contrafund's large asset base, which is now in the same league as Magellan.

So far, Danoff has made a smooth transition to the contrarian approach, and he may also benefit from the timing of this move. With the domestic stock market on the high end of its valuation range, buying out of favor stocks would seem prudent. Furthermore, this strategy can work well for a large fund like Contrafund. Because out-of-favor stocks are less volatile, there's usually more time available to accumulate a significant position.

PENELOPE DOBKIN

Penny Dobkin joined Fidelity in 1981 as an analyst following banks, savings and loans, financial services companies, and real estate investment trusts. Before joining Fidelity, Dobkin was an equity research analyst specializing in the retail industry at Aetna Life and Casualty. She received a bachelor of arts degree in English and an MBA in finance, both from the University of Connecticut.

As one of Fidelity's more experienced international managers, Dobkin has demonstrated an ability to exceed the indexes while keeping risk low. While running Europe Fund between October 1986 and December 1990, Dobkin returned 12.7 percent per year versus an 11.9 percent annual gain for the Morgan Stanley Europe index. At Worldwide (which began in May 1990) she returned 9.1 percent per year compared to 8.8 percent for the Morgan Stanley World Index. Dobkin achieved these results with broad diversification and relatively high cash levels (20 percent is not unusual), both of which have made for a low-risk posture.

Her current assignment, Worldwide, remains an excellent choice for international diversification without the anxiety of high volatility. Dobkin usually underweights the U.S. market relative to her index, making this fund more like a foreign fund than a global fund. In recent years, underweighting the U.S. has held her back, but in the years ahead it may allow her to outperform by a wider margin.

BETTINA DOULTON

Bettina Doulton joined Fidelity in 1986 as a research associate. She received a bachelor of arts degree in mathematics from Boston College in 1986.

From 1987 through 1990, she served as a research assistant for Magellan. For the next two years, she was an equity analyst following the gaming and lodging industries. In 1991, she began following the auto and tire businesses and became an assistant for Equity-Income. She also managed Select Automotive in 1993, helping to make it one of the better performing Selects that year.

In June 1993 she was assigned to VIP Equity-Income for almost three years. During that period, she provided a return of 18.9 percent per year, versus 17.0 percent for the S&P 500. Doulton also ran one of Fidelity's broker-sold funds during the same period, and her good track record led to an additional assignment at Value Fund between March 1995 and March 1996. During that year she trailed the S&P 500 28.2 percent to 32.2 percent, although most other Fidelity funds lagged during this period too. In addition to running two other broker-sold funds, Doulton manages the equity side of Puritan and the entire portfolio of Equity-Income II as of late 1996.

Doulton seems to have an excellent eye for value and seems to favor financial stocks more than other sectors. She leans toward a domestic-only approach, which has helped so far but could hold her back in future years if foreign markets make up for lost time. At any rate, Puritan and Equity-Income II remain excellent choices for growth and income investors.

JOHN HICKLING

John Hickling joined Fidelity in 1982 as a research analyst covering the biotechnology and medical technology industries. He received a bachelor's degree in economics from Bowdoin College in 1981.

Hickling is Fidelity's most experienced international manager. Often running two or more funds at the same time, he has racked up multiyear fund management experience in just about every world market.

Hickling has shown an ability to outperform the indexes during both bullish and bearish conditions. Between January 1987 and November 1993 (almost seven years), he delivered a 9.3 percent annualized return at International Growth & Income, while the Morgan Stanley EAFE index returned just 4.8 percent per year.

Hickling managed Pacific Basin between May 1990 and December 1991, a 21-month period during which the Japanese market underwent a massive sell-off. Even though his cash position was relatively low, Pacific Basin declined only 6.3 percent on an annualized basis, compared to a loss of 22.0 percent per year for the Morgan Stanley Pacific index. Later he ran Japan Fund between June 1993 and September 1994. During those 15 months, the fund logged at 9.0 percent annualized gain versus a 6.9 percent increase for the TOPIX, an index of Japanese stocks. While running Europe Fund between January 1991 and July 1992, Hickling did stumble a bit, returning 5.7 percent per year versus 9.6 percent for the Europe index. While running Overseas Fund between January 1993 and March 1996 he returned 15.6 percent versus 16.3 percent for the EAFE.

Hickling is once again managing International Growth & Income, the fund he originally ran with great results. One characteristic that sets Hickling apart is his ability to keep turnover and expenses on the low side. He tends to structure his mix of countries relatively close to the makeup of the index he seeks to beat. Then he looks for attractive stocks within each country and attempts to hold them for long-term growth. Many international managers make the mistake of buying and selling securities the same way they would in a domestic fund, which can be very expensive. Hickling sets himself up for success by avoiding unnecessary trades.

STEVEN KAYE

Steven Kaye joined Fidelity in 1985 as an analyst covering the pharmaceuticals, biotechnology, and photography industries. Before joining Fidelity, Kaye spent two years as a research analyst at Strategic Planning Associates in Washington, D.C. He received a bachelor of arts degree in political economics from John Hopkins University in 1981 and an MBA in finance from the Wharton School at the University of Pennsylvania in 1985.

Kaye managed Select Energy Services and Select Health Care from the beginning of 1986 until the start of 1990. He also ran Select Biotechnology from the beginning of 1986 until May 1989. His first major fund assignment was Blue Chip Growth. From October 1990 through the end of 1992 he returned 31.4 percent annually versus 21.9 percent for the S&P 500. He then moved to Growth & Income at the beginning of 1993, where he has returned 18.4 percent per year compared to 16.2 percent for the S&P 500 (as of mid-1996). He kept Growth & Income's risk about 15 percent lower than the S&P 500.

Kaye understands pharmaceuticals and biotech stocks quite well, and he seems to have a good ability to sense when a particular stock or industry is too expensive. Whether in a growth-oriented or value-oriented role, Kaye has shown a proven ability to pick good stocks.

As is the case with Will Danoff and Contrafund, Growth & Income is in the same league as Magellan. As such, Kaye won't be able to boost returns much by holding small- to medium-size companies. However, if his experience at Blue Chip Growth is any guide, Kaye should still do quite well in the large-cap arena.

BRADFORD LEWIS

Brad Lewis joined Fidelity as an equity research analyst in 1985. Before that, he was an aviator with the U.S. Navy for six years. He received a bachelor of science degree in operations analysis from the Naval Academy at Annapolis in 1977 and an MBA from the Wharton School of the University of Pennsylvania in 1985.

Lewis is part computer programmer and part fund manager. Whereas other Fidelity managers rely on analysts and researchers to point them in the direction of outperforming stocks, Lewis turns to his computer. He uses quantitative models to identify attractive stocks based on fundamental figures, economic factors, and marketplace pricing trends.

Once an attractive list of stocks is developed, Lewis then uses other programs to develop a portfolio suitable for the fund he is dealing with. Disciplined Equity is structured to maintain similar risk as the S&P 500 and must keep a mix of industries similar to the index. Stock Selector is allowed to be a little more venturesome. It too invests mainly in S&P 500 stocks, but it is allowed to overweight industry groups and take on foreign positions to increase total return. Small Cap Stock is the most aggressive, investing in the Russell 2000 universe of smaller companies. Lewis has also helped set up and optimize quantitative models for Diversified International and Fidelity Fifty.

Lewis has had mixed results so far. Disciplined Equity, which has been around since late 1988, has returned 17.7 percent per year versus 16.0 percent for the S&P 500 (as of mid-1996). Stock Selector has done better, although it hasn't been around as long and it had the advantage of starting right at the bottom of the 1990 sell-off. Since September 1990, Stock Selector has gained 22.0 percent annually versus 18.3 percent for the index. Small Cap Stock, on the other hand, has languished. Since June 1993, this fund has returned 12.2 percent annually, versus 18.3 percent for the Russell 2000 index. Lewis also had problems with a foreign model he helped develop for Diversified International, but three years later he and Greg Fraser introduced some changes that have made that fund a winner since early 1995.

The opportunity with quantitative techniques is significant, but it's no small task trying to choose which variables to follow and program the computer to interpret the data in a way that adds value.

Lewis has amassed considerable expertise during his time at Fidelity, and there has been significant improvement with each major change in his models. Lewis may not be too far away from developing powerful models that rival Fidelity's traditional approach for stock selection.

ROBERT STANSKY

Bob Stansky joined Fidelity in 1983 as a research analyst. Before that, he was a research assistant in the fixed income department of Kidder, Peabody & Company. He received a bachelor of science degree in 1978 from Nichols College in Dudley, Massachusetts, and an MBA from New York University in 1983. He is also a Certified Public Accountant.

Stansky was a research assistant for Magellan from 1984 to 1987. He managed Select Defense & Aerospace before a long-term assignment at Growth Company. Between March 1987 and May 1996 (a period of just over nine years), he returned 18.0 percent per year versus 14.6 percent for the S&P 500. He was assigned to Magellan in May 1996.

Stansky is an excellent fit for his latest assignment. During his years at Growth Company, he focused mainly on large-cap growth stocks, which is exactly what he'll have to do at Magellan. He prefers stockpicking to sector bets and tends to move in and out of his positions gradually—ideal for a mammoth fund like Magellan. Finally, he's not the type of manager that will generate a lot of controversy. No doubt Fidelity will appreciate that after seeing the press go after Jeff Vinik with a level of scrutiny formerly reserved only for major political leaders.

Shareholders should be pleased with Stansky. He probably won't exceed the market indexes by as much as he did at

Growth Company, but over the long run he should be able to outperform the S&P 500 by at least a few percentage points annually.

BETH TERRANA

Beth Terrana joined Fidelity in 1983 as a securities analyst in the retail and apparel industries as well as an assistant manager to Equity-Income. Before joining Fidelity, she was assistant vice president of fixed income at Putnam Management Company for three years. Prior to that, she was an assistant manager at Morgan Guaranty Trust Company. Terrana received a bachelor of science degree from the State University of New York, Binghamton, in 1977 and an MBA from Harvard Business School in 1983.

Terrana is one of Fidelity's more experienced growth and income managers, with about nine years of market-beating performance on her record. Her first mainstream assignment was Growth & Income at the end of 1985. From March 1986 (when the fund was first available) through October 1990, Terrana returned 12.2 percent per year versus 10.1 percent for the S&P 500. Then she managed Equity-Income until July 1993, gaining an average of 24.6 percent per year compared to 18.8 percent for the S&P 500. Thereafter at Fidelity Fund, Terrana has returned 18.3 percent annually through mid-1996, matching the return for the S&P 500 (many funds underperformed during this time because the S&P 500 was unusually strong relative to small-cap, mid-cap, and foreign stocks).

Terrana holds a balanced mix of stocks and industries and usually carries a risk level that's similar to the S&P 500. Her investment style at Fidelity Fund is very similar to the approach she used when running Growth & Income. Over time, I suspect she will exceed the S&P 500 while maintaining similar risk.

JOEL TILLINGHAST

Joel Tillinghast joined Fidelity in 1986 as an analyst covering the tobacco, coal, natural gas, personal care products, and appliance industries. Before then, he spent four years as a financial futures research analyst at Drexel Burnham Lambert in Chicago. He began his investment career in 1980 as an equity analyst with Value Line Investment Survey. Tillinghast received a bachelor of arts degree in economics from Wesleyan University in Connecticut in 1980 and an MBA from the Kellogg School of Management at Northwestern University in 1983.

After putting in some time as assistant manager of Fidelity OTC, Tillinghast became manager of Low-Priced Stock when it was introduced near the end of 1989. From day one this fund has focused on the small-cap value segment of the market, a less-analyzed group of stocks that contains many opportunities if you know where to look. Tillinghast and his team have been able to find them. Through mid-1996, Low-Priced Stock has returned 19.4 percent annually versus 14.0 percent for the Russell 2000. That alone would be impressive, but it was achieved against a backdrop of high cash levels (typically 20 to 40 percent) over the last five years.

The combination of a high cash level, a focus on small-cap value, and a highly diversified portfolio (over 700 stocks) makes for a very low risk level. In fact, Low-Priced Stock usually has less volatility than many growth and income funds, let alone its growth-oriented cousins.

Like other successful managers, Tillinghast has attracted too much capital. Although $4 billion isn't anywhere near as large as some, keeping this fund invested in small-cap stocks is still a major challenge. Increasingly, Tillinghast and his team are looking outside the domestic market for bargain stocks. As of mid-1996, about one-third of the fund's stock holdings are outside the U.S., with Canadian issues accounting for the lion's share.

Tillinghast's performance isn't likely to be as strong in the years ahead, but when you consider Low-Priced Stock's low risk score it stands out as a very sensible fund in a market where stock valuations have become excessive.

GEORGE VANDERHEIDEN

George Vanderheiden joined Fidelity in 1971 as a research analyst. Prior to that, he was a securities analyst with John Hancock Insurance Company for three years. He received a bachelor of arts degree in economics from Colby College in 1968 and an MBA from Boston University in 1972.

Vanderheiden was named manager of Destiny I around the end of 1980, and 15½ years later is still at the helm. He has managed through four bearish periods and six major rallies, returning 19.3 percent annually ($1,000 in Destiny I at the beginning of Vanderheiden's tenure would be worth over $15,000 as of mid-1996). During the same period, the S&P 500 returned 15.0 percent per year. At age 50, Vanderheiden clearly rates as Fidelity's most experienced and most successful stockpicker.

Until recently, there wasn't any easy way for retail fund investors to take advantage of Vanderheiden's skills. Thanks to the reorganization in March 1996, investors can now benefit by purchasing Asset Manager: Growth. Although this fund usually has a modest position in cash and 20 to 30 percent in bonds, the stock portion of the fund is the responsibility of Vanderheiden and will typically be a close match to Destiny I's stock holdings. Although Asset Manager: Growth may not perform quite as well as Destiny I over the long run, I suspect it will consistently outperform the S&P 500 while carrying less risk than the index.

14

The VIP Alternative

Sold under the name Retirement Reserves, Fidelity's Variable Insurance Products (VIPs) offer an investment alternative that may be appropriate for some investors, although this program is not a panacea for avoiding taxes. Restricted choices and an annual insurance fee of 1 percent could reduce your long-term investment performance by one to two percentage points per year compared with a mutual fund approach. That may not seem like much, but it erases the advantage of tax deferral for all but those portfolios invested for growth over a period of ten years or more.

A key consideration is the capital gains tax rate. Currently at a federal maximum of 28 percent, a lower rate would reduce the attractiveness of variable annuities. At 20 percent or lower the performance advantage of annuities would disappear for most investors.

Variable annuities resemble mutual funds in most respects, but they are structured as life insurance to qualify for their favorable tax status. Putting money into the VIP family is like making a non-deductible IRA contribution, except that there is no limit on the amount you may invest and there is no requirement for payroll-based income. Once your money is invested, you must wait until age 59½ to make withdrawals or you'll face an IRS penalty of 10 percent. Compared to an

IRA, however, you can keep your money in the VIP family longer before you must make automatic withdrawals. The tax code allows you to keep your money in an annuity account until age 85 (unless the original investment came from a previous qualified retirement plan, in which case the usual age of 70½ still applies).

When you do finally take money out of an annuity account, you are taxed at regular income rates (currently up to 39.6 percent federal) on all investment gains. Under the current tax code, your withdrawals are taxed until you have taken out an amount equal to the investment gains you have realized. After that, the original amount can come out with no additional tax liability (unless the original investment was rolled over from a qualified retirement plan, in which case it also is fully taxed).

An alternative withdrawal approach is to convert your investment to a lifetime income stream. This approach allows you to pull out a portion of the original investment along with the gains, helping to cut down on the tax bite. It can be done without penalty at any age, but once you annuitize you no longer have the flexibility of making withdrawals only when you need them.

In either withdrawal scenario, the fact that high-bracket investors are taxed above the 28 percent long-term capital gains rate presents a slight disadvantage compared to holding mutual funds in a regular account. Because of this, investors in the top brackets are not likely to realize much of an advantage with an annuity account unless their money is invested for growth over a period of more than 15 years.

FIDELITY VIP PORTFOLIOS

When you join Fidelity's Retirement Reserves program, you are allowed to move around among ten different portfolios. There are no switching fees, but telephone exchanges are limited to 18 per year. If you make your exchanges in writing, there is no limit. All money in the account is levied with a

1 percent annual fee for the insurance features. If you pull your money out within five years (by withdrawal or through a tax-free transfer to another insurance company), there is a redemption fee of up to 5 percent. During the first year, it runs the full 5 percent of assets, but it drops 1 percentage point per year to reach zero after the fifth year.

Following are the choices that are available, listed in increasing order of risk.

VIP Money Market

VIP Money Market seeks as high a level of current income as is consistent with the preservation of capital and liquidity; it invests in high-quality U.S. dollar-denominated money market instruments. The portfolio's yield will fluctuate.

This portfolio is one of the better-performing money markets in the variable annuity industry. Still, it gets left behind in comparison to regular money market mutual funds, which don't get trimmed by the annual insurance fee. For that reason, this portfolio makes sense only for VIP money that hasn't been put to work in other portfolios or for money that is earmarked to be withdrawn in the near future.

VIP Investment Grade Bond

VIP Investment Grade Bond was started in December 1988 and seeks high current income consistent with preservation of principal. It invests primarily in broad range of investment-grade fixed-income securities; the portfolio maintains a weighted average maturity of ten years or less.

This portfolio, like Short-Term Bond, was hurt by the peso decline in late 1994 and early 1995. Today it is run as a regular domestic bond fund with a primary focus on government notes and investment grade corporate debt.

Again, this portfolio makes sense only as a temporary holding place, perhaps for withdrawals that will be made in the next three years or for money being dollar cost averaged into a growth-oriented position. It makes no sense to invest your entire VIP balance in this fund, since your after-tax return could easily be higher in a regular taxable bond fund (or a tax-free muni for high-bracket investors).

VIP High Income

VIP High Income started in September 1985, and it seeks high current income. It invests primarily in high-yielding lower-rated, fixed-income securities. Growth of capital is also considered in security selection.

Fidelity has a good team of analysts in the junk bond arena, and this portfolio should continue to reflect that expertise (more on this in Chapter 7, under Capital & Income). In combination with other choices, it can make a nice addition to a growth and income or income strategy. Over the long term, expect total return to be similar to that of the S&P 500, with volatility running about half as much.

VIP II Asset Manager

VIP II Asset Manager was started in September 1989, and it seeks high total return with reduced risk over the long term by allocating its assets among stocks, bonds, and short-term fixed-income instruments.

The portfolio management team includes the same players that now run Asset Manager on the mutual fund side. The portfolio has a neutral mix of 40 percent stocks, 40 percent bonds, and 20 percent short-term (cash positions and bonds having a maturity of less than three years are considered "short-term" holdings).

Despite a poor 1994 showing, this portfolio is a good long-term choice for a growth and income portfolio. If you want to stay ahead of the S&P 500, however, you should probably move up in risk to Asset Manager: Growth.

VIP II Asset Manager: Growth

Introduced at the beginning of 1995, this portfolio's objective is maximum total return over the long run by allocation of assets among stocks, bonds, and short-term instruments of U.S. and foreign issuers, including emerging markets.

This portfolio also has the same management team as its mutual fund twin, and it will typically hold about 70 percent or more in the stocks that George Vanderheiden chooses. The portfolio has a neutral mix of 65 percent stocks, 30 percent bonds, and 5 percent short-term. I expect that over the long run this portfolio will outperform the S&P 500 with slightly less risk.

VIP Equity-Income

VIP Equity-Income was started in October 1986. Its objective is reasonable income by investing at least 65 percent of assets in income-producing equity securities. The fund seeks a yield that exceeds that of the S&P 500; capital appreciation is secondary.

Before June 1993 this portfolio lagged slightly behind mutual fund equivalents Equity-Income and Equity-Income II, but it improved under ex-manager Bettina Doulton. Current manager Andy Offit doesn't have much of a track record as of this writing, but has trailed his mutual fund counterparts.

VIP II Index 500

This portfolio started in August 1992, and it seeks investment results that correspond to the total return of the common stocks that compose the S&P 500.

Like Market Index on the mutual fund side, this portfolio has been quite accurate in mimicking the S&P 500; the only problem is that the management fee and the 1 percent annual annuity fee will subtract about 1.3 percentage points from its annual performance.

This portfolio might be a good choice if the alternatives were not run by Fidelity managers, but they are, and there's a good chance that over time it will lag behind VIP Equity-Income, VIP II Asset Manager: Growth, VIP II Contrafund, and VIP Growth.

VIP II Contrafund

Introduced in early 1995, VIP II Contrafund has the objective of capital appreciation from undervalued companies undergoing positive changes and turnarounds. It is a clone of the popular mutual fund and is also managed by Will Danoff.

Danoff's proven ability as a stockpicker makes this portfolio one of the more attractive offerings in the VIP group. Compared with its mutual fund counterpart, it has the advantage of smaller size but carries the burden of the 1 percent annual annuity charge. This portfolio is another solid bet for outperforming the S&P 500 over time.

VIP Overseas

Introduced in January 1987, VIP Overseas seeks long-term capital appreciation; it invests primarily in foreign securities of issuers whose principal business activities are outside of the United States.

VIP Overseas has concentrated on the major foreign markets in Europe and Japan; the portfolio has not held any significant position in emerging countries.

New manager Rick Mace has a respectable record on Fidelity's mutual fund side; time will tell if he will be able to improve this portfolio's lackluster track record.

VIP Growth

Introduced in October 1986, VIP Growth seeks capital appreciation; it invests primarily in common stocks, although it is not restricted to any one type of security. Larry Greenberg, who also runs Growth Company on the mutual fund side, has been managing this portfolio since April 1991. Like Growth Company, VIP Growth concentrates on domestic growth companies. Throughout most of Greenberg's tenure, the fund has maintained a heavy emphasis in the technology sector.

Although this portfolio is one of the more risky choices in the group, Fidelity's strong research capabilities and Greenberg's stockpicking skills could make it one of the better long-term performers in the group.

VIP PORTFOLIOS

The VIP model portfolios published in *Fidelity Monitor* are my preferred approach for investing in Fidelity's VIP family, but the portfolios in Figure 14 should provide similar long-term returns.

Portfolio A is designed for a growth-oriented approach. Holdings are 50 percent VIP Contrafund, 25 percent VIP Asset Manager: Growth and 25 percent VIP Growth. My ten-year total return estimate for this split is 12 percent per year after deducting the 1 percent annual insurance fee. This mix of funds could decline 25 percent or more in a bear market.

Portfolio B is for global growth. It holds 40 percent VIP Contrafund, 30 percent VIP Overseas, and 30 percent VIP Asset Manager: Growth. This approach is a little less risky than Portfolio A, but it will probably grow at a slightly lower rate over the long run. I expect a ten-year return of 11 percent per year after fees, with potential losses of 20 percent or more in a bear market.

Portfolio C is for growth and income. With a mix of 50 percent VIP Asset Manager, 25 percent VIP Equity-Income, and 25 percent VIP High Income, this portfolio should provide a ten-year return in the neighborhood of 10 percent per year after fees. In a bear market, this portfolio could decline 15 percent.

If you are investing for a long-term growth rate of less than 10 percent per year, you'll probably be better off in regular taxable mutual funds. That way, you'll avoid the 1 percent annual insurance fee, and you'll have more to choose from.

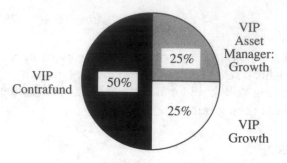

Portfolio A: Growth

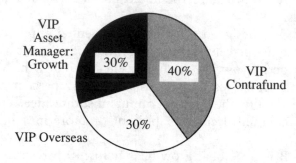

Portfolio B: Worldwide Growth

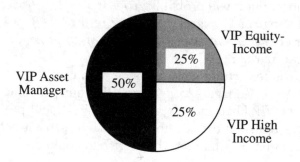

Portfolio C: Growth & Income

Figure 14   VIP portfolios.

15

Question and Answer Forum

One of my columns in *Fidelity Monitor* features my responses to the questions that subscribers ask. Over the years, I've covered quite a bit of ground with this column, and I've found it useful for addressing topics that don't always fit into the context of the regular columns. This chapter includes some of the more commonly asked questions. Because many *Fidelity Monitor* subscribers will be reading this book, I have included some questions that relate directly to the newsletter service.

I received a proxy ballot for a fund I own shares in, and it was very confusing. What should I vote for?

Typical proxy measures include electing the board of directors and okaying the choice of the fund's accounting firm. With Fidelity funds these are routine items that present no concerns.

Sometimes the fund is making fundamental changes to its investment limitations, a procedure that may sound risky but is usually aimed at increasing the manager's flexibility. I usually vote yes on these because I figure that Fidelity can manage risk in a responsible way. If you disagree, you can vote no or move to a fund with tighter restrictions. These types of changes are usually approved.

Finally, the fund may be requesting a change to the management contract. If the management fee will be equal to or lower than the old contract (Fidelity will clearly indicate if this is the case), I vote yes. If the new contract will increase fees, I vote no, assuming that Fidelity will manage the fund to its best ability regardless of the fee structure. Usually these measures pass anyway, in which case you can always cast one final vote by selling your shares. I made such a move in the *Fidelity Monitor* Growth model after the management fee for Trend nearly doubled in late 1993, but situations like that are unusual. Trend's previous management contract from the 1960s was a deal that was too good to last. In the future, I suspect that competition will force Fidelity and other fund companies to keep management fees competitive. One example of this was the small reduction in fees for Puritan and Asset Manager funds in 1996, and there may be more to come. In general, Fidelity expenses are just below average in the industry.

I became nervous and moved my investments to a money market fund. Since then the market has moved up. Should I get back in?

Unfortunately, your situation is common. It illustrates how market timing seldom works out very well in practice. If you want to get back into growth funds, consider doing it over time. Divide the amount you want to invest by 8, and make quarterly purchases over a two-year period. This approach reduces the risk of loss if the market sells off, and it should reduce your tendency to jump out of the market because you won't be fully exposed to stocks for almost two years.

You may also want to consider lowering your risk level. The very fact that you were nervous indicates that you took on more risk than you were comfortable with. If you were originally invested for aggressive growth, try dollar cost averaging into some regular growth funds. If you were originally in growth funds, try dollar cost averaging into a growth and income fund. Although your long-term potential is lower when you drop down in risk, you'll probably be better off in the long run because you won't be jumping out of the market at the wrong time.

Does Fidelity limit how much you can put into a fund?

Fidelity has standard trading limits that are different for each fund, based on the fund's total assets. Usually the telephone representative can tell you the limit if you ask; typically it runs about 1 percent of the fund's total assets per day (per hour on the Selects). For most funds, 1 percent of assets is a huge sum, but for some of the smaller Selects you can trip the limit on a $50,000 trade. During market hours, you can usually get permission to exceed the limit. The rep can connect you to the specialty trading group, which will check with fund management for clearance. If you are turned down, you can choose a similar but larger fund or make multiple trades to obtain the desired position.

As of mid-1996, many Fidelity funds have lagged the S&P 500 for almost three years. Why shouldn't I just go with an index fund?

Interestingly, Fidelity funds went through a similar lagging period in the mid-1980s when the S&P 500 outperformed most other asset classes. Indexing to the S&P 500 has been a self-fulfilling prophecy over the last few years, with an estimated $600 billion now following this passive approach. The result is a lot of high-priced S&P 500 stocks, as evidenced by a mid-1996 price-to-earnings ratio of 20 for the index. The stage is set for mid-caps, small-caps, and foreign stocks to outperform the S&P 500 for the next decade. Fidelity funds should do quite well in this kind of environment.

How can I get more information on your newsletter service?

For a free trial issue and information, call 800-397-3094 or write *Fidelity Monitor*, P.O. Box 1270, Rocklin, CA 95677.

Do you offer a managed account service? How does it work?

I am the chief investment strategist (the person who picks the funds and the mix) for Weber Asset Management. Clients with accounts of $100,000 or more can have their portfolio managed for an annual fee of 1.2 percent on diversified fund positions (the fee can be higher for Select holdings). With this approach, exchanges are made for you in a Fidelity brokerage account set up in your name. Your portfolio is kept only in Fidelity mutual funds, and each time a trade is made you get a confirming statement. As of mid-1996 we have $80 million under management.

For an information package on this service, call 800-438-3863 or write to Weber Asset Management, 1983 Marcus Avenue #221, Lake Success, NY 11042.

I always thought that investors in high tax brackets should just put everything into municipals to minimize taxes. Why should I take on the tax consequences of taxable distributions from a growth fund?

In the end, what counts is how fast your portfolio grows after you pay the tax bill. Whereas a municipal bond fund will give you tax-free income, its long-term after-tax return is not likely to be much greater than 6 percent per year. Even in the top tax brackets, I think most Fidelity growth funds are capable of delivering a long-term after-tax return of about 8 percent annually. Although a municipal bond fund has less short-term risk than a growth fund, the growth fund is still the best way to build wealth if you are investing for the long haul.

What do you think about using margin to increase your long-term return with growth funds?

In a brokerage account it is possible to use margin, or borrowed money, to own more shares of a fund than you could buy outright. (This practice is not possible with retirement accounts.) For stock funds the limit is 50 percent, meaning that for a $20,000 purchase you must put up at least $10,000. You pay interest on the extra $10,000 that you borrow.

There's a very simple reason why I don't like margin. In a nutshell, the problem is that margin magnifies losses more than it magnifies gains. As an extreme example, a 50 percent loss will wipe you out. Even under normal market fluctuations, margin can reduce your long-term return. Suppose you are fully margined, having bought $20,000 worth of a market index fund by putting up $10,000. First the market goes up 15 percent, making your shares worth $23,000. Upon reestablishing full margin, you now own $26,000 in shares. Then the market falls 20 percent. After selling to get back to a 50 percent margin position, you own $15,600 in shares. Then the market goes up 15 percent, and you close out your position. Your final balance is $10,140. After deducting the margin interest, you have a net loss. In comparison, you would have realized a 6 percent gain if you had simply bought and held the index fund itself.

Margin would work great if stock funds moved up in a straight line, allowing only gains to be magnified. Unfortunately, that doesn't happen in the real world.

I heard that Fidelity offers a service in which Select funds can be sold short in a Fidelity brokerage account. What do you think of this?

I don't recommend it. Even during a market downturn, it's very difficult to make any money with a strategy of borrowing and selling short Select shares with the idea of buying them back at a lower price. There are three things working against you in this situation:

- You are going against the market. For any random period of time, the odds of being right when betting against the market are only about 33 percent.
- You are betting against the fund manager. In the long run, most Selects outperform market averages, which further reduces your chance of making a profit in a short position.
- Brokerage expenses on the trades and interest paid on the borrowed shares can wipe out the profit even if you do realize an occasional gain.

Granted, there may seem to be times when shorting looks attractive despite these handicaps. When those times occur, however, you probably won't find many shares available for shorting. Fidelity limits short positions to $2 million per day per Select, and if that limit hasn't been reached single customers are limited to 12 percent of shares available. Furthermore, the technology Selects, which have the greatest potential for a rapid short-term decline, are not included in the pool of Selects eligible for shorting.

Are you concerned that the popularity of mutual funds could lead to a massive bear market if investors get in the mood to sell at the same time?

Contrary to the impression the media presents, mutual fund investors are not a nervous group waiting to bail out at the first sign of trouble. Most did not sell during the 1973–74 bear market; they waited several years until their losses were recovered. During the 1987 crash, the percentage of mutual fund assets redeemed was much smaller than the selling activity on the institutional side. During the 1990 sell-off, the net outflow from funds was tiny. In 1994, thanks to increased 401(k) participation, many stock funds experienced net inflows throughout the correction periods.

Perhaps mutual fund investors think longer term because they are not overly concerned about the results in the current quarter. Or maybe it's because they have other things going on in their lives and they are not watching the market every day. It could even be that they aren't as compelled to try to outsmart the market because they don't have a boss they are trying to impress. Whatever the reason, mutual fund investors as a group are relatively mature and do not panic out of the market the way institutional investors usually do.

As mutual funds play an increasingly dominant role in the financial markets, I think they are more likely to have a stabilizing effect on the stock market rather than a destabilizing effect.

Is it true that early investors get a better price when a large number of investors are rushing to buy a particular mutual fund?

You might be thinking about a closed-end fund (which acts like a stock). With regular open-end mutual funds, the price is set by the value of the underlying assets. In order for buying activity to push up the price, it would have to push up the price of all underlying stocks held. That's not likely unless the amount of capital involved is very large and the fund manager is putting it to work as fast as he or she can. Even then, the effect would be considerably less dramatic than the same amount of money chasing an individual stock.

I was looking at Select Health Care, but I decided not to buy it because of the high share price. Will there be a better time to get in?

A mutual fund's share price is irrelevant. Select Health Care could be holding cheap stocks, expensive stocks, or even cash, and its share price (NAV) would still be higher than that of other funds because of events that occurred from 1988 to 1991.

The only thing a high share price means is that the fund went through a period in its history where gains were robust and cash inflows were strong. Under these conditions, a lack of selling activity reduces distributions to very modest amounts. During a situation like this, almost all investment gains become fully reflected in the share price.

Ultimately the fund returns to a normal pattern of payouts, and the price stops moving up. Years later, the share price may remain high relative to other funds (unless Fidelity elects to do a split), but chances are that most of the stock holdings are different. The share price itself tells nothing about whether the fund's assets are cheap or expensive.

I want to sell Equity-Income and buy Short-Term Bond because I'll need the money for this year's tax bill. However, I don't want to miss out on Equity-Income's year-end distribution. What should I do?

Unlike a dividend stock, you don't "miss out" by selling a mutual fund before its Ex-date. With stock funds, all stock dividends and capital gains are fully reflected in the share price at all times. For bond funds, any regular income you've earned is always pro-rated on a daily basis and distributed when you sell.

Waiting until after the payout doesn't benefit you because the share price drops by an amount equal to the distribution. The value of your holdings is not affected by the distribution; you simply own more shares at a lower price.

From a tax standpoint, it usually doesn't matter if you sell before or after the Ex-date if you plan to sell before the end of the year anyway. However, if you are in a tax bracket higher than 28 percent and have held the fund for more than a year, you should sell before the Ex-date to avoid taking an unnecessary distribution of short-term gains and income.

Why are the Dow and S&P 500 year-to-date figures published in Fidelity Monitor higher than the ones I read in the newspaper?

Our total return figures assume reinvested stock dividends, which typically add around two to three percentage points per year. Many newspapers mislead investors by ignoring the dividends when they report gains or losses for the Dow and the S&P 500. The total return figures we report are consistent with other mutual fund tracking services such as Morningstar and Lipper.

Why don't you cover Fidelity's Advisor funds?

The Fidelity Advisor funds are a group of funds designed to be sold with a load by stockbrokers. (Some of these funds include 12(b)-1 fees in their expense ratio.) If you are buying through a stockbroker, these funds are probably a lot better than the alternatives. However, they provide no significant advantage over Fidelity's retail funds, which are sold directly to the public at a maximum 3 percent load.

I have a large portfolio, and each year I have to sell some of it to pay the taxes on the distributions generated in the previous year. When is the best time to do that?

Statistically speaking, the best time is right before you have to pay the IRS. Because your investments are growing over the long run, you'll realize an advantage more often than not if you wait as long as possible. If your taxes are due on April 15, you'll also benefit from the stock market's seasonal tendency. Between November and April, stocks usually perform better than during the other half of the year. By selling in early April, you have the best chance for paying the tax bill with the least take on your investment portfolio.

Is there any advantage to using a Fidelity brokerage account for purchasing Fidelity funds?

The enhanced USA package comes with a wide variety of services, and the core account is able to do almost everything a bank checking account can do. A Fidelity brokerage account is convenient if you have other investments (stocks, bonds, etc.) you want consolidated in a single account, or if you want access to mutual funds from other companies.

If you don't need any of this, you can simply purchase Fidelity funds directly from Fidelity. That way, you'll probably end up with less paperwork and statements to deal with.

Is it safe to have all my investments with Fidelity?

I do. Each Fidelity mutual fund is actually a separate financial entity that hires Fidelity Management & Research (FMR) to manage the portfolio. Actual fund assets are held with the custodian (usually a bank holding company), where they are protected against insolvency. If Fidelity were to fail, all Fidelity funds would have to hire a new management company, but the assets would still be there. Redemptions might be heavy and performance might deteriorate, but at least you would have access to your money.

Can I invest in Fidelity funds if I live out of the country?

Yes, but if you don't already have a Fidelity account you might have to find someone else to send you the prospectus for the first fund you buy. That's because some foreign countries have laws barring solicitations by U.S. mutual fund companies, and a prospectus constitutes solicitation.

As long as you can deal in U.S. funds, Fidelity can mail statements and redemption checks just as it would to a domestic address. Fidelity maintains international toll-free numbers in most developed countries, and you can usually call collect if a toll-free number isn't available in your country. (The toll-free international numbers are also handy if you take a vacation overseas.)

If you are a foreigner living in the United States or a foreigner living in a foreign country, you can invest in Fidelity funds, but certain withholding taxes will apply on all redemptions and nonreinvested distributions. The withholding percentage depends on your citizenship. Typically it's 30 percent.

Although Fidelity investors outside the United States are a small group compared to domestic account holders, they can be found all over the globe. *Fidelity Monitor* is mailed to more than 20 different countries, with Canada being the most common outside the United States.

How can I find a complete list of a fund's current holdings?

A complete listing of a fund's portfolio can be found in the annual or semiannual report. If you own shares in the fund, it should be mailed to you automatically. Otherwise, you can request a copy from Fidelity.

Keep in mind that fund managers make trades every day. By the time you get the report, some of the fund's portfolio is likely to have changed. There's really no way to find out exactly what a fund is holding at a given point in time. Fidelity makes it a point not to release a fund's holdings for about 40 days to prevent other fund companies from profiting from its research efforts.

Has Fidelity ever blocked investor trades? Will I have any problems if I try to follow your *Fidelity Monitor* newsletter models?

Fidelity has, on occasion, closed certain funds to new investors when the inflow of cash became difficult to manage. Low-Priced Stock went through this twice during its early years, and in 1987 Growth Company and Contrafund were closed for a few weeks when subscribers to a popular market timing newsletter stampeded into both funds. (A few years later, Fidelity actually sent letters to these investors informing them that future trades with this service would be blocked.)

Since our goal at *Fidelity Monitor* is for our subscribers to follow our models without restrictions, we give Fidelity advance notice to allow the affected fund managers to anticipate the flow of dollars. On the occasion that a Fidelity fund manager has voiced concern, we have changed the timing or amount of the trade to find an acceptable common ground. Because we consider the fund managers, and because all of our trades are within Fidelity's fund group, Fidelity probably won't ever have reason to restrict our recommended switches.

Are newsletter subscriptions and managed account fees deductible expenses?

It depends. Both of these fall into a category called miscellaneous deductions, which includes investment fees, the cost of a safe deposit box, tax advice and preparation fees, subscriptions to professional and investment-related publications, depreciation on computer equipment used for monitoring investments, dues to professional societies, employment-related education, job search expenses, union dues, and a few other things.

Unfortunately, you are allowed to deduct only the portion of these expenses that exceed 2 percent of your adjusted gross income (AGI). Suppose your AGI is $40,000. That means only expenses above and beyond $800 are deductible. Some investors try to bunch their miscellaneous expenses in alternate years, making it easier to exceed the 2 percent threshold. For example, you can take out two-year subscriptions to publications and have your accountant bill you ahead of time on tax preparation every other year.

How would the investment landscape change if Congress were to pass a bill to reduce the tax rate on long-term capital gains?

If the reduction were significant (such as a cut in the top rate from 28 percent to less than 20 percent), variable annuities and retirement accounts could become less attractive for many investors. In addition, the pressure would be on for everyone (including mutual fund managers) to hold profitable positions for at least one year in order to qualify for the lower rate.

GLOSSARY

Advisor   The individual or organization who is hired to manage a mutual fund's investments.

After-Tax Return   The net return on a mutual fund position after income taxes have been paid on the distributions of dividends and capital gains.

Aggressive Growth   An investing style (or fund) which seeks to maximize returns by taking on more risk than the market. The usual approach is to buy stocks in fast-growing, smaller companies.

Alpha   A measure of how much a fund exceeds its predicted performance based on its beta and the gain or loss for the S&P 500 over a specified period. Domestic stock funds with high Alpha scores usually indicate a talented manager or an overweighted industry group that is performing well.

AMT   (Alternative Minimum Tax) A separate income tax system which applies whenever the total tax due under AMT rules is higher than the tax due under the normal rules. Taxpayers usually become subject to AMT when their regular income taxes are significantly reduced by passive losses, excessive deductions for investment expenses, or by various other tax shelters.

AMT Paper   Municipal bonds (or short-term municipal notes) whose interest is taxable for taxpayers subject to AMT. These debt securities usually provide slightly more income than regular muni bonds because there is less demand for them.

Annual Report   A yearly document sent to shareholders that provides fund performance figures and lists all of the fund's holdings at the close of the fund's fiscal year.

Annualized Return (or Average Annual Total Return)   The compound annual rate at which the total return would be realized over a specified period.

Asset Allocation   The practice of allocating a portfolio between different asset classes (usually stocks, bonds, and cash) based on a desired level of overall risk.

Average Maturity   See *Weighted Average Maturity*.

Basis Point   A one-hundredth of one percentage point. For example, 50 basis points is equivalent to one-half of one percentage point.

Beta   A measure of a fund's volatility relative to the S&P 500. A fund with a beta of 0.5 can be expected to gain or lose 0.5 percent for a 1.0 percent gain or loss in the S&P 500 index. Beta is useful for estimating the impact of the domestic stock market on a fund. However, Beta is not a good indicator of overall risk unless the fund's R-squared is relatively high. For funds with an R-squared of less than 75 percent, relative volatility is generally a better measure of overall risk.

Blue Chip   Refers to a stock of a large, well-established company. Blue Chips generally grow at a slower rate than mid-caps or small caps, but usually hold up better in an economic downturn.

Book Value   The worth of a corporation based on standard accounting rules (assets less liabilities).

Bond   A debt security which promises the bondholder a string of specified interest payments and the repayment of principal at maturity.

Brokerage Account   An account which can be used for consolidating a wide variety of investments into one holding place. Certain terms and conditions apply depending on the brokerage company that provides the account.

Brokerage Commission   The cost of executing a trade when selling or buying a security (also applies to selling or buying a fund from a brokerage account, unless the fee is waived as part of a network program).

Capital Gain   The gain (or loss) realized on the price of a security that has been sold. The gain (or loss) is considered short-term if the security was held less than 1 year, otherwise it is considered long-term. As part of a mutual fund distribution, the capital gain components represent the capital gains the fund has realized in selling securities.

Carryforward Losses   A loss on the sale of securities which is carried forward from a previous tax year. In a stock-oriented mutual fund, a large carryforward loss may allow the fund to absorb future capital gains, eliminating the need for a distribution for a few years.

Cash Position   The percentage of short-term notes (or repurchase agreements) held by a fund.

Closed-End Fund   A mutual fund which can only be bought or sold in the secondary market once the initial offering is completed. This type of fund is listed and traded like an individual stock, and usually sells at a premium or discount to its actual net asset value.

Convertible Security   Typically a bond (or preferred stock) which can be converted to common stock under certain conditions.

Cost Basis   The amount of money paid to accumulate a mutual fund position (or a position in an individual security), including any load fees and transaction costs. Once sold, the selling price less the cost basis is the capital gain (or loss).

Coupon Rate   The interest a bond pays on its par value when first issued.

Credit Rating   An assessment of a company's ability to repay principal and interest on its bonds. The judgment is made by a credit rating agency such as Standard & Poor's or Moody's. Top-rated corporations are considered AAA or Aaa, and those with excessive credit risk are usually not rated at all (nonrated bonds are often referred to as "junk bonds").

Credit Risk   The risk of default by the issuer of a bond. In a mutual fund, credit risk is secondary to interest-rate risk but can still play a key role in junk bond funds (the entire junk bond market can sell off if the market believes credit risk is going up for a large percentage of companies).

Custodian   The entity responsible for holding a mutual fund's actual stock certificates, bonds, and other assets for safekeeping. Usually a bank holding company.

Derivative   A security with returns that are linked in a specified way to an underlying security or index of securities.

Disclosure   The obligation of a mutual fund to clearly state historical performance, risks and potential risks, limitations, fee structure, compensation to the advisor, and any other factors which may affect performance. These items are discussed in a fund's prospectus.

Distribution   A payout of income, short-term capital gains, or long-term capital gains from a fund's asset base.

Diversification   Investing in many different securities so that a large loss in a single security will not have much impact on the portfolio as a whole. A diversified portfolio does not usually protect against losses from market-related declines. For example, a growth fund with several hundred stocks could still decline 25–30 percent in a bear market.

Dividends   For a stock, the return of a portion of profits to the shareholders. For mutual funds, this is the income portion of a distribution. Most bond and money market funds compute dividends daily and make payouts on a monthly basis.

Dividend Yield   The annualized rate at which dividends are posted to shareholder accounts. For an individual stock, the percent return of the stock's dividend payouts (over the last 12 months) divided by its share price. The aggregate dividend yield of the S&P 500 has been a closely watched indicator of stock valuations, but is becoming outdated by the increasing popularity of stock buybacks.

Dollar Cost Averaging   Investing a fixed amount of money at regular intervals. This is considered a low-risk approach to investing in stocks because you end up buying more shares when prices are low and fewer when prices are high. Lacking this kind of disciplined approach, most investors tend to do the opposite.

Duration   A measure of a bond fund's interest rate sensitivity. For example, a duration of 5 means that, other factors being equal, an across-the-board one percentage point increase in interest rates would cause a 5 percent decline in share price.

Equity   Ownership interest in a corporation operated for profit. Value is determined by supply and demand in the market, and is affected by earnings, dividends paid, stock buyback programs, assets owned, rate of growth, competition, takeover potential, breakup value, burden of regulation, and other factors.

Equity-Income   An investing style (or fund) seeking conservative growth from a strategy of investing in dividend stocks. The risk level of such an approach is slightly less than that of the S&P 500.

Exchange   Selling one mutual fund and buying another within the same fund family or network program. Exchanges represent taxable transactions unless they are made within a retirement account.

Exchange Fee   A charge for making a switch from one fund to another.

Excise Distribution   A special dividend payout on a bond fund which, unlike regular dividends, reduces the fund's share price.

Ex-date   The date of record on which a fund distribution reduces the fund's share price by an amount equal to the value of the distribution.

Expense Cap   A voluntary limit on a fund's expenses, usually put in place on new bond and money market funds to result in an above average yield and accelerate sales of the fund. Typically the fund's management company absorbs any expenses in excess of the cap. Expense Caps can be changed or eliminated without notice to shareholders.

Expense Ratio   The cost of running the fund expressed as annual percentage of total fund assets. Does not include the cost of brokerage commissions on securities the fund buys and sells.

Expense Waiver   A temporary agreement by a fund's management company to absorb all costs of running the fund. Can be eliminated without notice to shareholders.

401(k)   A corporate retirement plan that allows employees to decide (up to IRS limits) how much to contribute and which investment vehicle(s) to use. The employer decides on which choices to make available to employees. Most medium and large corporations offer 401(k) plans, but the range of choices varies widely.

403(b)   Similar to a 401(k) plan, but designed for nonprofit organizations. Most 403(b) programs allow for more choices than do 401(k)s.

Front-End Load   The sales charge which goes to the management company before the remaining dollars go to work in the fund being purchased.

Fund Network   A mutual fund purchasing program, usually offered by a brokerage company. Several brokerages waive transaction fees for funds that are part of their program.

Future   A contract to buy or sell a security, index, or commodity at a set price at a future date.

Gain Factor   A number representing the growth of a fund which, when multiplied by the original investment, will show the final value of the investment.

Ginnie Mae Fund   A fund that invests in government bonds which are backed by mortgages. Compared to Treasuries, the credit risk and yield are usually slightly higher. These funds tend to hold up better than other government bond funds when rates are rising, but because of prepayment risk they don't gain as much when rates are on a decline.

Growth   An investing style (or fund) seeking long-term growth from stocks. Usually the risk level of such an approach is slightly higher than that of the S&P 500.

Growth and Income   An investing style (or fund) seeking conservative growth from stocks, with a portion of the portfolio allocated to income-producing securities, typically dividend stocks or bonds. Usually the risk level with this approach is less than that of the S&P 500.

Growth Stock   An equity security of a company whose revenue and earnings are expected to grow faster than the economy over the long run.

Hedging   The practice of buying currency contracts or using other means to reduce or eliminate the effect of exchange-rate fluctuations on a foreign security.

Index   An unmanaged collection of securities that can be used to compare the results of an actively managed portfolio. For example, domestic growth funds usually aim to exceed the S&P 500 stock index.

Inflation   The average annual rate at which the cost of goods and services increase relative to the nation's currency.

Interest-Rate Risk   The risk that a bond will decline in price if interest rates go up (it is not an issue if you plan to hold the bond to maturity). In most bond funds, interest-rate risk is the dominant risk factor, because unlike credit risk it is not reduced through diversification.

Intermediate-Term   A period of time (or an average maturity) of more than three but less than ten years.

Investment Advisor   See *Advisor.*

Investment Grade   Generally refers to corporate bonds that carry ratings above BB (Standard & Poor's) or Bb (Moody's). This represents the mainstream market for corporate debt.

IRA (Individual Retirement Account)   An account with special tax status that permits certain types of investments and allows them to compound on a tax-deferred basis. Contributions are deductible under certain conditions, and usually there is a 10 percent penalty that applies if the money is taken out of the account before the owner reaches age 59 $^1/2$.

Junk Bonds   Corporate bonds that are not rated or carry a rating of BB and below (Standard & Poor's) or Bb and below (Moody's). Because of their greater credit risk, these bonds generally yield 2 to 5 percentage points more than government bonds with a similar maturity.

Junk Bond Yield Spread   The difference in yield between junk bonds and similar maturity government bonds.

Keogh   An employer retirement plan similar to a IRA but with unique rules governing contribution amounts.

Liquidity   The speed in which a security can be converted to cash without having to reduce the price below market value.

Load   See *Front-End Load.*

Long-Term   A period of time (or an average maturity) of ten years or more.

Management Fee   The money a fund pays to its advisor for managing the fund's investments.

Manager   The individual (or team) responsible for a mutual fund's performance. Typically, this person supervises or does the actual buying and selling of securities held in the fund's portfolio.

Margin   The practice of borrowing to purchase more shares in a security than could be purchased directly. Margin magnifies both gains and losses, but losses are magnified more than gains.

Market Capitalization   The worth of a corporation calculated by multiplying its stock price times total shares outstanding.

Market Timing   Attempting to buy stocks or stock funds when the broad market is moving higher, and holding cash when the market is declining. While this approach can reduce the average risk in a portfolio, it seldom improves long-term returns.

Maturity   The date when a bond's interest payments terminate and the principal is to be returned to the bondholder.

Mid-Cap   A stock with a market capitalization of more than $300 million but less than $3 billion (these limits can be wider under other definitions).

Momentum   The tendency for a security to keep moving in the direction it currently is going.

Moving Average   An average of a specified number of adjusted NAV data points over fixed intervals of time. For example, some technical traders sell a fund when its current price drops below its 39-week moving average, and buy when it moves back above. Use of moving averages is popular with market timing systems.

Municipal Bonds   Debt securities issued at the state or local level to finance public works. Interest earned is exempt from federal income tax, and in the state where the bond is issued interest is typically exempt from state income taxes as well.

Net Asset Value (NAV)   The mutual fund equivalent of share price. The mutual fund company's calculation of the total market value of all securities owned by the fund, divided by the total number of shares outstanding. This figure is typically calculated once each day after the market's close, except for Fidelity Selects, which are priced hourly.

No-Load   A fund which is sold without a front-end load.

Objective   The purpose for which a fund exists; the fund's goal.

Offering Price (or Asking Price)   In a no-load fund, the net asset value. In a load fund, the net asset value plus the front-end sales charge.

Open-End Fund   Refers to the most common type of mutual fund where shares can be bought or redeemed directly from the fund company (all of the funds discussed in this book are open-end funds).

Option   A contract that grants the right to buy or sell a specific security, index, or commodity at a set price up until a specified date.

Performance The return that you realize while owning shares in a fund.

Price-Book Ratio The ratio of a corporation's share price divided by its book value per share.

Price-Sales Ratio The ratio of a corporation's share price divided by its revenue per share. Not generally used for evaluating financial stocks and others Where sales are not well defined

Price-Earnings Ratio The ratio of a corporation's share price divided by its earnings per share (usually over the last 12 months). This valuation indicator is not defined for companies with zero earnings or with a net loss, and is not useful for evaluating firms near breakeven. Generally speaking, stocks selling at multiples below the expected rate of earnings growth are considered undervalued. For example, a stock with a P/E of 8 and expected earnings per share growth of 12 percent per year would be considered a good buy.

Price-Sales Ratio The ratio of a corporation's share price divided by its revenue per share. Not generally used for evaluating financial stocks and others where sales are not well defined.

Prospectus A legal document which states historical performance, risks and potential risks, limitations, fee structure, compensation of the advisor, and any other factors which may affect performance. Unless you buy through a brokerage account, a fund company is required to ask if you have read the prospectus before they can legally sell you shares in the fund.

Proxy A measure allowing mutual fund shareholders to vote on board members, fee structure, investment limitations, selection of an accounting firm, and other fundamental items that can affect the fund's operation.

Quantitative Approach A method of investing based on mathematical calculations that has been tested against historical data to optimize performance. Some quantitative models are based on neural nets (complex computer programs which "learn" patterns over time).

R-Squared A statistical calculation which indicates how much a fund's performance correlates with a particular index, usually the S&P 500. A figure of 1.00 (or 100 percent) indicates perfect correlation, whereas 0.00 indicates that there is no correlation (although rare, it is possible for a fund to have a negative R-squared if it moves opposite the market).

Realized Gain The capital gain realized from the sale of a security.

Redemption The act of selling mutual fund shares back to the management company for the purpose of switching to another fund or having the money returned to the shareholder.

Redemption Fee A charge against the money being redeemed out of the fund. Some funds charge a redemption fee until the money has been in the fund for a specified length of time; this practice discourages investors from jumping in and out of the fund based on short-term trends.

Reinvested Distribution The automatic purchase of additional shares (of the same fund) when a distribution is paid. Retirement accounts are automatically set up with this structure, and it is a common choice for regular taxable accounts.

REIT A Real Estate Investment Trust. A company that invests in real estate properties and returns income and profits to shareholders.

Relative Volatility A general measure of risk which is computed from a fund's monthly, weekly, or daily gains and losses over a specified interval of time. It is usually computed by taking the standard deviation of the gains and losses (a statistical calculation) and normalizing to the S&P 500. Thus, a fund with price fluctuations equivalent to the index will be 1.00. Relative volatility is similar to beta for funds that are highly correlated to the index.

Risk   The probability that an investment could experience a substantial decline in value.

Risk-Adjusted Return   An indicator which reduces a fund's total return by the amount of risk it takes on, allowing an apples-to-apples comparison of a wide variety of different securities. Funds with high risk-adjusted returns in the past tend to be above average performers in the future.

Rollover IRA   An account which is set up to receive a lump-sum pension, a 401(k) payout, or some other type of qualified retirement distribution. When the transfer is made directly from the previous plan administrator to the financial institution of choice, the taxpayer pays no taxes and gains direct control over how his or her nest egg is invested.

S&P 500   Standard and Poor's composite index of 500 stocks, a capitalization-weighted index that gives the most weight to companies with the greatest total market valuation. The index has existed since 1925 and does not include the reinvestment of stock dividends; as a result the dividends must be figured back in when calculating total return.

SEC 30-Day Yield   A method of calculating a bond fund's yield which is specified by the SEC. It is based on yield-to-maturity, with hedging activities excluded from the calculation. It is only an estimate of the actual income you will receive on a monthly basis, and with certain foreign bond funds it can substantially overstate the actual income that is earned. Fund companies are required to calculate bond fund yield using this approach.

Sector Fund   A fund which invests in the stocks of a specific industry or group of industries.

Security   A financial instrument such as a short-term note, a bond, a share of stock, or a derivative.

Share Price   See *Net Asset Value (NAV)*.

Sharpe Ratio   A calculation used to determine the relative risk-adjusted returns of various funds or investments. Starting with a population of gains and losses (usually daily, weekly, or monthly), you compute the average gain of a security (or fund) and subtract the average gain of a "riskless" investment (usually 90-day T-bills). The result is then divided by the standard deviation of the gains and losses of the security.

Short-Term   A period of time (or an average maturity) of less than three years.

Soft Dollars   Money used to pay for goods and services that comes out of the commissions paid for selling or buying securities (or from the price spread between buyer and seller on a purchased security). Soft Dollars are typically "rebated" back to the fund's management company and are used to purchase computer equipment, quote systems, research reports, and other things that would otherwise show up in a fund's expense ratio. The practice is legal, but skirts disclosure rules (it causes a fund's expense ratio to be understated, even though shareholders are still paying the bill). Fund companies may be required to disclose these purchases at some point in the future.

Stock   See *Equity.*

Switch   See *Exchange.*

Taxable Equivalent Yield   Used to compare a municipal bond fund with a taxable bond fund. Figured by dividing the yield of the municipal fund by the quantity of one minus your federal tax bracket in decimal form. For a state-specific fund, divide the yield by [(1 − Federal tax bracket) × (1 − State tax bracket)].

Total Return   The percentage gain or loss in a fund over a specified interval with distributions reinvested. Unless specified, total return figures usually do not reflect load fees or redemption charges.

Transfer Agent   An organization that keeps the records of the fund's shareholders, and handles the paperwork for shares that are bought and sold.

Treasuries   Bonds or notes issued and backed directly by the U.S. Government. Credit risk is considered to be near zero because the

U.S. government can always raise taxes, sell more bonds, or print more currency to satisfy an obligation.

Turnaround A company with poor profitability which has taken steps to improve its bottom line.

Turnover Ratio The rate at which securities are bought and sold within a fund's portfolio. A 100 percent turnover is equivalent to replacing every security over a year's time, but could also mean that a fund kept one-half of its portfolio and replaced the other 50 percent twice during the course of a year.

12b-1 Fee An annual fee taken from a fund's asset base and used to pay for sales and marketing expenses.

Unrealized Gain The appreciation of a security which will become taxable after the security is sold.

Value An investing style (or fund) seeking long-term growth from value stocks. Usually the risk level of such an approach is slightly lower than that of the S & P 500.

Value Stock An equity security of a company whose worth is determined more by dividends and underlying assets than by its potential for growth of earnings

Variable Annuity An investment with special tax treatment (similar to that of a nondeductible IRA) which works somewhat like a mutual fund account; it offers life insurance features and charges an annual fee for them.

Wash Sale When selling at a loss in a regular taxable account, the sale of a security 30 days prior to or after the purchase of a substantially identical asset. In the event of a wash sale you are not allowed to deduct the loss, but you can add it to your cost basis to offset the gain on a future sale.

Weighted Average Maturity The average maturity of a fund's bond holdings in years, weighted in proportion to their dollar value. Generally speaking, the longer the average maturity, the greater the sensitivity to interest rates.

Yield The annual rate of interest or dividends paid as a percentage of the security's current price (also see SEC 30-day Yield and

Dividend Yield).

Yield Curve   A plot of interest rates versus maturity for Treasury notes and bonds. A steep curve indicates a large spread between short-term and long-term interest rates. A flat curve means rates are similar regardless of the period you invest for, and an inverted curve means short-term rates are higher than long-term interest rates.

Yield to Maturity   A method of calculating bond yield that takes into account the fact that bonds selling at a discount or premium to their par value will return to par as they approach their maturity.

APPENDIX A

Growth Funds - 1977 Return

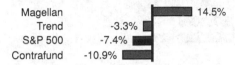

Magellan	14.5%
Trend	-3.3%
S&P 500	-7.4%
Contrafund	-10.9%

Growth Funds - 1978 Return

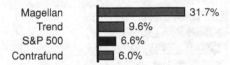

Magellan	31.7%
Trend	9.6%
S&P 500	6.6%
Contrafund	6.0%

Growth Funds - 1979 Return

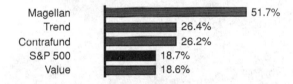

Magellan	51.7%
Trend	26.4%
Contrafund	26.2%
S&P 500	18.7%
Value	18.6%

Growth Funds - 1980 Return

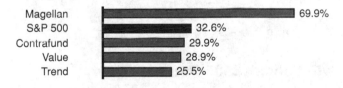

Magellan	69.9%
S&P 500	32.6%
Contrafund	29.9%
Value	28.9%
Trend	25.5%

Growth Funds - 1981 Return

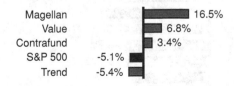

Magellan	16.5%
Value	6.8%
Contrafund	3.4%
S&P 500	-5.1%
Trend	-5.4%

Growth Funds - 1982 Return

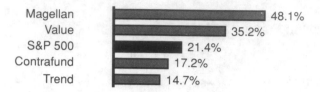

Magellan	48.1%
Value	35.2%
S&P 500	21.4%
Contrafund	17.2%
Trend	14.7%

Growth Funds - 1983 Return

Magellan	38.6%
Value	32.3%
Trend	26.6%
Contrafund	23.3%
S&P 500	22.4%

Growth Funds - 1984 Return

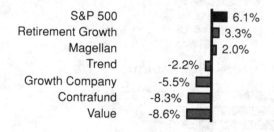

S&P 500	6.1%
Retirement Growth	3.3%
Magellan	2.0%
Trend	-2.2%
Growth Company	-5.5%
Contrafund	-8.3%
Value	-8.6%

Growth Funds - 1985 Return

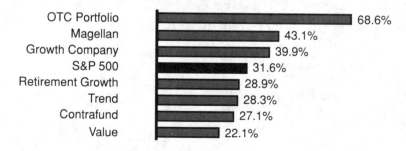

OTC Portfolio	68.6%
Magellan	43.1%
Growth Company	39.9%
S&P 500	31.6%
Retirement Growth	28.9%
Trend	28.3%
Contrafund	27.1%
Value	22.1%

Growth Funds - 1986 Return

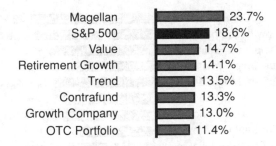

Magellan	23.7%
S&P 500	18.6%
Value	14.7%
Retirement Growth	14.1%
Trend	13.5%
Contrafund	13.3%
Growth Company	13.0%
OTC Portfolio	11.4%

Growth Funds - 1987 Return

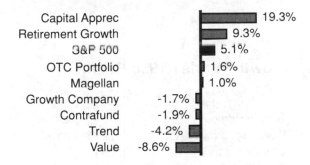

Capital Apprec	19.3%
Retirement Growth	9.3%
S&P 500	5.1%
OTC Portfolio	1.6%
Magellan	1.0%
Growth Company	-1.7%
Contrafund	-1.9%
Trend	-4.2%
Value	-8.6%

Growth Funds - 1988 Return

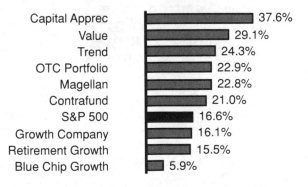

Capital Apprec	37.6%
Value	29.1%
Trend	24.3%
OTC Portfolio	22.9%
Magellan	22.8%
Contrafund	21.0%
S&P 500	16.6%
Growth Company	16.1%
Retirement Growth	15.5%
Blue Chip Growth	5.9%

Growth Funds - 1989 Return

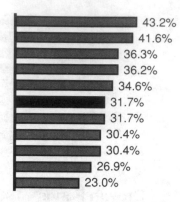

Fund	Return
Contrafund	43.2%
Growth Company	41.6%
Disciplined Equity	36.3%
Blue Chip Growth	36.2%
Magellan	34.6%
S&P 500	31.7%
Trend	31.7%
Retirement Growth	30.4%
OTC Portfolio	30.4%
Capital Apprec	26.9%
Value	23.0%

Growth Funds - 1990 Return

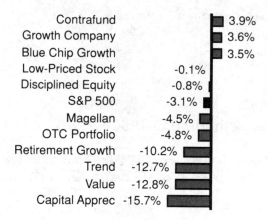

Fund	Return
Contrafund	3.9%
Growth Company	3.6%
Blue Chip Growth	3.5%
Low-Priced Stock	-0.1%
Disciplined Equity	-0.8%
S&P 500	-3.1%
Magellan	-4.5%
OTC Portfolio	-4.8%
Retirement Growth	-10.2%
Trend	-12.7%
Value	-12.8%
Capital Apprec	-15.7%

Growth Funds - 1991 Return

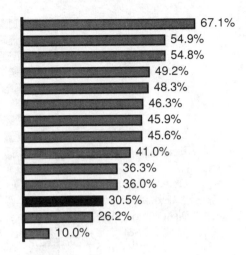

Emerging Growth	67.1%
Contrafund	54.9%
Blue Chip Growth	54.8%
OTC Portfolio	49.2%
Growth Company	48.3%
Low-Priced Stock	46.3%
Stock Selector	45.9%
Retirement Growth	45.6%
Magellan	41.0%
Trend	36.3%
Disciplined Equity	36.0%
S&P 500	30.5%
Value	26.2%
Capital Apprec	10.0%

Growth Funds - 1992 Return

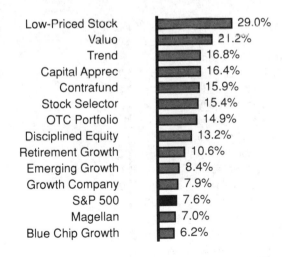

Low-Priced Stock	29.0%
Value	21.2%
Trend	16.8%
Capital Apprec	16.4%
Contrafund	15.9%
Stock Selector	15.4%
OTC Portfolio	14.9%
Disciplined Equity	13.2%
Retirement Growth	10.6%
Emerging Growth	8.4%
Growth Company	7.9%
S&P 500	7.6%
Magellan	7.0%
Blue Chip Growth	6.2%

Growth Funds - 1993 Return

Fund	Return
Capital Apprec	33.4%
New Millennium	24.7%
Magellan	24.7%
Blue Chip Growth	24.5%
Value	22.9%
Retirement Growth	22.1%
Contrafund	21.4%
Low-Priced Stock	20.2%
Emerging Growth	19.9%
Trend	19.2%
Growth Company	16.2%
Stock Selector	14.0%
Disciplined Equity	13.9%
S&P 500	10.1%
OTC Portfolio	8.3%

Growth Funds - 1994 Return

Fund	Return
Blue Chip Growth	9.9%
Value	7.6%
Low-Priced Stock	4.8%
Dividend Growth	4.3%
Fidelity Fifty	4.0%
Disciplined Equity	3.0%
Capital Apprec	2.5%
S&P 500	1.3%
New Millennium	0.8%
Stock Selector	0.8%
Retirement Growth	0.1%
Emerging Growth	-0.2%
Contrafund	-1.1%
Magellan	-1.8%
Growth Company	-2.2%
OTC Portfolio	-2.7%
Small Cap Stock	-3.3%
Trend	-6.7%

Growth Funds - 1995 Return

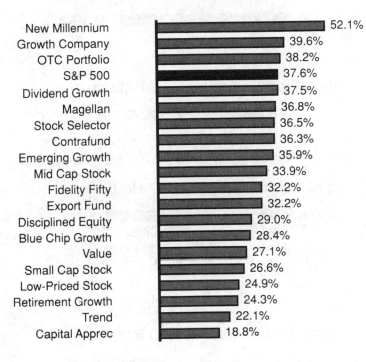

Fund	Return
New Millennium	52.1%
Growth Company	39.6%
OTC Portfolio	38.2%
S&P 500	37.6%
Dividend Growth	37.5%
Magellan	36.8%
Stock Selector	36.5%
Contrafund	36.3%
Emerging Growth	35.9%
Mid Cap Stock	33.9%
Fidelity Fifty	32.2%
Export Fund	32.2%
Disciplined Equity	29.0%
Blue Chip Growth	28.4%
Value	27.1%
Small Cap Stock	26.6%
Low-Priced Stock	24.9%
Retirement Growth	24.3%
Trend	22.1%
Capital Apprec	18.8%

International Funds - 1985 Return

Overseas
78.7%

International Funds - 1986 Return

Overseas
69.3%

International Funds - 1987 Return

Pacific Basin	25.0%
Overseas	18.4%
Europe	14.9%
Int'l Growth & Inc	8.3%

International Funds - 1988 Return

Canada	19.5%
Int'l Growth & Inc	11.6%
Pacific Basin	10.5%
Overseas	8.3%
Europe	5.8%

International Funds - 1989 Return

Europe	32.3%
Canada	27.0%
Int'l Growth & Inc	19.1%
Overseas	16.9%
Pacific Basin	11.4%

International Funds - 1990 Return

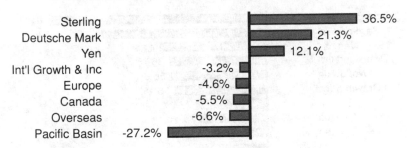

Sterling	36.5%
Deutsche Mark	21.3%
Yen	12.1%
Int'l Growth & Inc	-3.2%
Europe	-4.6%
Canada	-5.5%
Overseas	-6.6%
Pacific Basin	-27.2%

International Funds - 1991 Return

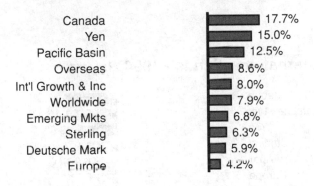

Canada	17.7%
Yen	15.0%
Pacific Basin	12.5%
Overseas	8.6%
Int'l Growth & Inc	8.0%
Worldwide	7.9%
Emerging Mkts	6.8%
Sterling	6.3%
Deutsche Mark	5.9%
Europe	4.2%

International Funds - 1992 Return

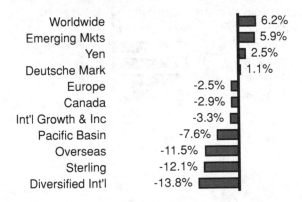

Worldwide	6.2%
Emerging Mkts	5.9%
Yen	2.5%
Deutsche Mark	1.1%
Europe	-2.5%
Canada	-2.9%
Int'l Growth & Inc	-3.3%
Pacific Basin	-7.6%
Overseas	-11.5%
Sterling	-12.1%
Diversified Int'l	-13.8%

International Funds - 1993 Return

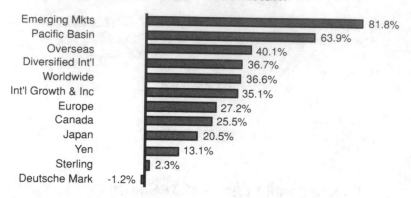

Emerging Mkts	81.8%
Pacific Basin	63.9%
Overseas	40.1%
Diversified Int'l	36.7%
Worldwide	36.6%
Int'l Growth & Inc	35.1%
Europe	27.2%
Canada	25.5%
Japan	20.5%
Yen	13.1%
Sterling	2.3%
Deutsche Mark	-1.2%

International Funds - 1994 Return

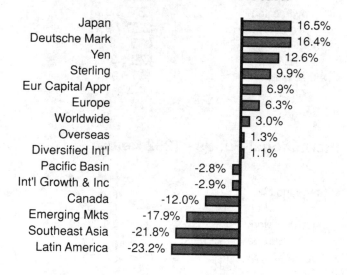

Japan	16.5%
Deutsche Mark	16.4%
Yen	12.6%
Sterling	9.9%
Eur Capital Appr	6.9%
Europe	6.3%
Worldwide	3.0%
Overseas	1.3%
Diversified Int'l	1.1%
Pacific Basin	-2.8%
Int'l Growth & Inc	-2.9%
Canada	-12.0%
Emerging Mkts	-17.9%
Southeast Asia	-21.8%
Latin America	-23.2%

International Funds - 1995 Return

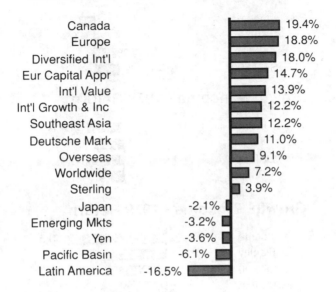

Canada	19.4%
Europe	18.8%
Diversified Int'l	18.0%
Eur Capital Appr	14.7%
Int'l Value	13.9%
Int'l Growth & Inc	12.2%
Southeast Asia	12.2%
Deutsche Mark	11.0%
Overseas	9.1%
Worldwide	7.2%
Sterling	3.9%
Japan	-2.1%
Emerging Mkts	-3.2%
Yen	-3.6%
Pacific Basin	-6.1%
Latin America	-16.5%

Growth & Income - 1977 Return

Equity-Income	5.0%
Puritan	0.8%
Fidelity	-3.3%
S&P 500	-7.4%

Growth & Income - 1978 Return

Equity-Income	11.4%
Fidelity	9.4%
S&P 500	6.6%
Puritan	4.5%

Growth & Income - 1979 Return

Equity-Income	30.8%
Fidelity	18.7%
S&P 500	18.7%
Puritan	14.8%

Growth & Income - 1980 Return

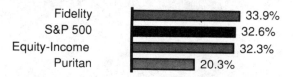

Fidelity	33.9%
S&P 500	32.6%
Equity-Income	32.3%
Puritan	20.3%

Growth & Income - 1981 Return

Puritan	10.8%
Equity-Income	9.5%
Fidelity	-3.3%
S&P 500	-5.1%

Growth & Income - 1982 Return

Equity-Income	34.6%
Fidelity	34.5%
Puritan	29.1%
S&P 500	21.4%

Growth & Income - 1983 Return

Equity-Income	29.2%
Puritan	25.9%
Fidelity	22.4%
S&P 500	22.4%

Growth & Income - 1984 Return

Puritan	10.6%
Equity-Income	10.5%
S&P 500	6.1%
Fidelity	1.5%

Growth & Income - 1985 Return

S&P 500	31.6%
Puritan	28.7%
Fidelity	27.7%
Equity-Income	25.1%

Growth & Income - 1986 Return

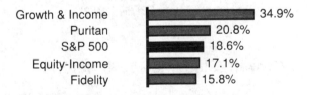

Growth & Income	34.9%
Puritan	20.8%
S&P 500	18.6%
Equity-Income	17.1%
Fidelity	15.8%

Growth & Income - 1987 Return

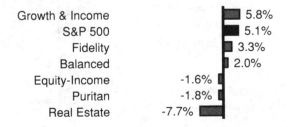

Growth & Income	5.8%
S&P 500	5.1%
Fidelity	3.3%
Balanced	2.0%
Equity-Income	-1.6%
Puritan	-1.8%
Real Estate	-7.7%

Growth & Income - 1988 Return

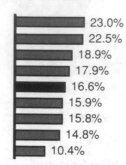

Growth & Income	23.0%
Equity-Income	22.5%
Puritan	18.9%
Fidelity	17.9%
S&P 500	16.6%
Convertible Sec	15.9%
Balanced	15.8%
Utilities Income	14.8%
Real Estate	10.4%

Growth & Income - 1989 Return

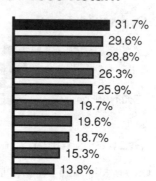

S&P 500	31.7%
Growth & Income	29.6%
Fidelity	28.8%
Convertible Sec	26.3%
Utilities Income	25.9%
Balanced	19.7%
Puritan	19.6%
Equity-Income	18.7%
Asset Mgr	15.3%
Real Estate	13.8%

Growth & Income - 1990 Return

Asset Mgr	5.4%
Utilities Income	1.9%
Balanced	-0.5%
Convertible Sec	-2.9%
S&P 500	-3.1%
Fidelity	-5.1%
Puritan	-6.4%
Growth & Income	-6.8%
Real Estate	-8.7%
Equity-Income	-14.0%

Growth & Income - 1991 Return

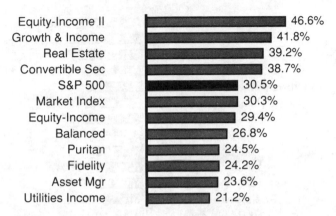

Equity-Income II	46.6%
Growth & Income	41.8%
Real Estate	39.2%
Convertible Sec	38.7%
S&P 500	30.5%
Market Index	30.3%
Equity-Income	29.4%
Balanced	26.8%
Puritan	24.5%
Fidelity	24.2%
Asset Mgr	23.6%
Utilities Income	21.2%

Growth & Income - 1992 Return

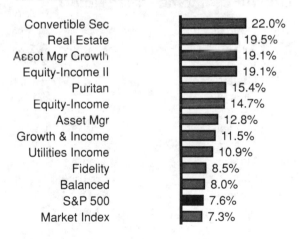

Convertible Sec	22.0%
Real Estate	19.5%
Asset Mgr Growth	19.1%
Equity-Income II	19.1%
Puritan	15.4%
Equity-Income	14.7%
Asset Mgr	12.8%
Growth & Income	11.5%
Utilities Income	10.9%
Fidelity	8.5%
Balanced	8.0%
S&P 500	7.6%
Market Index	7.3%

Growth & Income - 1993 Return

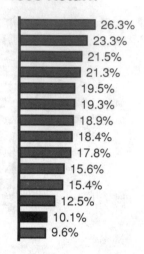

Asset Mgr Growth	26.3%
Asset Mgr	23.3%
Puritan	21.5%
Equity-Income	21.3%
Growth & Income	19.5%
Balanced	19.3%
Equity-Income II	18.9%
Fidelity	18.4%
Convertible Sec	17.8%
Utilities Income	15.6%
Asset Mgr Inc	15.4%
Real Estate	12.5%
S&P 500	10.1%
Market Index	9.6%

Growth & Income - 1994 Return

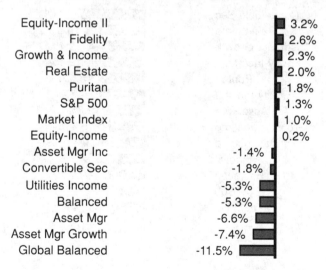

Equity-Income II	3.2%
Fidelity	2.6%
Growth & Income	2.3%
Real Estate	2.0%
Puritan	1.8%
S&P 500	1.3%
Market Index	1.0%
Equity-Income	0.2%
Asset Mgr Inc	-1.4%
Convertible Sec	-1.8%
Utilities Income	-5.3%
Balanced	-5.3%
Asset Mgr	-6.6%
Asset Mgr Growth	-7.4%
Global Balanced	-11.5%

Growth & Income - 1995 Return

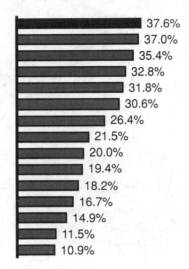

S&P 500	37.6%
Market Index	37.0%
Growth & Income	35.4%
Fidelity	32.8%
Equity-Income	31.8%
Utilities Fund	30.6%
Equity-Income II	26.4%
Puritan	21.5%
Asset Mgr Growth	20.0%
Convertible Sec	19.4%
Asset Mgr	18.2%
Asset Mgr Inc	16.7%
Balanced	14.9%
Global Balanced	11.5%
Real Estate	10.9%

Bond Funds - 1977 Return

Invest Grade Bond
Intermediate Bond

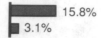

15.8%
3.1%

Bond Funds - 1978 Return

Capital & Income
Intermediate Bond
Invest Grade Bond

4.0%
3.1%
1.4%

Bond Funds - 1979 Return

Intermediate Bond
Capital & Income
Invest Grade Bond

7.2%
4.7%
1.2%

Bond Funds - 1980 Return

Intermediate Bond
Gov't Securities
Capital & Income
Invest Grade Bond

10.5%
6.7%
4.4%
2.3%

Bond Funds - 1981 Return

Intermediate Bond
Gov't Securities
Capital & Income
Invest Grade Bond

12.4%
10.5%
6.9%
3.9%

Bond Funds - 1982 Return

Capital & Income
Invest Grade Bond
Gov't Securities
Intermediate Bond

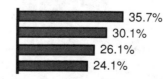

35.7%
30.1%
26.1%
24.1%

Bond Funds - 1983 Return

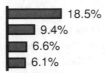

Capital & Income	18.5%
Intermediate Bond	9.4%
Invest Grade Bond	6.6%
Gov't Securities	6.1%

Bond Funds - 1984 Return

Intermediate Bond	13.6%
Invest Grade Bond	11.8%
Gov't Securities	11.3%
Capital & Income	10.5%

Bond Funds - 1985 Return

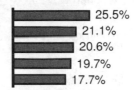

Capital & Income	25.5%
Invest Grade Bond	21.1%
Intermediate Bond	20.6%
Mort. Securities	19.7%
Gov't Securities	17.7%

Bond Funds - 1986 Return

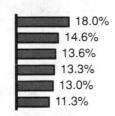

Capital & Income	18.0%
Gov't Securities	14.6%
Invest Grade Bond	13.6%
Intermediate Bond	13.3%
GNMA Portfolio	13.0%
Mort. Securities	11.3%

Bond Funds - 1987 Return

Global Bond	19.1%
Short-Term Bond	4.0%
Mort. Securities	2.7%
Intermediate Bond	2.0%
Capital & Income	1.3%
GNMA Portfolio	1.2%
Gov't Securities	1.1%
Invest Grade Bond	0.1%

Bond Funds - 1988 Return

Capital & Income	12.6%
Invest Grade Bond	7.9%
Intermediate Bond	7.2%
GNMA Portfolio	7.2%
Mort. Securities	6.7%
Gov't Securities	6.4%
Short-Term Bond	5.7%
Global Bond	3.7%

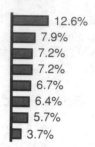

Bond Funds - 1989 Return

Spart Gov't Inc	15.2%
GNMA Portfolio	13.9%
Mort. Securities	13.6%
Invest Grade Bond	13.0%
Gov't Securities	12.6%
Intermediate Bond	11.8%
Short-Term Bond	10.5%
Spart Ltd Mat Gov	10.3%
Global Bond	7.9%
Capital & Income	-3.2%

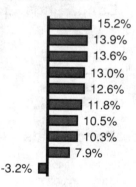

Bond Funds - 1990 Return

Global Bond	12.3%
GNMA Portfolio	10.5%
Mort. Securities	10.4%
Gov't Securities	9.5%
Spart Gov't Inc	9.2%
Spart Ltd Mat Gov	9.1%
Intermediate Bond	7.5%
Invest Grade Bond	6.1%
Short-Term Bond	5.8%
Capital & Income	-3.9%

Bond Funds - 1991 Return

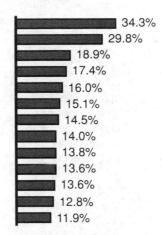

Spart High Inc	34.3%
Capital & Income	29.8%
Invest Grade Bond	18.9%
Spart Long-Term	17.4%
Gov't Securities	16.0%
Spart Gov't Inc	15.1%
Intermediate Bond	14.5%
Short-Term Bond	14.0%
Spart GNMA	13.8%
Mort. Securities	13.6%
GNMA Portfolio	13.6%
Global Bond	12.8%
Spart Ltd Mat Gov	11.9%

Bond Funds - 1992 Return

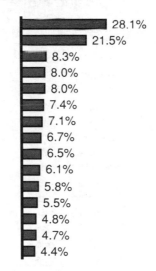

Capital & Income	28.1%
Spart High Inc	21.5%
Invest Grade Bond	8.3%
Spart Long-Term	8.0%
Gov't Securities	8.0%
Short-Term Bond	7.4%
Spart Gov't Inc	7.1%
GNMA Portfolio	6.7%
Spart GNMA	6.5%
Intermediate Bond	6.1%
Spart Ltd Mat Gov	5.8%
Mort. Securities	5.5%
ST World Income	4.8%
Short-Int. Gov't	4.7%
Global Bond	4.4%

Bond Funds - 1993 Return

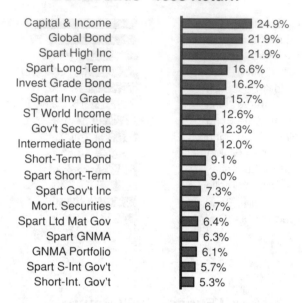

Capital & Income	24.9%
Global Bond	21.9%
Spart High Inc	21.9%
Spart Long-Term	16.6%
Invest Grade Bond	16.2%
Spart Inv Grade	15.7%
ST World Income	12.6%
Gov't Securities	12.3%
Intermediate Bond	12.0%
Short-Term Bond	9.1%
Spart Short-Term	9.0%
Spart Gov't Inc	7.3%
Mort. Securities	6.7%
Spart Ltd Mat Gov	6.4%
Spart GNMA	6.3%
GNMA Portfolio	6.1%
Spart S-Int Gov't	5.7%
Short-Int. Gov't	5.3%

Bond Funds - 1994 Return

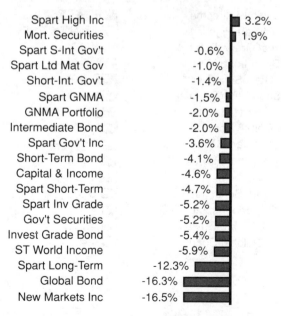

Spart High Inc	3.2%
Mort. Securities	1.9%
Spart S-Int Gov't	-0.6%
Spart Ltd Mat Gov	-1.0%
Short-Int. Gov't	-1.4%
Spart GNMA	-1.5%
GNMA Portfolio	-2.0%
Intermediate Bond	-2.0%
Spart Gov't Inc	-3.6%
Short-Term Bond	-4.1%
Capital & Income	-4.6%
Spart Short-Term	-4.7%
Spart Inv Grade	-5.2%
Gov't Securities	-5.2%
Invest Grade Bond	-5.4%
ST World Income	-5.9%
Spart Long-Term	-12.3%
Global Bond	-16.3%
New Markets Inc	-16.5%

Bond Funds - 1995 Return

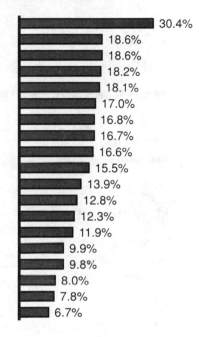

Spart Long-Term	30.4%
Spart Inv Grade	18.6%
Spart High Inc	18.6%
Spart Gov't Inc	18.2%
Gov't Securities	18.1%
Mort. Securities	17.0%
Capital & Income	16.8%
Spart GNMA	16.7%
GNMA Portfolio	16.6%
Invest Grade Bond	15.5%
Spart Ltd Mat Gov	13.9%
Intermediate Bond	12.8%
Spart S-Int Gov't	12.3%
Short-Int. Gov't	11.9%
Spart Short-Term	9.9%
Short-Term Bond	9.8%
New Markets Inc	8.0%
ST World Income	7.8%
Global Bond	6.7%

Muni Bond Funds - 1977 Return

Municipal Bond
Municipal Income   -0.1%
 7.5%

Muni Bond Funds - 1978 Return

Municipal Income   -0.1%
Ltd Term Muni   -3.6%
Municipal Bond   -6.3%

Muni Bond Funds - 1979 Return

Municipal Income   1.3%
Ltd Term Muni   0.5%
Municipal Bond   -1.9%

Muni Bond Funds - 1980 Return

Ltd Term Muni   -6.5%
Municipal Income   -12.6%
Municipal Bond   -18.1%
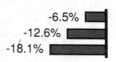

Muni Bond Funds - 1981 Return

Ltd Term Muni   -2.9%
Municipal Income   -6.0%
Municipal Bond   -10.2%

Muni Bond Funds - 1982 Return

Municipal Bond   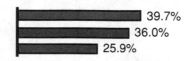 39.7%
Municipal Income   36.0%
Ltd Term Muni   25.9%

Muni Bond Funds - 1983 Return

Municipal Income	12.7%
Ltd Term Muni	9.9%
Municipal Bond	9.2%

Muni Bond Funds - 1984 Return

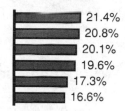

Municipal Income	9.9%
Ltd Term Muni	9.9%
Municipal Bond	9.0%
MA Muni	8.5%

Muni Bond Funds - 1985 Return

Municipal Income	21.4%
NY Muni	20.8%
Municipal Bond	20.1%
MA Muni	19.6%
Ltd Term Muni	17.3%
CA Muni	16.6%

Muni Bond Funds - 1986 Return

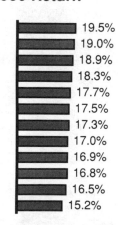

Municipal Bond	19.5%
MI Muni	19.0%
Municipal Income	18.9%
Insured Muni	18.3%
Aggressive	17.7%
CA Muni	17.5%
NY Insured	17.3%
MN Muni	17.0%
MA Muni	16.9%
NY Muni	16.8%
OH Muni	16.5%
Ltd Term Muni	15.2%

Muni Bond Funds - 1987 Return

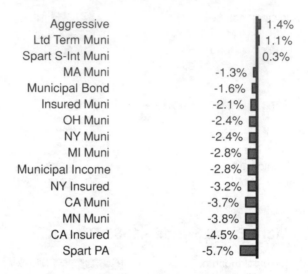

Aggressive	1.4%
Ltd Term Muni	1.1%
Spart S-Int Muni	0.3%
MA Muni	-1.3%
Municipal Bond	-1.6%
Insured Muni	-2.1%
OH Muni	-2.4%
NY Muni	-2.4%
MI Muni	-2.8%
Municipal Income	-2.8%
NY Insured	-3.2%
CA Muni	-3.7%
MN Muni	-3.8%
CA Insured	-4.5%
Spart PA	-5.7%

Muni Bond Funds - 1988 Return

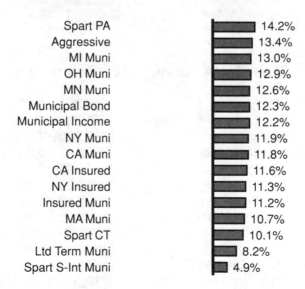

Spart PA	14.2%
Aggressive	13.4%
MI Muni	13.0%
OH Muni	12.9%
MN Muni	12.6%
Municipal Bond	12.3%
Municipal Income	12.2%
NY Muni	11.9%
CA Muni	11.8%
CA Insured	11.6%
NY Insured	11.3%
Insured Muni	11.2%
MA Muni	10.7%
Spart CT	10.1%
Ltd Term Muni	8.2%
Spart S-Int Muni	4.9%

Muni Bond Funds - 1989 Return

Fund	Return
Municipal Income	11.4%
Spart CT	10.4%
Spart NJ	10.3%
MI Muni	10.2%
OH Muni	10.0%
Spart PA	9.8%
CA Muni	9.7%
Municipal Bond	9.6%
Aggressive	9.5%
Insured Muni	9.5%
NY Muni	9.3%
MA Muni	9.3%
MN Muni	9.2%
NY Insured	9.1%
CA Insured	8.8%
Ltd Term Muni	7.8%
Spart S-Int Muni	6.3%

Muni Bond Funds - 1990 Return

Fund	Return
Municipal Income	0.5%
Spart CA	8.2%
OH Muni	7.5%
Aggressive	7.5%
MA Muni	7.4%
MN Muni	7.2%
Spart PA	7.2%
Spart NJ	7.1%
Insured Muni	7.1%
CA Insured	7.0%
Ltd Term Muni	7.0%
CA Muni	7.0%
Municipal Bond	6.9%
Spart CT	6.7%
Spart S-Int Muni	6.4%
NY Insured	6.2%
MI Muni	5.2%
NY Muni	5.1%

Muni Bond Funds - 1991 Return

Fund	Return
Spart NY	14.4%
NY Muni	13.4%
Spart Muni Inc	12.7%
Spart PA	12.5%
NY Insured	12.5%
Spart NJ	12.3%
MI Muni	12.0%
Municipal Bond	11.9%
Ltd Term Muni	11.9%
Aggressive	11.8%
Insured Muni	11.6%
Spart CA	11.5%
OH Muni	11.5%
MA Muni	11.3%
CA Insured	11.0%
Spart CT	10.6%
Municipal Inc	10.2%
CA Muni	10.2%
Spart S-Int Muni	8.8%
MN Muni	8.5%

Muni Bond Funds - 1992 Return

Fund	Return
MI Muni	9.5%
Spart NY	9.5%
MA Muni	9.3%
Aggressive	9.2%
CA Insured	9.2%
Spart PA	9.1%
NY Muni	9.0%
Municipal Bond	8.9%
Spart CA	8.8%
CA Muni	8.7%
Spart NJ	8.7%
OH Muni	8.7%
NY Insured	8.6%
Spart Muni Inc	8.4%
Municipal Inc	8.4%
Spart CT	8.2%
Ltd Term Muni	8.2%
Insured Muni	7.9%
MN Muni	7.6%
Spart S-Int Muni	6.2%

Muni Bond Funds - 1993 Return

Fund	Return
Spart FL	14.9%
Spart Muni Inc	14.3%
Spart CA	14.0%
Insured Tax Free	13.9%
MI Muni	13.8%
CA Insured	13.8%
Aggressive	13.6%
CA Muni	13.4%
Spart NY	13.4%
Spart PA	13.2%
Municipal Bond	13.2%
Municipal Inc	13.1%
Spart NJ	13.1%
Spart CT	13.0%
MA Muni	12.9%
NY Muni	12.9%
NY Insured	12.8%
OH Muni	12.6%
MN Muni	12.4%
Ltd Term Muni	12.2%
Spart S-Int Muni	7.1%

Muni Bond Funds - 1994 Return

Spart S-Int Muni	-0.1%
Spart NY Int	-4.3%
Spart CA Int	-4.7%
Ltd Term Muni	-4.8%
Spart PA	-5.0%
Spart Intermed	-5.1%
OH Muni	-5.5%
Spart NJ	-5.8%
Aggressive	-5.8%
MN Muni	-5.9%
MA Muni	-6.1%
Spart Aggressive	-6.1%
Spart FL Muni	-6.8%
Spart CT	-7.0%
Municipal Inc	-7.5%
MI Muni	-7.5%
Spart MD Muni	-7.5%
Spart Bond Strat	-7.7%
Insured Muni	-7.7%
NY Insured	-8.0%
NY Muni	-8.0%
Spart Muni Inc	-8.1%
Spart NY	-8.3%
Municipal Bond	-8.6%
CA Muni	-8.8%
Spart CA	-9.0%
CA Insured	-10.2%

Muni Bond Funds - 1995 Return

Fund	Return
NY Muni	19.6%
CA Insured	19.5%
CA Muni	19.2%
Spart NY	19.1%
Spart CA	19.0%
Insured Muni	18.7%
Spart FL	18.6%
Spart Muni Inc	18.6%
NY Insured	18.5%
Spartan AZ	18.5%
Municipal Bond	18.2%
MA Muni	18.1%
Spart MD	17.8%
Spart Aggressive	17.7%
Spart PA	17.4%
Spart CT	17.1%
Spart Bond Strat	16.6%
OH Muni	16.4%
Muni Income	16.2%
MN Muni	16.0%
MI Muni	15.4%
Spart NJ	15.4%
Spart CA Int	15.1%
Aggressive	14.9%
Ltd Term Muni	14.9%
Spart NY Int	14.4%
Spart Int	14.4%
Spart S-Int Muni	8.5%

Money Markets - 1979 Return

FDIT   11.9%

Money Markets - 1980 Return

Cash Reserves   12.9%
FDIT   12.8%

Money Markets - 1981 Return

Cash Reserves   17.2%
FDIT   17.0%

Money Markets - 1982 Return

Cash Reserves   13.0%
FDIT   12.8%
U.S. Gov't Reser   11.5%

Money Markets - 1983 Return

FDIT   8.9%
Cash Reserves   8.8%
U.S. Gov't Reser   8.6%

Money Markets - 1984 Return

Cash Reserves   10.2%
FDIT   10.1%
U.S. Gov't Reser   9.8%

Money Markets - 1985 Return

FDIT   7.9%
Cash Reserves   7.9%
U.S. Gov't Reser   7.8%

Money Markets - 1986 Return

Select MM	6.6%
Cash Reserves	6.5%
FDIT	6.5%
U.S. Gov't Reser	6.4%

Money Markets - 1987 Return

Cash Reserves	6.4%
FDIT	6.1%
U.S. Gov't Reser	6.0%
Select MM	6.0%

Money Markets - 1988 Return

Cash Reserves	7.3%
FDIT	7.2%
Select MM	7.1%
U.S. Gov't Reser	7.0%

Money Markets - 1989 Return

Select MM	9.0%
FDIT	9.0%
Cash Reserves	9.0%
U.S. Gov't Reser	8.8%
Spart U.S. Treas	8.3%

Money Markets - 1990 Return

Spart MM	8.4%
Spart U.S. Treas	7.9%
FDIT	7.8%
Cash Reserves	7.8%
Select MM	7.8%
U.S. Gov't Reser	7.7%

Money Markets - 1991 Return

Spart MM	6.2%
Spart U.S. Treas	6.1%
Spart U.S. Gov't	6.1%
Cash Reserves	6.0%
FDIT	5.8%
Select MM	5.8%
U.S. Gov't Reser	5.7%

Money Markets - 1992 Return

Spart MM	4.0%
Spart U.S. Gov't	3.8%
Cash Reserves	3.8%
Spart U.S. Treas	3.7%
FDIT	3.6%
Select MM	3.5%
U.S. Gov't Reser	3.4%

Money Markets - 1993 Return

Spart MM	3.1%
Cash Reserves	2.9%
Spart U.S. Gov't	2.8%
FDIT	2.8%
Spart U.S. Treas	2.7%
Select MM	2.7%
U.S. Gov't Reser	2.6%

Money Markets - 1994 Return

Spart MM	4.1%
Cash Reserves	4.0%
Spart U.S. Gov't	3.9%
FDIT	3.9%
U.S. Gov't Reser	3.9%
Select MM	3.7%
Spartan US Treas	3.7%

Money Markets - 1995 Return

Spart MM	▮ 5.8%
Spart U.S. Gov't	▮ 5.7%
Cash Reserves	▮ 5.7%
Select MM	▯ 5.7%
FDIT	▮ 5.7%
U.S. Gov't Reser	▯ 5.6%
Spartan US Treas	▯ 5.4%

Muni MM Funds - 1981 Return

Municipal MM   7.0%

Muni MM Funds - 1982 Return

Municipal MM   7.1%

Muni MM Funds - 1983 Return

Municipal MM   5.0%

Muni MM Funds - 1984 Return

Municipal MM   5.8%
MA Muni MM   5.2%

Muni MM Funds - 1985 Return

Municipal MM   5.2%
CA Muni MM   5.0%
NY Muni MM   4.9%
MA Muni MM   4.7%

Muni MM Funds - 1986 Return

Municipal MM   4.5%
CA Muni MM   4.5%
MA Muni MM   4.2%
NY Muni MM   4.2%

Muni MM Funds - 1987 Return

Municipal MM   4.3%
Spart PA MM   4.3%
CA Muni MM   4.1%
MA Muni MM   4.0%
NY Muni MM   3.8%

Muni MM Funds - 1988 Return

Spart PA MM	5.0%
Municipal MM	4.9%
CA Muni MM	4.8%
MA Muni MM	4.6%
NY Muni MM	4.5%

Muni MM Funds - 1989 Return

NJ Muni MM	6.4%
Spart PA MM	6.3%
Municipal MM	6.0%
MA Muni MM	5.9%
CA Muni MM	5.8%
NY Muni MM	5.5%

Muni MM Funds - 1990 Return

Spart PA MM	6.0%
OH Muni MM	5.9%
Spart CA MM	5.9%
CT Muni MM	5.7%
NJ Muni MM	5.7%
Municipal MM	5.6%
MA Muni MM	5.3%
CA Muni MM	5.2%
NY Muni MM	5.1%

Muni MM Funds - 1991 Return

Spart CA MM	4.6%
Spart NJ MM	4.6%
Spart PA MM	4.6%
OH Muni MM	4.5%
MI Muni MM	4.5%
Municipal MM	4.4%
CT Muni MM	4.4%
Spart NY MM	4.3%
NJ Muni MM	4.1%
MA Muni MM	4.0%
CA Muni MM	4.0%
NY Muni MM	3.9%

Muni MM Funds - 1992 Return

Spart Muni MM	3.3%
Spart CA MM	3.0%
Spart CT MM	3.0%
Spart NJ MM	2.9%
Spart PA MM	2.9%
Municipal MM	2.9%
OH Muni MM	2.8%
Spart MA MM	2.7%
NJ Muni MM	2.7%
Spart NY MM	2.7%
MI Muni MM	2.7%
CA Muni MM	2.6%
CT Muni MM	2.6%
NY Muni MM	2.5%
MA Muni MM	2.2%

Muni MM Funds - 1993 Return

Spart Muni MM	2.5%
Spart FL MM	2.5%
Spart CA MM	2.4%
Spart PA MM	2.2%
Municipal MM	2.2%
Spart CT MM	2.1%
OH Muni MM	2.1%
Spart NJ MM	2.1%
Spart NY MM	2.0%
CA Muni MM	2.0%
MI Muni MM	2.0%
Spart MA MM	2.0%
NJ Muni MM	1.9%
CT Muni MM	1.9%
NY Muni MM	1.9%
MA Muni MM	1.7%

Muni MM Funds - 1994 Return

Fund	Return
Spart CA MM	2.8%
Spart Muni MM	2.8%
Spart NJ MM	2.7%
Spart PA MM	2.6%
Spart FL MM	2.6%
Municipal MM	2.5%
OH Muni MM	2.5%
MI Muni MM	2.4%
Spart NY MM	2.4%
Spart CT MM	2.4%
CA Muni MM	2.4%
CT Muni MM	2.3%
NJ Muni MM	2.3%
NY Muni MM	2.3%
Spart MA MM	2.3%
MA Muni MM	2.2%

Muni MM Funds - 1995 Return

Fund	Return
Spart AZ MM	3.9%
Spart Muni MM	3.7%
Spart CA MM	3.7%
Spart NJ MM	3.7%
Spart PA MM	3.6%
Spart FL MM	3.6%
Municipal MM	3.5%
OH Muni MM	3.5%
Spart NY MM	3.5%
Spart CT MM	3.4%
MI Muni MM	3.4%
NY Muni MM	3.3%
NJ Muni MM	3.3%
Spart MA MM	3.3%
CA Muni MM	3.3%
CT Muni MM	3.3%
MA Muni MM	3.2%

Select Funds - 1982 Return

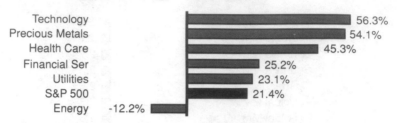

Technology	56.3%
Precious Metals	54.1%
Health Care	45.3%
Financial Ser	25.2%
Utilities	23.1%
S&P 500	21.4%
Energy	-12.2%

Select Funds - 1983 Return

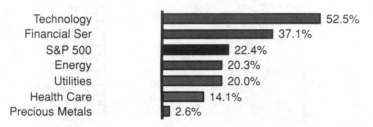

Technology	52.5%
Financial Ser	37.1%
S&P 500	22.4%
Energy	20.3%
Utilities	20.0%
Health Care	14.1%
Precious Metals	2.6%

Select Funds - 1984 Return

Utilities	20.9%
Financial Ser	18.0%
S&P 500	6.1%
Energy	2.4%
Health Care	-1.1%
Technology	-16.9%
Precious Metals	-26.1%

Select Funds - 1985 Return

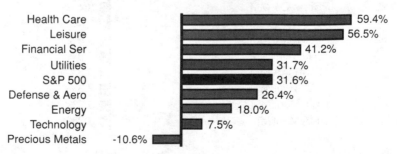

Health Care	59.4%
Leisure	56.5%
Financial Ser	41.2%
Utilities	31.7%
S&P 500	31.6%
Defense & Aero	26.4%
Energy	18.0%
Technology	7.5%
Precious Metals	-10.6%

Select Funds - 1986 Return

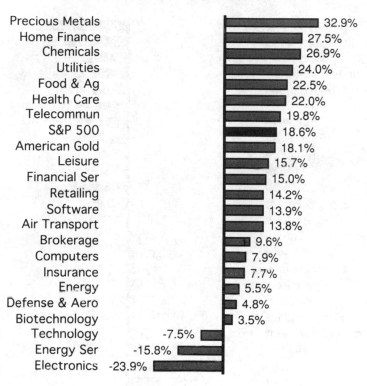

Precious Metals	32.9%
Home Finance	27.5%
Chemicals	26.9%
Utilities	24.0%
Food & Ag	22.5%
Health Care	22.0%
Telecommun	19.8%
S&P 500	18.6%
American Gold	18.1%
Leisure	15.7%
Financial Ser	15.0%
Retailing	14.2%
Software	13.9%
Air Transport	13.8%
Brokerage	9.6%
Computers	7.9%
Insurance	7.7%
Energy	5.5%
Defense & Aero	4.8%
Biotechnology	3.5%
Technology	-7.5%
Energy Ser	-15.8%
Electronics	-23.9%

Select Funds - 1987 Return

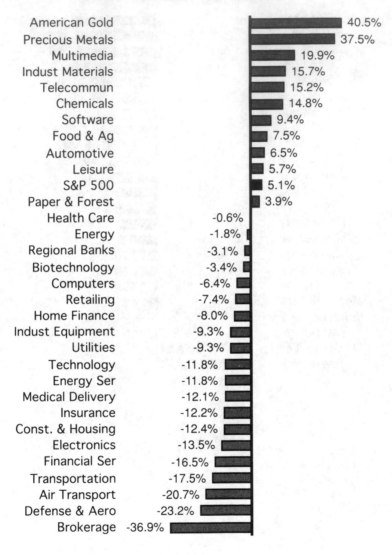

Fund	Return
American Gold	40.5%
Precious Metals	37.5%
Multimedia	19.9%
Indust Materials	15.7%
Telecommun	15.2%
Chemicals	14.8%
Software	9.4%
Food & Ag	7.5%
Automotive	6.5%
Leisure	5.7%
S&P 500	5.1%
Paper & Forest	3.9%
Health Care	-0.6%
Energy	-1.8%
Regional Banks	-3.1%
Biotechnology	-3.4%
Computers	-6.4%
Retailing	-7.4%
Home Finance	-8.0%
Indust Equipment	-9.3%
Utilities	-9.3%
Technology	-11.8%
Energy Ser	-11.8%
Medical Delivery	-12.1%
Insurance	-12.2%
Const. & Housing	-12.4%
Electronics	-13.5%
Financial Ser	-16.5%
Transportation	-17.5%
Air Transport	-20.7%
Defense & Aero	-23.2%
Brokerage	-36.9%

Select Funds - 1988 Return

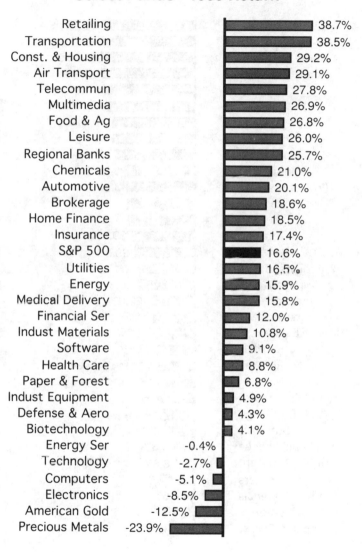

Fund	Return
Retailing	38.7%
Transportation	38.5%
Const. & Housing	29.2%
Air Transport	29.1%
Telecommun	27.8%
Multimedia	26.9%
Food & Ag	26.8%
Leisure	26.0%
Regional Banks	25.7%
Chemicals	21.0%
Automotive	20.1%
Brokerage	18.6%
Home Finance	18.5%
Insurance	17.4%
S&P 500	16.6%
Utilities	16.5%
Energy	15.9%
Medical Delivery	15.8%
Financial Ser	12.0%
Indust Materials	10.8%
Software	9.1%
Health Care	8.8%
Paper & Forest	6.8%
Indust Equipment	4.9%
Defense & Aero	4.3%
Biotechnology	4.1%
Energy Ser	-0.4%
Technology	-2.7%
Computers	-5.1%
Electronics	-8.5%
American Gold	-12.5%
Precious Metals	-23.9%

Select Funds - 1989 Return

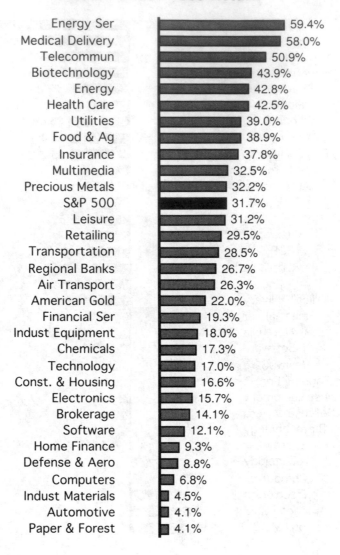

Energy Ser	59.4%
Medical Delivery	58.0%
Telecommun	50.9%
Biotechnology	43.9%
Energy	42.8%
Health Care	42.5%
Utilities	39.0%
Food & Ag	38.9%
Insurance	37.8%
Multimedia	32.5%
Precious Metals	32.2%
S&P 500	31.7%
Leisure	31.2%
Retailing	29.5%
Transportation	28.5%
Regional Banks	26.7%
Air Transport	26.3%
American Gold	22.0%
Financial Ser	19.3%
Indust Equipment	18.0%
Chemicals	17.3%
Technology	17.0%
Const. & Housing	16.6%
Electronics	15.7%
Brokerage	14.1%
Software	12.1%
Home Finance	9.3%
Defense & Aero	8.8%
Computers	6.8%
Indust Materials	4.5%
Automotive	4.1%
Paper & Forest	4.1%

Select Funds - 1990 Return

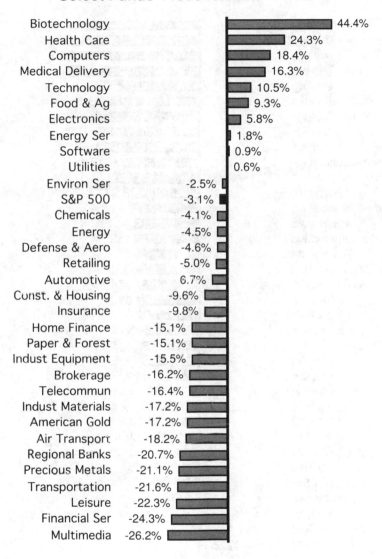

Fund	Return
Biotechnology	44.4%
Health Care	24.3%
Computers	18.4%
Medical Delivery	16.3%
Technology	10.5%
Food & Ag	9.3%
Electronics	5.8%
Energy Ser	1.8%
Software	0.9%
Utilities	0.6%
Environ Ser	-2.5%
S&P 500	-3.1%
Chemicals	-4.1%
Energy	-4.5%
Defense & Aero	-4.6%
Retailing	-5.0%
Automotive	-6.7%
Const. & Housing	-9.6%
Insurance	-9.8%
Home Finance	-15.1%
Paper & Forest	-15.1%
Indust Equipment	-15.5%
Brokerage	-16.2%
Telecommun	-16.4%
Indust Materials	-17.2%
American Gold	-17.2%
Air Transport	-18.2%
Regional Banks	-20.7%
Precious Metals	-21.1%
Transportation	-21.6%
Leisure	-22.3%
Financial Ser	-24.3%
Multimedia	-26.2%

Select Funds - 1991 Return

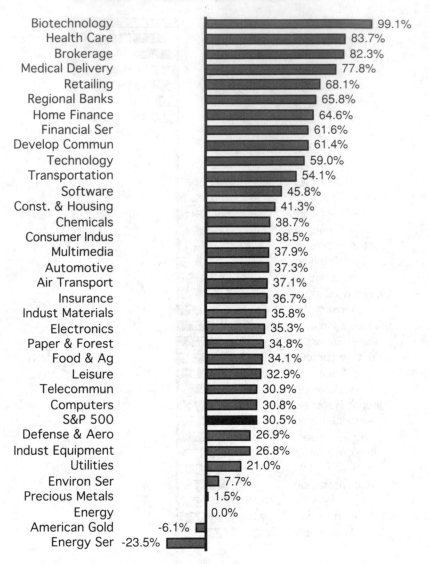

Biotechnology	99.1%
Health Care	83.7%
Brokerage	82.3%
Medical Delivery	77.8%
Retailing	68.1%
Regional Banks	65.8%
Home Finance	64.6%
Financial Ser	61.6%
Develop Commun	61.4%
Technology	59.0%
Transportation	54.1%
Software	45.8%
Const. & Housing	41.3%
Chemicals	38.7%
Consumer Indus	38.5%
Multimedia	37.9%
Automotive	37.3%
Air Transport	37.1%
Insurance	36.7%
Indust Materials	35.8%
Electronics	35.3%
Paper & Forest	34.8%
Food & Ag	34.1%
Leisure	32.9%
Telecommun	30.9%
Computers	30.8%
S&P 500	30.5%
Defense & Aero	26.9%
Indust Equipment	26.8%
Utilities	21.0%
Environ Ser	7.7%
Precious Metals	1.5%
Energy	0.0%
American Gold	-6.1%
Energy Ser	-23.5%

Select Funds - 1992 Return

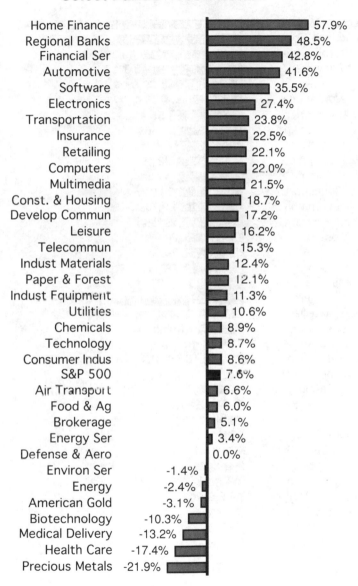

Home Finance	57.9%
Regional Banks	48.5%
Financial Ser	42.8%
Automotive	41.6%
Software	35.5%
Electronics	27.4%
Transportation	23.8%
Insurance	22.5%
Retailing	22.1%
Computers	22.0%
Multimedia	21.5%
Const. & Housing	18.7%
Develop Commun	17.2%
Leisure	16.2%
Telecommun	15.3%
Indust Materials	12.4%
Paper & Forest	12.1%
Indust Equipment	11.3%
Utilities	10.6%
Chemicals	8.9%
Technology	8.7%
Consumer Indus	8.6%
S&P 500	7.6%
Air Transport	6.6%
Food & Ag	6.0%
Brokerage	5.1%
Energy Ser	3.4%
Defense & Aero	0.0%
Environ Ser	-1.4%
Energy	-2.4%
American Gold	-3.1%
Biotechnology	-10.3%
Medical Delivery	-13.2%
Health Care	-17.4%
Precious Metals	-21.9%

Select Funds - 1993 Return

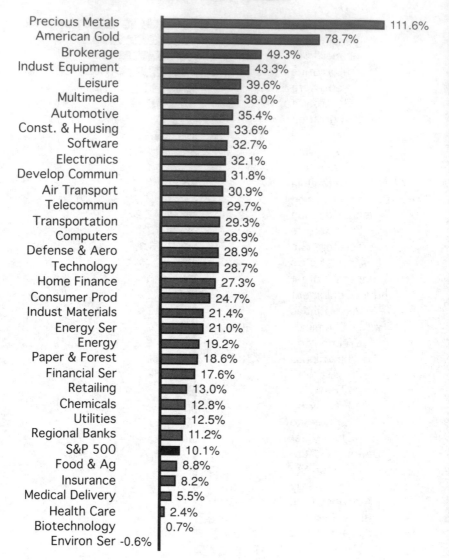

Fund	Return
Precious Metals	111.6%
American Gold	78.7%
Brokerage	49.3%
Indust Equipment	43.3%
Leisure	39.6%
Multimedia	38.0%
Automotive	35.4%
Const. & Housing	33.6%
Software	32.7%
Electronics	32.1%
Develop Commun	31.8%
Air Transport	30.9%
Telecommun	29.7%
Transportation	29.3%
Computers	28.9%
Defense & Aero	28.9%
Technology	28.7%
Home Finance	27.3%
Consumer Prod	24.7%
Indust Materials	21.4%
Energy Ser	21.0%
Energy	19.2%
Paper & Forest	18.6%
Financial Ser	17.6%
Retailing	13.0%
Chemicals	12.8%
Utilities	12.5%
Regional Banks	11.2%
S&P 500	10.1%
Food & Ag	8.8%
Insurance	8.2%
Medical Delivery	5.5%
Health Care	2.4%
Biotechnology	0.7%
Environ Ser	-0.6%

Select Funds - 1994 Return

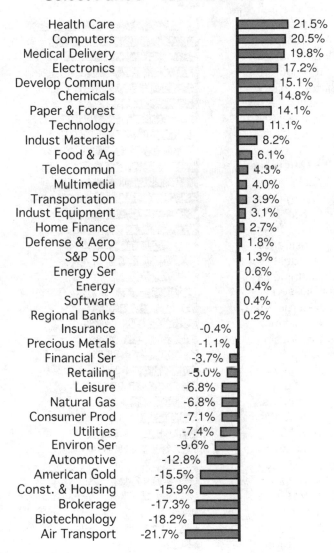

Health Care	21.5%
Computers	20.5%
Medical Delivery	19.8%
Electronics	17.2%
Develop Commun	15.1%
Chemicals	14.8%
Paper & Forest	14.1%
Technology	11.1%
Indust Materials	8.2%
Food & Ag	6.1%
Telecommun	4.3%
Multimedia	4.0%
Transportation	3.9%
Indust Equipment	3.1%
Home Finance	2.7%
Defense & Aero	1.8%
S&P 500	1.3%
Energy Ser	0.6%
Energy	0.4%
Software	0.4%
Regional Banks	0.2%
Insurance	-0.4%
Precious Metals	-1.1%
Financial Ser	-3.7%
Retailing	-5.0%
Leisure	-6.8%
Natural Gas	-6.8%
Consumer Prod	-7.1%
Utilities	-7.4%
Environ Ser	-9.6%
Automotive	-12.8%
American Gold	-15.5%
Const. & Housing	-15.9%
Brokerage	-17.3%
Biotechnology	-18.2%
Air Transport	-21.7%

Select Funds - 1995 Return

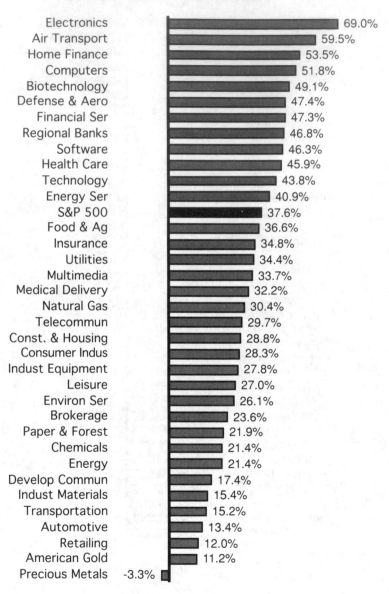

Electronics	69.0%
Air Transport	59.5%
Home Finance	53.5%
Computers	51.8%
Biotechnology	49.1%
Defense & Aero	47.4%
Financial Ser	47.3%
Regional Banks	46.8%
Software	46.3%
Health Care	45.9%
Technology	43.8%
Energy Ser	40.9%
S&P 500	37.6%
Food & Ag	36.6%
Insurance	34.8%
Utilities	34.4%
Multimedia	33.7%
Medical Delivery	32.2%
Natural Gas	30.4%
Telecommun	29.7%
Const. & Housing	28.8%
Consumer Indus	28.3%
Indust Equipment	27.8%
Leisure	27.0%
Environ Ser	26.1%
Brokerage	23.6%
Paper & Forest	21.9%
Chemicals	21.4%
Energy	21.4%
Develop Commun	17.4%
Indust Materials	15.4%
Transportation	15.2%
Automotive	13.4%
Retailing	12.0%
American Gold	11.2%
Precious Metals	-3.3%

VIP Portfolios - 1989 Return

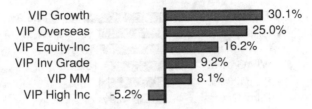

VIP Growth	30.1%
VIP Overseas	25.0%
VIP Equity-Inc	16.2%
VIP Inv Grade	9.2%
VIP MM	8.1%
VIP High Inc	-5.2%

VIP Portfolios - 1990 Return

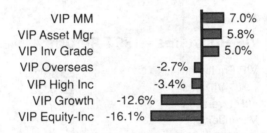

VIP MM	7.0%
VIP Asset Mgr	5.8%
VIP Inv Grade	5.0%
VIP Overseas	-2.7%
VIP High Inc	-3.4%
VIP Growth	-12.6%
VIP Equity-Inc	-16.1%

VIP Portfolios - 1991 Return

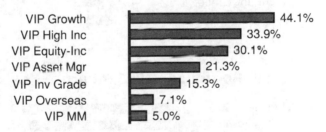

VIP Growth	44.1%
VIP High Inc	33.9%
VIP Equity-Inc	30.1%
VIP Asset Mgr	21.3%
VIP Inv Grade	15.3%
VIP Overseas	7.1%
VIP MM	5.0%

VIP Portfolios - 1992 Return

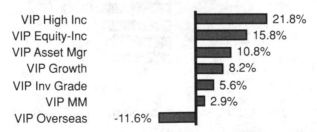

VIP High Inc	21.8%
VIP Equity-Inc	15.8%
VIP Asset Mgr	10.8%
VIP Growth	8.2%
VIP Inv Grade	5.6%
VIP MM	2.9%
VIP Overseas	-11.6%

VIP RETURNS ARE NOT ADJUSTED FOR THE 1%/YEAR ANNUITY FEE

VIP Portfolios - 1993 Return

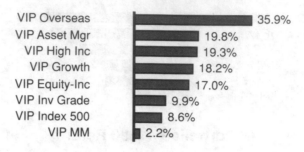

VIP Overseas	35.9%
VIP Asset Mgr	19.8%
VIP High Inc	19.3%
VIP Growth	18.2%
VIP Equity-Inc	17.0%
VIP Inv Grade	9.9%
VIP Index 500	8.6%
VIP MM	2.2%

VIP Portfolios - 1994 Return

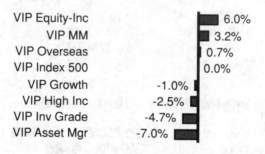

VIP Equity-Inc	6.0%
VIP MM	3.2%
VIP Overseas	0.7%
VIP Index 500	0.0%
VIP Growth	-1.0%
VIP High Inc	-2.5%
VIP Inv Grade	-4.7%
VIP Asset Mgr	-7.0%

VIP Portfolios - 1995 Return

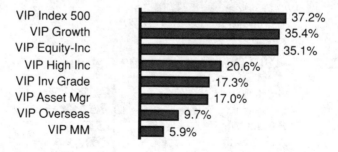

VIP Index 500	37.2%
VIP Growth	35.4%
VIP Equity-Inc	35.1%
VIP High Inc	20.6%
VIP Inv Grade	17.3%
VIP Asset Mgr	17.0%
VIP Overseas	9.7%
VIP MM	5.9%

VIP RETURNS ARE NOT ADJUSTED FOR THE 1%/YEAR ANNUITY FEE

APPENDIX B

The numbers listed below are those most commonly used by Fidelity customers. In case you prefer to conduct business in person, I've also listed the locations of Fidelity's network of investor centers.

PHONE NUMBERS
(available 24 hours unless otherwise indicated)

800-544-8888	Mutual fund information, prospectuses, and sales information
800-544-6666	Mutual fund service (general number with menu of choices)
800-544-7777	Mutual fund exchanges and redemptions
800-544-5555	Mutual fund price quotes, account balances, and transactions
800-544-1877	Tax information line
800-544-4774	Retirement specialists
800-544-3455	Portfolio Advisory Services (9 A.M. to 6 P.M. EST weekdays)
800-544-0118	TDD hearing-impaired Service (9 A.M. to 9 P.M. EST weekdays)
800-544-8666	Fidelity Brokerage account assistance
800-544-7272	Fidelity Brokerage product information
800-544-3939	Fidelity Brokerage trades

800-544-5670	Spanish-speaking representatives (EST business hours)
800-544-9697	FundsNetwork
800-544-5115	Spartan Brokerage Service
800-847-0342	Stock / fund research reports (8 A.M. to 9 P.M. EST weekdays)
801-534-1910	International Service (collect calls accepted)
800-544-4702	Annuity specialists (EST business hours)
800-634-9361	Annuity Service Center
800-258-5759	Charitable services (EST business hours)
800-544-9797	To reach investor center near you (business hours)

INVESTOR CENTER LOCATIONS

Arizona

Scottsdale
7373 North Scottsdale Rd.,
  Suite 182A

California

Campbell/San Jose
851 East Hamilton Ave.,
  Suite 100

Glendale
527 North Brand Blvd.

Irvine
The Atrium
19100 Von Karman Ave.,
  Suite 180
Los Angeles—Century City
10100 Santa Monica Blvd.,
  Suite 100

Los Angeles—Downtown
811 Wilshire Blvd., Suite 150

Palo Alto
251 University Ave.

Sacramento
1760 Challenge Way,
  Suite 200

San Diego
Hazard Center Office Tower
7676 Hazard Center Dr.,
  Suite 210

San Francisco
455 Market St., Suite 100

San Rafael
960 Northgate Dr., Suite 101

Walnut Creek
1400 Civic Dr.

Woodland Hills
300 Canoga Ave.,
  Suite 1001

Colorado

Denver
Dome Tower
1625 Broadway, Suite 110

Connecticut

West Hartford
Town Center
29 South Main St., Suite 402

New Haven
One Century Tower
265 Church St.

Stamford
300 Atlantic St.

Delaware

Wilmington
222 Delaware Ave., Suite 5

Florida

Boca Raton
Tower Shops at the Sanctuary
4400 North Federal Hwy.

Coral Gables
90 Alhambra Place

Ft. Lauderdale
4090 North Ocean Blvd.
  (Route A1A)

Naples
Northern Trust Bank Building
4001 Tamiami Trail, North,
  Suite 102

Orlando/Longwood
The Longwood Village
  Shoppes
1907 West State Road 434,
  Suite 1907

Palm Beach Gardens
The Harbour Financial Center
2401 PGA Blvd., Suite 186

Sarasota
8065 Beneva Rd., South,
  Suite 2

St. Petersburg
Crosswinds Center
2000 66th St., North

Georgia

Atlanta—Buckhead
3525 Piedmont Rd., N.E.
Piedmont Center
Building 8, Suite 215

Atlanta—Dunwoody
Northpark Town Center
1000 Abernathy Rd.
Building 400

Hawaii

Honolulu
AMFAC Center
700 Bishop St., Ground
  Floor

Illinois

Chicago—Loop
1 North Franklin, Suite 100

Chicago—North
215 East Erie St.

Deerfield
Corporate 500 Complex
540 Lake Cook Rd., Suite 115

Oak Brook
Oak Brook Regency Towers
1415 West 22nd St.

Schaumburg
Santa Fe Building
1700 East Golf Rd.,
   Suite 150

Louisiana

New Orleans
Place St. Charles
201 St. Charles Ave.,
   Suite 132

Maine

Portland
Three Canal Plaza

Maryland

Bethesda
7401 Wisconsin Ave.

Towson
Towson Commons
1 West Pennsylvania Ave.

Massachusetts

Boston—Back Bay
470 Boylston St.

Boston—Financial District
21 Congress St.
25 State St.

Braintree
Plaza Executive Center
300 Granite St., Suite 102

Burlington
44 Mall Rd., Suite 100

Worcester
416 Belmont St., Route 9

Michigan

Birmingham
280 North Woodward Ave.

Southfield
Franklin Plaza
29155 Northwestern
   Highway

Minnesota

Minneapolis—Edina
7600 France Ave. South,
   Suite 110

Missouri

Kansas City
The Plaza Steppes
700 West 47th St., Suite 120

Ladue
8885 Ladue Rd., Suite 1

St. Louis
St. Louis Place
200 North Broadway,
   Suite 120

New Jersey

Morristown
56 South St.

Paramus
501 Route 17, South

Short Hills
505 Millburn Ave., Suite 3

New York

Garden City
1050 Franklin Ave., Suite 115

Melville
999 Walt Whitman Rd.

New York—Financial
   District
71 Broadway, Main Level

New York—Park Avenue
350 Park Ave.

New York—Rockefeller
   Center
1271 Avenue of the Americas

White Plains
10 Bank St., Suite 100

North Carolina

Charlotte
Two Coltsgate
4611 Sharon Rd.,
   Suite 125

Durham
2200 West Main St.
Erwin Square

Ohio

Chagrin
Eton Collection
28699 Chagrin Blvd.

Cincinnati
600 Vine St., Suite 108

Cleveland—Downtown
1903 East Ninth St.

Oregon

Portland
One Financial Center
121 S.W. Morrison St.,
   Suite 100

Pennsylvania

Philadelphia
Mellon Bank Center
1735 Market St.

Pittsburgh
Union Trust Building
439 Fifth Ave., Suite 157

Tennessee

Memphis
Clark Tower Building
5100 Poplar Ave., Suite 112

Texas

Austin
The Arboretum
10000 Research Blvd.,
   Suite 214

Dallas
Park Cities Tower
7001 Preston Rd.,
   Suite 140

Houston—North
19740 1H
45 North Spring

Houston—Galleria
2701 Drexel Dr.

Houston—West
1155 Dairy Ashford,
   Suite 104

Las Colinas
400 East Las Colinas Blvd.,
   Suite 120

San Antonio
14100 San Pedro, Suite 110

Utah

Salt Lake City
215 South State St.,
   Suite 130

Vermont

Burlington
Courthouse Plaza,
199 Main St.

Virginia

Tysons Corner
Greensboro Park
8180 Greensboro Dr.

Washington

Bellevue
One Bellevue Center
411 108th Ave., N.E.

Seattle
511 Pine Street

Washington, D.C.
The Suffridge Building
1775 K St., N.W.

Wisconsin

Milwaukee—Brookfield
595 North Barker Rd.,
   Suite 400

INDEX